'Everybody Has to Cry Sometime' Parts 1 & 2.

by

John Kenneth Rodgers

www.fast-print.net/store.php

EVERYBODY HAS TO CRY SOMETIME
PARTS 1 & 2

A catalogue record for this book is available from the British Library

ISBN 978-178035-650-1

First published 2013 by
FASTPRINT PUBLISHING
Peterborough, England.

Contents

Chapter One

"Who are you for a Rodgers?"

'The Family' was already bigger than average, as my mum and dad had provided me with three big sisters and two big brothers before I bawled my way into this world on 6th January 1957. Lillian, Jim, Marlene, Elaine and Bobby were already filling nappies and charging through their infancy and early childhood. We were not rich and famous, but we all had at least double-barrelled names – Christian names, that is.

Lillian was therefore Lilian Davidson;

Jim – James Allan;

Marlene – Marlene Anne;

Elaine – Elaine Elizabeth;

Bobby – Robert Leslie;

and me, John Kenneth.

My mum liked proper names and I suppose it was a sign of respect for existing or previous members from both sides of the family. Names were handed down like good clothes; they could even coincide with some great event or be borrowed from some highly respected person outwith the family.

Names, like times also change and hand me down names, like clothes become unfashionable. Old, 'respectable' names have been eclipsed by the new media, sports and pop personalities. This has bred a clutch of Kylies, Charlenes, Dannies, Brads, Mels, Romeos and the likes.

In the fifties and sixties, forenames might have given you a sense of who some of your relatives were, but it was your surname which marked out your potential character and standing in the community. The cry was, "Who are you for a Rodgers?"

I didn't know then, but I know now that for Rodgers we were the product of the soil and hard toil. There was no blue blood, no knights and no nouveau riche to ease the rigours of the earlier centuries. The occupations of our ancestors confirmed we were "ordinary common folk."

On my dad's side, we stretched back to Arthur Curragh ,a farm labourer in Ireland, whose son, William, emigrated to Scotland during the mid-1800s (like thousands of others who left the Emerald Isle in face of the potato famine).

The Curragh's, from around Auchinleck, and the Rodgers, from Cumnock, formed my father's side of the family, allied to the Watts and the Hardies, who originated from Aberdeenshire.

On my mother's side, the alliances centred around the Allan's from Larkhall and the Davidson's from Hamilton. Basically, we were three parts Scottish and one part Irish, with an American strain 'thrown out' for good measure, and now living in Wyoming and beyond.

There were no exotic job titles then and in the main, our male ancestry consisted of farm labourers, coal miners, furnace labourers, iron miners, wood forester, gas man, labourer, dairyman and crofters. Our place in the social strata of the day was really borne out by the registered occupations of our female ancestors – they were variously described as general servant (domestic), domestic servant, housekeeper, estate worker, domestic nurse, domestic servant (cook), dairymaid, housekeeper and cotton weaver.

The most 'upmarket' occupations in our ancestry included a cinder molter (presumably part of the iron industry); a silk weaver around 1881 and a caustic soda maker in 1923. Various 'scholars' are also listed but the curiosity 'value' lies in our past association with the Murrays, who were described as 'bank agents,' and in particular, Bentley Murray (c1870), who appeared not to have a job, but had "income derived from dividends." The 'dividends,' if they existed, were never passed on to the Allan's or Rodgers' – instead we inherited a work ethic and a sense of pride in being able to work and make it (whatever 'it' was) on our own merits.

In more recent times, I never knew my mum's mum, but my grandpa was John Allan, aka Wee Jock. Big or bigger families were pretty much the norm back then and my mum had three brothers, John, Tom and Willie, and three sisters, Margaret, Molly and Annie. The brothers were all characters in their own right and Margaret, Molly and Annie were quiet and loving sisters.

The real character in my mum's family, apart from my mum, was undoubtedly "Wee Jock," a miner from Lanarkshire. In his later years, he frequently came to visit us from his home in Low Waters, Hamilton. He liked the peace and quiet of the Darvel countryside and would often arrive at weekends dressed in a dark tweed-style suit with a pipe and matches in the right-hand jacket pocket and chunks of cheese in the left. I never really understood the chunks of cheese in his left pocket, but when he and my dad would return from the pub after a few pints and haufs, the cheese was gone! He was always up bright and early the next day with no sign of a hangover. I don't think Wee Jock ever visited Spain, but I suppose the cheese was the equivalent of 'tapas' in the pocket.

Loudoun Hill is situated about a mile to the east of Darvel, on the old A71 road to Edinburgh. It is a 'volcanic plug' and history has it as the site of a Roman fort. It is also reputed to have been the site of numerous battles, including those fought by our "Braveheart," William Wallace; Robert the Bruce; and the Covenanters.

The Loudoun Hill Inn ("The Inns"), the scene of many a boozy session, also lies on the A71 and nowadays, droothy climbers quench their thirst and celebrate getting to the summit with a quick pint.

It transpires that Wee Jock had seen a few battle sites himself and was a veteran of World War I. He had served in his 'local' Regiment, the Cameronians (Scottish Rifles), whose HQ was at 129 Muir Street, Hamilton.

In the Great War, the Regiment served in France, Flanders, Macedonia, Egypt and Palestine, and the 7th Battalion was the last to evacuate Gallipoli.

Having survived the Battle of the Somme and the Great War, wee Jock became a miner in Lanarkshire. The miners rows were out of town and meant an eight mile walk for mum, as a young girl, to the school in Low Quarter , Hamilton.

Serving and surviving two World Wars did not save the Cameronians from a review of Regiments and Wee Jock proudly attended the disbanding of the Cameronians on 14 May 1968. After 279 years of wartime exploits, a peacetime military review achieved what wartime enemies couldn't – they killed off the Cameronians.

None of my grandpa's wartime exploits came from him, nor my mum and dad. They emerged from a chance meeting with a local worthy at the top of Loudoun Hill, who asked the inevitable, "Who are you for a Rodgers?"

Even after retiring from the pits, Wee Jock took up a job as a night watchman.

Late at night or early morning calls usually meant bad news and I remember the early morning call on 4 April 1973, when my mum was told he had been found dying in a cabin, "defending" the steelworks.

Not to be outdone in the family size front, my dad had four brothers – Jim, Peter, David and William, and two sisters – Rhoda and Annie.

Jimmy and Ina were my grandparents on my dad's side and I can remember visiting them on a couple of occasions at Saltcoats. Jimmy grew tomatoes and had 'budgies.' The tomatoes were not just any tomatoes – they were yellow, just like some of his budgies. Yellow tomatoes in the 1960s were a bit like gay men – you didn't see a lot of them, but when you did, they stood out a mile. This of course was in the days when the mention of 'gay' did not mean you were homophobic.

Jimmy, like 'Wee Jock,' was a real character. In his late teens and early twenties, he had gone to America and worked as a 'hired hand' moving from farm to farm to secure work. His wanderlust ended when he returned to Scotland after the First World War and married Williamina Watt Hardy – thankfully, Ina for short. He retired to his budgies and yellow tomatoes after completing his job as a Foreman with Shell Mex. Apart from his sojourns to America, his other claim to fame was as a follower of junior football club, Saltcoats Victoria for over forty years – he must have been a patient man!

We were therefore ordinary people with no hidden fortunes, but equally, there were no shady dealings, debts or abject poverty. Times were hard, but seemed happy with no real sense of sadness or grief, which develops with age and through time, friendship and love.

Like many kids, I don't have a vivid recollection of my earliest real memories. The first three or four years of life I suppose are like Alzheimer's in reverse – you build up the brain power and strength to progressively learn and remember things, as opposed to losing your brain power and forgetting things. In short, I don't really remember anything until after we moved to Darvel in 1959.

Darvel is a small town in East Ayrshire, in South West Scotland, with about 3,000 inhabitants. It is the most easterly of the three 'Irvine Valley' towns of Galston, Newmilns and Darvel,all of which straddle the river Irvine as it meanders its way to the sea on the Ayrshire coast.

It's a pretty anonymous town, with probably three main claims to fame. It is the birthplace of Sir Alexander Fleming, who discovered penicillin; Sammy Cox, the Rangers and Scotland footballer, hailed from Darvel; and up until the arrival of foreign imports and cheaper overseas labour in the late 1980s/early 1990s, it had a thriving lace and textile manufacturing industry, which rivalled that of Nottingham in England.

Anonymous or not, there was an inherent sense of pride in Darvel (or at least, in Darvel of old), as recalled by local resident, Val McKay (age 96):

"Dear Sir

Did you know that at one time Darvel had an outdoor curling club? It was situated in an old stone building at the top of what we called the "Pond Brae," a continuation of Jamieson Road. It had two ponds, one for curling and one for skating. We had no world champions but the pleasure and competition was there for both curlers and skaters. Darvel also had a quoiting club which had a senior and junior Scottish champion among its members. There were three tennis clubs in Darvel at one time, one of which, Darvel Gowanbank, held the Singles and Doubles Championships of Ayrshire. The other two were in Priestland. We also had a nine hole golf course at Loudounhill where the sand quarry is now. There was a Darvel burgh band which competed with the best bands in England and eventually won the British Band Championship at Crystal Palace. There was even a Boys' Brigade Pipe Band.

John Campbell, a keen athlete and manager of the Darvel branch of the Clydesdale Bank, was responsible for starting the Darvel Athletic Club. We had over 20 members at the start. The club house was the one handed over by the curling club and was a bit primitive. It had an outside shower we used after training. Tuesday and Thursday were training nights but on Saturday some of us competed in local sports and actually won prizes. One member went further afield and won at Powder Hall.

Sadly these features of Darvel life of the 1920s and 1930s are all away now – the curling club owing to the vagaries of the Scottish weather and the rest just due to lack of interest.

Incidentally, the John Campbell mentioned became Sir John for services rendered and signed his name on all Clydesdale Bank notes after he became Chairman of the Clydesdale Bank."[1]

---

[1] *Source – Autumn 2002 issue of the Valley Advertiser*

Pride in the past, however, does not necessarily relate to faith in the future of Darvel or any town or city. The past can be fondly remembered, but not lived in.

People remember insults and compliments in about equal measure and that is why my first real memory of the past is of being wheeled down the street in a big, black pram by my sister, Lilian. Elderly residents would peer into the pram and would regularly remark, "Oh she's a lovely wee lassie with her blonde, curly hair." I think it was then I decided to get a haircut and walk more!

My first wee sister came along in 1959 and she was, and is, the inimitable Yvonne – Yvonne Lorraine Margaret to be precise. No TV then, but my mum and dad still managed to conjure up a sensual-sounding French name with my Aunt Margaret.

My mum and dad were and are a real double-act and with over fifty years of marriage, they are a real polished double-act.

Mum is the most practical, honest, caring and beautiful person. Mrs Baxter hasn't a look-in when it comes to making soup, as mum's is the best in the world. She cares so much for the family that it hurts. She would like to take every pain and hurt suffered by her children and shoulder them. She would have your cold, flu, your broken bones, your tears and grief and what do you get in return? A real mum without comparison.

In stereotypical terms mum was the gatherer; she gathered money, friends , love and affection and the whole family.

This intense caring meant that family setbacks and incidents which other parents would regard as fairly trivial in the scale things, were a serious source of concern to mum.

Dad was the hunter; the provider, the comedian, a shooter and a fisher. He was also a piper and, as part of the Ardrossan & Saltcoats and then Darvel Pipe Bands, he played at Marymass in Irvine, gala days and Burns' Suppers. He couldn't read music, but he mastered playing the pipes and we would often fall asleep to the skirl of the bagpipes and in his most modern phase, this included a wee tune by the Pipes & Drums of the Royal Scots Dragoon Guards, "Amazing Grace," and also Paul McCartney and Wings' "Mull of Kintyre." A dab hand at darts, he and Sam Dunlop were the double-handed champions of Ayrshire in their day.

In her early teens, my mum 'went into service' with the Dean family. She was a housemaid and surrogate mother all rolled into one in the home of the Deans, where she stayed for five years. It's an association and affection which continues to this day, through visits and cards to celebrate birthdays and anniversaries, the most recent of which was the now Mrs Brownlie's ninetieth birthday, on 31 October 2004.

In 1996, Mrs Brownlie exclaimed, in the story of her life,

"I was left, at 32, after nine wonderfully happy years, with Ian who was six months old, and Margaret just four. Dr Steel immediately brought me Lily, our wonderful Lily, who at 16 nursed the baby as her own and stayed with us daily for almost five years. She spoiled everyone, including me! She went on to have ten (actually eleven) *children of her own, and is as wonderful today as ever, living happily with her husband Robert, in Darvel, with two middle-aged sons who see no reason to leave home!!! And I'm not surprised!"*

Beyond that period of 'domestic service' my mum has always been a mum whom you could neither pay by the hour, or for the love, care and affection she produces.

After and early spell as a fireman, my dad became a Council worker. Following a bout of TB, the outdoor work helped to improve his health and fitness. Periods of work with the Councils in Ardrossan and Saltcoats, Dreghorn and Springside, were followed by the longest posting to Darvel in Kilmarnock & Loudoun/East Ayrshire. Loyalty and enjoyment of his job meant an accumulation of over forty years' service with 'the Council' by the time my dad retired.

These were the backgrounds of the characters whose world's collided, resulting in marriage in 1948, at the age of 24, and who remain the 'matriarch' and 'patriarch' to the family.

Both mum and dad have worked like "Trojans" all their lives and really did embrace the old work ethic. Both agreed "there would be 'nothing on tick' in this house." The 'Store Quarter' was a wee bit of an exception, but even then, everything was paid at the end of the quarter. Our Co-operative Dividend number was originally 902 and when business and customer numbers were booming, the number changed to 3902.

Boom turned to bust for the Co-operative shops in Darvel and now all but the fruit shop, which masquerades as a Ladbrokes 'betting shop,' have succumbed to the wooden-window syndrome – they've been 'boarded up.'

Before the advent of ASDAs, Morrisons, Safeway, Sainsburys and Tesco, Darvel and many a Scottish town had its Co-op (store) Bakers, Butchers, Fruit Shop, Hardware and Drapery; separate shops but co-operatives. The socialist roots of the Co-operative movement couldn't halt the movement out of town and out of fashion until the late 1990s. It's ironic that many of the major 'multiples' now offer what the Co-op offered in its heyday – the Co-op 'van' or store-boy delivered your orders to the door. Yesterday's 'van' has been replaced by order on-line via the superhighway. With more in-store value and community values, the Co-op is making a comeback – a comeback that's too late to save the sandstone buildings that once proudly proclaimed, "*Darvel Industrial Co-operative Society Limited – Instituted 1840*."

Economics were pretty simple back then and without the aid of Keynesian or Monetarist Theories, my mum and dad worked out that if we couldn't afford it, we didn't have it, and yet we didn't really want for anything. Most families were the same, with the exception of the 'upwardly mobile' and the 'never works, never wants' brigade.

In season, pheasants, partridge, ducks, pigeons, rabbits, hare and trout were all in plentiful supply, as dad was a good shot and fisher. After teaching us to fish in the local 'burns,' the River Irvine and the Glen, we progressed to the Avon at

Drumclog and the Clyde as it flows through the Clyde Valley in Lanarkshire.

We grew potatoes, turnips, carrots, brussels, cabbages and peas and although we were never anything like self-sufficient, it all helped. For relatively poor people, we had a 'rich man's diet,' but we never reached the stage of saying, "Aw no pheasant again!"

"Hillcrest," Manse Brae, Darvel – otherwise known as the new cemetery, was where we stayed and sat in 'perfect peace and isolation,' above the rest of the town. My dad was the Cemetery Superintendent, or 'gravedigger' as the folks in Darvel would have it. In his early days as the new 'gravedigger,' my dad was in one of those, "Who are you for a Rodgers" conversations with a couple of old biddies down the street, when the topic came round to good bones to make soup. My dad's offer to get them 'some good bones' for soup was hastily rejected when the who are you for a Rodgers question was answered by, "I'm the new gravedigger."

My uncles and aunts used to love coming to visit us in Darvel. There was Jim and Dot in the Ford Consul, Duncan and Annie in the Ford Anglia, Rhoda and Barclay, William and Mary, Tom and John on the bus, and Willie 'six-guns' and his entire family on the motor bike and side car – it seems there were a lot of cowboys in East Kilbride where Uncle 'William' stayed?! In the absence of money and before the advent of the people carrier, my mum and dad never owned a car, so it was 'Shank's pony' for us. It was never something we queried – we didn't have a car and we didn't need one – we were 'visited' not 'visitors.'

Visits and weekend stays by Aunt Annie and Uncle (big) Duncan meant the girls, Marlene , Elaine and Yvonne vacated their room for the bed settee in the living room. The settee folded down to a double bed and we had plenty of bed linen but on occasion blankets could be a problem especially in winter ; so it was that the grey and the black coats would emerge from the press opposite the pantry in the kitchen. These muckle great coats were the eiderdowns of their day.

Complete with my curly blond locks, it came time to go to the primary school – the 'wee school.' This involved a two mile return journey each day which, even then I realised would be a real chore for my mum to do day in and day out, especially with Yvonne and Davy (David Gordon) now on the scene. By the second day at school, I boldly declared my independence, and from now on, my mum needn't accompany me to and from school each day.

Some kids cried on their first days at school, but this was short-lived, and the race was on to see who would be the next world racing driving champion by running round the school buildings at playtime. Would it be Jim Clark? Stirling Moss? Aka Stoory, Beefy, Edgar, Kerr or wee Kenny.

Halloween was usually a good time at the primary, as there was a party with games and dookin' for apples. My head was in the pale filled with water as I bit into the biggest apple of the lot – success? Chuffed with myself, I gorged it down and an hour or so later, made my independent way up the road to 'Hillcrest.' By the time I reached John Aird's lace factory at Glen Brig, my stomach was doing 'wheelies.' I would hold it in until I came to the wooded area at Manse Brae (well bears shit in woods, and there would be doken leaves to wipe my bum). The best laid plans of a wee Ayrshire boy went aft aglay with the first squirt of diarrhoea, followed by a 'meltdown' which escaped from my pants and made a lava flow down my legs, below my short trousers. Independent or what? The final ignominy was sitting in the sink getting washed and explaining to mum that, although her wee boy could walk up the dangerous road himself, he couldn't control his bowels.

Christmas was also usually a good time at the primary (a party, pantomime or play, but no big soor apples to induce involuntary shiting). So it was that the P4 Nativity Play got under way, 'choreographed' by Mrs McFarlane and Mrs Smith. Sitting (yes, **sitting**) cross-legged on the wooden floor,

I was suddenly aware that things had "stopped" and I was being beckoned to join the 'cast' backstage. One of the Wise Men had taken appendicitis and I had been called off the 'subs' bench' to present myrrh to Mary and Joseph for the baby Jesus. It was over in a flash and I think I fluffed my lines, all six words.

There is and was something ironic about being born on Epiphany and my role in the Nativity Play. My mum had always stressed I had been born on Epiphany but, to me, that was the day that Christmas decorations came down and we returned to school after the holidays, rather than the day the Wise Men from the East reached Jesus in Bethlehem.

These 'happy days' were not tainted with sadness or grief or any sense of being poor. Even pain was a short, sharp sensation which didn't last, but which is literally etched on my head.

The rocking horse at the big park was a source of great fun and fascination to a boy of five. Curious as to how it worked, I ventured closer and closer as the horse was rocked on its axis by some older kids. The higher it went, the closer I got, and the more I learned about how it worked, until wallop! Blood was streaming from my head through my blond hair. A hurried visit to the doctors and the split head was mended but the rocking horse was no longer a winner for me. Off came the curly blond locks of hair which had been matted with blood.

Darvel once boasted its very own Roxy Picture House (cinema), which stood next to Paterson's, later Struther's fruit shop. The picture house showed its last western in the early sixties. (I don't think it was "Gone With the Wind"). But as one picture house door closed, another opened, as we used to sneak into the building which was a haven for playing in when it was wet and cold (and it was frequently wet and cold in Darvel). The rows of chairs and curtains and ropes all provided a stage for us to play on. That was, until we emerged from the dark recesses under the stage with our nostrils full of the smell of shite. Someone had been caught short, and emptied his or her bowels under the stage. The empty Darvel picture house became out of bounds, but there was still the 'flea pit' or Rex in Newmilns (which was demolished in 2002), that was if the Darvel crew were brave enough to enter into 'Apache territory.' Whilst Glasgow and bigger Scottish cities had a 'gang culture' in the 1960s and 1970s, smaller Scottish towns had 'town rivalries' which, whilst not acute, could still merit a 'doing' if you were in the wrong place at the wrong time.

The Junior Secondary was the next step on the educational ladder. Unfortunately, there were also a few snakes at the 'big school' and snakes had to be confronted or avoided. Avoidance was not my strong point, then or now, but I wasn't town-wise, never mind street-wise. In Scotland, the smaller you are, the harder you have to try and prove you're 'big.' 'Wee man' can be a term of endearment or an insult and a challenge to be 'big.' Who says it, and how it is said, is critical. A fight here and a fight there soon established the 'wee man's' credibility, to the point where I became the Henry Kissinger of my year. I got in more trouble stopping or preventing fights than I did from being in them. It wasn't really a case of me being really 'hard,' and more that other kids (with fewer brothers and sisters) got fed up fighting the Rodgers family, as the first flurry of fists was followed by a declaration of *"If you beat him you'll have to fight me next...., and me next...., and me next,"* by Bobby, Marlene and Elaine.

From the 'splendid isolation' of Hillcrest, school offered a collective and competitive challenge, or at least, that's how I rationalise my approach looking back. I was a country boy playing catch-up with the kids from the town, who already knew and had played with each other. School was an opportunity to learn and develop and get involved in new activities; it was a time to shape yourself and your future, or so it seemed to me. While other kids 'plunked' the school, I reckoned if I've got to be here, I'm going to give it my best shot. There were others more gifted and talented that me, but I got 'stuck in,' and the reward was attendance at the annual prize-giving ceremony, to collect certificates of merit and excellence and books in recognition of being in the first three of the class. Ironically, apart from a passing glance, these books were never read and like many of yesterday's mementos, have been packed and stacked in the attic.

School was more than books and lessons, there were games and sports. Sport was also a real passion for me and Recreation Park, the home of the mighty but skint Darvel Juniors was the scene of my first game of 'organised' football for the school. Mrs Young took the team and it was rumoured that if you left your y-fronts on under you shorts, she came into the dressing room and personally removed them. We crushed Crossroads 8-0 and we were all real Scotsmen under our shorts! Football really was the national sport then and we played morning, noon and night on the public parks with our jumpers down for makeshift goals. The rivalry between the top of the town – myself, my brother Bobby, Jim Browning, Ricky McNaughton, Munger, Jack Collins and Cat Houston (funnily enough he wasn't a goalkeeper) and the bottom of the town – Beefy (who went on to play in goals for Motherwell – I suppose someone has to do it?!), Stoory, Dung, Grimley and Sammy Cox (grandson of the legendary Rangers and Scotland player, Sammy Cox), was reflected in various clashes at Kate Ross's, down by the big park. These were fraught affairs, which usually ended in a fracas or fight; sometimes me and Bobby as 'brothers-in-arms,' and sometimes involving me and him as 'brothers-in-battle,' especially when I scored an own goal to give the bottom of the town victory. This was pre-Bosman days and the fixture fizzled out as players moved house and loyalties and friendships got mixed/blurred or maybe, just maybe, we got older and acquired other interests.

Up until the early 1960s, the family revolved around those brothers and sisters in front of me. By the time I had arrived at the 'wee school' all the others had gone to the 'big school' and by the time I reached the 'big school' my siblings had already left or were about to leave. There was a sense of chasing my brothers and sisters and never quite catching up with them and at the same time, not knowing if I really wanted to catch up with where they were going or what they were doing. As brothers and sisters in the country life and pursuits followed the seasons – fishing in the spring and summer; swimming in the river when it was really warm was popular and would be followed by building a fire and cooking potatoes on a stick in the warm embers until they were brown and burnt on the outside and white and fluffy in the middle. Occasionally, a can of beans on metal plates was the added ingredient and recipe for a full days outing. Late summer and autumn could involve helping out by lifting bales of straw and picking potatoes at local farms before a period of winter inactivity and near hibernation indoors in front of a coal fire. No central heating, no Game Boys, no computers and no mobiles – only each other for company and a laugh.

'Doing the shoes' became a rite of passage and by the time I was twelve it was my turn. Initially this was no problem as it was a bit of a chore but it was just cleaning and polishing the school shoes with the old Cherry Blossom or Kiwi polish. As the years progressed 'doing the shoes' became a decidedly dodgy business after Jim became a baker and Bobby a butcher. The ridges on the soles of Jim's shoes became filled with dough and the occasional raisin and worst still was the sawdust and bits of mince in the tread of Bobby's shoes. These foot odours came from well respected trades and are nothing to compare with the dogs' shit which fouls its way into every grove in modern day shoes and trainers. Life certainly didn't smell of roses in the 1960's but dog shit was not the curse of every pavement in every town.

Rural life was not idyllic but it did have its idiosyncrasies. In the coal house we had 'dross and brickets' to back up and fuel the fire and in amongst the black diamonds we had potatoe skins , potatoe skins! The goodness of the potatoe lies directly beneath the skin my mum would chant but we had some thick skinned potatoes and their role in life became the back up to the dross and brickets in the raeburn / stove. Nowadays they would be loaded for loaded restaurateurs to fuel our hunger and turn the noble tattie's outerskin to a delicacy.

With farms all around us we could live of the land; we could get 'double yokers' from Dunlop's farm . These were very large eggs and the equivalent of the poor wee brown hen expecting twins – they had two yokes. For thrupence a week (one pence) we would take our turns to deliver the eggs , double wrapped in brown paper bags to the Flannigan sisters in Green Street , Ethil and Margaret. Their names were old and their living room reflected a clean dullness that was decidedly pre 1960's. The visits and the double yokers became more infrequent as age and standardisation caught up with the sisters and the brown hen respectively.

Strang's farm was more modern; it was a piggery. Huge pigs in pens the equivalent of battery hens in cages stuck out their snouts to devour whatever was in the trough. Piglets ran to suckling mothers in families of 8, 9 and even ten in blissful ignorance of their fate and destiny with the plate.

The adult pig was caught and strung up at Strang's farm and ready for the killing. Dad shot it and the farmer slashed it from throat to groin and its entrails spilled on to the clean concrete for Jim to clear up. We had pork for a week and spare ribs before they ever became fashionable and therefore by definition expensive for what you were actually getting.

The rhythm of rural life was interspersed by the lure of the town. Playing the bagpipes and playing Darts were dad's passions. The brown pay-packet was handed over to my mum every Friday and in return for his toils my dad got a brown / bronze 'ten bob note ' (50 pence) . Gowanbank Hotel or the Black Bull Inn were the places to sharpen his skills with the arrows and his wit. In good weeks this might extend to another ten bob note for a pint on Saturday and the Monday night league game. Mum always gathered the brown pay packets and dealt out the money. It is a skill that is practiced weekly and comes as second nature except on one Christmas when inexplicably the empty brown pay packet remains in mum's hand and the green pound notes spark to life on the red hot coals on the open fire. Only a few green backs are retrieved from the fire as in distraught and despair mum's fingers burn.

For youths going down the town meant playing football, Newmarket ; going a 'plunder or experimenting with smoking – cigarettes for the inhalers and cinnamon sticks for those with asbestos lungs .

In summer nights Newmarket was common ; it was a hundred yard run over the front hedges of the gardens in Paterson Terrace. If that was a lung buster so too was running away from the aftermath on a failed plunder on local fruit trees and strawberry plants.

Even more of a lung buster was the smoking or failed (successful) attempts at smoking. Getting a 'single ' (fag) and a match was a major coup ; smoking it was the coup d'etat but failing that a cinnamon stick could be bought and lit and your credibility was still intact . Still intact until the first intake of smoke from the hollow stick and you realise your breathing fire – you're smoking a fuckin fire lighter and no bugger warned you; there was no notice on the packet and you've just tried to inhale raw flames and look cool – yeah right !

On the more solitary side there was little to beat fishing. At Hillcrest the grass cuttings from the regular cutting of the cemetery plots were pilled at the four corners of the cemetery . The bottom left hand corner was the favoured spot for digging worms for fishing but not just any worms, these were bramble worms with their distinctive whitish yellow rings around reddish bodies . These were much more attractive than dew worms, at least they were to the fish. These worms were perfect for catching brown trout on the rivers Avon , Glen and Irvine but not as perfect as a ' raspberry'.

The raspberry does not feature in the classic fishing guides as a bait for brown trout but it can be effective when you're in a jam, so to speak.

The river Irvine was fishing well in early August and with a little run on the water from a fresh shower I set off in search of a few brownies with my treasured bramble worms in a ' jeely jar'. They would do the trick or at least they might have done if they had not slipped from my pocket to freely feed the fish waiting downstream. All's lost with lost worms and I make my way up to the small bridge at Priestland to walk home wormless and fishless – that is until I spy some ripe raspberries on the other side of the river and decide to have a feed.

After six or eight raspberries the thought crosses my head that the small conical inside of the ripe raspberries look to me like a small white grub which the fish would eat. How would they look to the fish – let's try and see. Under the shade of the bridge I put the master-plan to test with two raspberries masquerading as grubs on the end of a size 12 hook. Two casts later and the big fish is hooked on raspberries. Playing a one pound trout on an eight foot rod under a six foot bridge gave the fish a fair chance but a wee bit of luck and invention and the big fellow was landed, sweet as you like.

The family was 'close in adversity' and would rally against the world, but we were not and are not the most expressive in terms of our affection for each other. The closeness of brotherly and sisterly relationships was set by age and sex differentials. We were brothers and sisters but probably didn't fully realise the value of blood ties in the face of friendships which were formed outwith the family. But in the 1960s, we were all young with little or no real sense of who we were as individuals, yet alone our relationships and values as a family.

We were not rich and famous, but we were a happy lot with a Mum and Dad who provided and cared for us. There were the occasional 'fall-outs,' 'rows' and a few 'skelps' here and there, but we knew a 'skelp' or belt from Dad was for our own good or we deserved it – that was normal to us. When we, five or six brothers and sisters, had caused a 'rammy,' the trick was not to be top of the heap but bottom of the heap, as this left less of you to be 'skelped.' The cry was '*that was your fault*' as calm and order was restored by Dad.

We didn't have a lot, but we had the love and support of Mum and Dad and nowadays, those seem to be exceptional traits, as 'star' after 'rising star' or 'falling star' seem to have managed it to 'the top' through and despite having parents from Hell. Still, I suppose some of these 'revelations' are true and I suppose some of these things sell books. Genuine abuse is as hard to comprehend and abhorrent as is abuse of the genuine.

Wiliam Watt: My Great, Great Grandfather in a Abraham Lincoln statesman-like pose.

Top: 'Wee Jock' (Bottom Left) preparing for The Great War
Bottom: Loudoun Hill, a volcanic plug to the east of Darvel

Left: Dad aged 5
Right: Dad 'the piper'

Mum and Dad – married on 31st March 1948

CHAPTER TWO

Friends, Football, Flares & France

Newmilns, like every Scottish town, has its 'character families,' and in this case, it was the home of the Ferries, the Gilmours, the Kilties, the Spences and Johnnie 'Borrie.' These 'characters' and 'character families' were not 'families from Hell,' but individuals and families with 'old-fashioned' 'character.'

Character could be a trait, talent or skill, which had come to characterise an individual or even the whole family. They were 'lovable rogues,' 'rough diamonds,' or simply 'gallus' – they had a bit of spirit, a sense of humour and a bit of get up and go about them – they were not 'beige people' who melted into life's canvas; they were upfront and admired, even if grudgingly admired. A lot of these characters still frequent the Valley, a bit greyer with age but still more colourful than their counterparts in yesteryear and still holding the attention of the younger generation, who recognise the story, if not the true character of the individual.

In 1969, the Newmilns Secondary School became home of the senior school pupils from Darvel. Junior Secondary Schools were on the way out and through consolidation and amalgamation of school rolls, new academies spawned. The Newmilns School has long since been demolished and is now the home of the dry ski slope, but it was there I encountered – "Wee Eck" (Alex Wallace), the history teacher. The pipe-smoking Wee Eck was well regarded, but nevertheless, prone to some micky-taking, including being locked out of his own class.

His entrance after one such lock-out was like a scene from Aladdin – huge puffs of 'chalk-dust' filled the air, or so it appeared, until the cry went up, "Sir, your pocket's on fire." He never again forced the door with his Swan Vestas matches in his jacket pocket, but he kept the same jacket, complete with leather patch over the 'smoking' pocket.

The big family became the biggest family in Darvel as, after Yvonne, Davy – David Gordon; Colin – Colin Cameron; Avril – Avril Allison Ogilvie, and finally, Graham – Graham Anderson, came along. We were then thirteen, including mum and dad – a football team plus two subs. I was slap-bang in the middle, with three elder sisters and two elder brothers; two younger sisters and three younger brothers. At the peak of our numbers at Hillcrest, the "boys' room" had a double bed, a single bed and two bunk beds, in order to sleep all six brothers. The girls' room was slightly less crowded as Lilian left the nest to marry at a fairly early age, so at it's peak, it really had only four occupants.

Hillcrest, like most houses then, had no central heating. Each room had a coal fire-place but only the living room and the Raeburn in the kitchen had coal in them to heat the whole house. 'Frosted glass' was therefore a winter feature of not just the bathroom window but all the bedrooms as the cold of winter was reflected in the icing of the windows on the inside!

TVs were pretty rare and colour TVs were rarer, but John Logie Baird's brilliance was reflected in the Rodgers' living room in colour in the late 1960s. 'Bill and Ben, the Flowerpot Men;' 'Tales from the Riverbank;' 'Andy Pandy,' gave way to 'Blue Peter;' 'Dixon of Dock Green;' 'The White Heather Club' and 'Para Handy,' and eventually, the advent of BBC2 and American TV shows like 'The High Chaparral.' TV was a great source of leisure and a bit of learning.

At work in the cemetery Dad took a great pride in seeing that the plots (grass) were cut neat and tidy and the rows of plots were as level as possible, by backfilling newer graves, which sunk when the earth recently returned to the graves compacted.

Helping my dad in the cemetery was a natural way of helping pay back my mum and dad's support. After all, if it was good enough for Rod Stewart, it was good enough for me. We could fill in a grave in about twenty-five minutes and have the wreaths neatly positioned, ready for the relatives and friends returning to see them. The heavy roller on the ATCO mower gave the grass those straight lines which you rarely see nowadays, except on bowling greens and some football pitches. The old tell-tale lines were erased as the roller mower succumbed to "less bother with a hover."

Filling in graves and cutting grass was a breeze, but digging a grave by hand was hard, sweaty work. Even in death I think I would get claustrophobic in my wooden suit and therefore, it's the crematorium for me (when I go!?!) A hole, six feet deep by around two feet wide at "the shoulders" is not much room to work in and the deeper you go, the harder it is to throw the dirt out. New graves go to six feet and 're-opens' to about four feet, six inches. I liked digging the graves but my dad would only let me dig down to about four feet before he would finish it off. Keen to finish off the digging for my dad, on a day he had hurt his back quite badly, I kept digging to finish the job. It was a 're-open' and I came to the lid of the coffin of the previous burial. This was obviously deep enough, so I started to 'square off the shoulders' and sides, when I suddenly dropped a good foot into the grave which filled with musty air. I was mortified and was out of the hole like a sprinter out of running blocks – only vertically. The lid of the first coffin, after twenty years in the ground, had given way – after that, I wasn't too keen to dig beyond four feet.

Mum went up and down the street every day, except Sunday, and 'lugged' messages all week. Friday, being pay day, was special and fruit and bars of 'five-boys chocolate' could be had. Instead of a fridge or a freezer, in those days we had a 'pantry.' It was the equivalent of a large walk-in wardrobe for storing food. Ground space would be used for potatoes (normally half a hundred weight, or fifty-six pounds, or twenty-five kilos in 'Euro currency'), carrots, turnips and other vegetables. The lower, cooler shelves would be reserved for meat and fish, and cereals and items used regularly would be at hand or eye level shelves for ease of use. Cooking was a major activity for my mum and most of it in the early days was done on the Raeburn, a sort of coal-fired cooker which also served to heat up the kitchen where, on the pulley, damp clothes would also be dried.

Food or fruit was the last thing on our minds when we received a huge parcel from my cousin William, who was serving with the RAF in Gan, an island in the Indian Ocean. But the bugger had downed a coconut, complete with husks, and sent it to us in a box. William is Margaret's boy (mum's sister) and he is a bit special, even if the coconut was a bit of an anti-climax – but I don't suppose there were many gift shops on Gan.

Kilmarnock Football Club versus Leeds United in the Fairs Cup in 1967 was the first senior football match I ever attended. Killie were at their peak and the ground seemed filled to capacity. The game passed me by as I jostled and jumped up and down – not in celebration of a goal, but in an effort to get a glance of the park and players. All seated stadiums definitely benefit the 'wee man.'

Adolescence is a funny thing and I think I knew I was in it when I paid more attention to the new French student teacher's legs than her lessons – and I liked French! It was then French ceased to be a language and became a kiss. It's about this time that boys experience 'learning difficulties' and girls experience difficult boys. Adolescence was all the more pronounced when we moved to Newmilns School and there were a whole new range of female faces and figures to contend with.

Discos at the Club (Darvel Juniors' Social Club, now demolished), Boy Scouts, Girl Guides and birthday parties all provided opportunities to slow dance to "Je t'aime", 10cc's "I'm Not In Love" etc, etc and have a good snog on the way home or to the bus stop. It was like underwater swimming, without the snorkel – you just held your breath and went for it.

Our immediate family reached its peak but we acquired an extended family as Lilian married wee Duncan McTavish. Marlene, after 'going out' with a few guys – including one who was deaf (I should add that he was deaf *before* he met Marlene) – married big Frank Best from Galston –now there's a change from wee Jock, wee Eck, wee Kenny! Elaine married Alistair McKie and that became an extended family in itself, as there were eight (Jack, Alistair, George, Andy, Margaret, Mary, Susan and Morag) in Alistair's immediate family. Jim and Jessie tied the knot on 26th September 1975 – a significant date for reasons yet to unfold. Too young to attend the first two weddings of Lilian and Duncan and Marlene and Frank, I was in Gowanbank Hotel in Darvel to see Elaine and Alistair married and at Crofthead Farm Restaurant for Jim and Jessie's wedding. Bobby and myself ended up legless at Jim and Jessie's 'do' as we raced 'hauf for hauf' and later adjourned to Hillcrest with the family only to throw up and awake to a massive hangover.

Even in the 1970s, Scotland was enlightened when it came to a question of where and when people could be married. Next to the 'Best Man,' the Minister was the 'main man' in terms of agreeing to particular locations for weddings.

Gowanbank Hotel was originally the ancestral home of the Morton's who were instrumental in establishing the lace manufacturing in Darvel.

Crofthead Farm and Restaurant is no more, as 'green belt' was buckled by houses to form part of the hamlet of Priestland.

The location of these marriages in a sense was absolutely meaningless – it was all about what was shared then between the bride and groom and how it would stand the test of time, fortune, family and forbearance that really mattered.

My mum is absolutely Christian in her values but literally had little time for those that Robert Burns epitomised in "Holy Willie's Prayer." Living the life was more important than being there on a Sunday and singing the song in your finest apparel. My mum of course would not actually say this, but I have no such sensitivities. That is not to say there were not and are not genuine Christian people about – even in Darvel. One of those was undoubtedly Mr Collins, who stayed at the Manse. He was the Minister who married most of our family. He was a *real* Christian, but a hellish driver, from whom even folk on crutches would refuse a lift!

As he drove along the road, he would attend to his flock – he would wave to Mrs Anderson; beckon to Johnnie James and move to greet the new Rodgers' baby on the other side of the road. God knows how he passed his test and God must have kept a powerful eye on him, because for all of his motoring meanderings, he was only involved in two minor accidents in his red Mini. Collins Court now stands near the centre of Darvel and is fittingly named in memory of Mr Collins, who is our, and Scotland's, longest-serving Parish Minister ever – and ever, Amen.

In 1971, I ventured to 'L.A.' as that was the year the brand, spanking (or belting) Loudoun Academy opened its doors (on 26 February 1971) to the cream of the learning talent from Darvel, Newmilns, Galston and Hurlford. If Galston was the "historical heart of Ayrshire and the home of the Campbells of Loudoun Castle," Hurlford struck fear into the heart of Ayrshire, and was the home of Big Joe Haining, Widzy, the Hamiltons and the McCanns. This is of course the stuff local legends are made of and Hurlford is the equal of any of the Irvine Valley towns. Perception is however reality and the perception was that Hurlford was viewed as a rough and tough town, but with good people in it, who had lovely daughters who were much sought after by 'gentlemen' from the 'higher-level' Valley towns – particularly Darvel?!

Apart from Elaine's stint at College, no Rodgers had stayed on at school beyond the earliest leaving date. There were jobs out there and the money was needed in the house. My decision to stay on at school was never questioned by mum and dad, just supported. In the scheme of things anyway, if I had left school then I would have been destined to become a 'candlestick maker;' after all, Bobby was a butcher with William Allans and Sons, Jim a baker with the Co-op, so that only left the one occupation according to the old nursery rhyme. On the female side of the family, Lilian had started a family of her own, Marlene worked in the lace industry in Jock Aird's factory, and Elaine became a Secretary within BMK in Kilmarnock (the once world renowned carpet makers).

Jobs were the last thing on my mind as we lined up against "The Jo's" (St Joseph's Academy, Kilmarnock) in the final of the Ayrshire Cup at Rugby Park, home of Kilmarnock FC. Big Jim McFadzean, one of the 1965 League Winners' legends, had decked us out in an old black and white hooped Ayr United strip, which reached my knees. On a winter's day it would have made a great "willie–warmer" but on a summer's evening it was a "sweater!" Still, some of us 'froze' on the evening and The Jo's deservedly won 3-0 with Paddy Brolly, Michael Joyce running the show. It was really hard to take the defeat but my days with Ernie 'Broon's' Youth Club football team should have prepared me for it. Penalty misses are even harder to take, especially when it is down to you and in the Youth Club Cup Final, I had missed a penalty to win the game, and Tony Wright missed the penalty to lose the game. The school Cup Final was worse than that, with family, friends and fellow pupils all turning out for the game. Still, we received a standing ovation at the assembly the next day.

Sport (unlike today it seems) featured very strongly in school life – everything from football, rugby, running, cross-country running, basketball, volleyball and even cricket. Everything but swimming, which was out of my league – forty-five feet of my fifty feet swimming badge was underwater and I think I walked twenty of those! Fortunately, the sports championship was decided on 'terra firma' and following on from John and Hugh Collins, Kenny Mann and myself became the Senior Boys Sports Champions in 1974. It was competitive 'stuff' - you ran a race to win it, not just to be in it. Other kids with less sporting prowess had talents to demonstrate, be it academically, in art, music, chess – these talents were honed and exhibited in a competitive environment, not in a world of over-protective 'everyone's a winner' mediocre mentality. Everyone's a winner if they compete and develop whatever talent they believe they have.

1973/4 was also a good year for football. As 16-year olds, Tony Wright and myself (that well-known penalty missing double act) joined Newmilns Vesuvius Amateurs. It was a star 'studded' line up, including Jackie and Benny Ferrie, Billy Fulton, John Guild, Billy and Andy McMillan, Rab Struthers, Jock Spence and James McAllister – among others. The mighty Knockentiber (the 'Tiber) were trounced 4-2 as Vesuvius lifted the Ayrshire Cup. Tony and me didn't feature (probably for fear of going to penalties), but "we were there," and we were part of it – including the celebrations in the Crown Hotel in Newmilns.

"We were there" was also the cry for the Scotland vs Czechoslovakia game in 1973, when big Jim Holton and Joe Jordan did the business and got Scotland through to the World Cup Finals. The experience of the hair on the back of your head standing on edge in national pride and fervour is one to be savoured, but someone pissing down the back of your jacket and legs is not (although the hot sensation at the start is not entirely unpleasant!).

Scarborough was the first place I went on holiday to, other than visiting relatives for one or two days. This was neither surprising nor disappointing – we would have needed a 10 or 12-berth caravan if we were all to go on holiday together. Steve Fullarton's (aka Big Steve) mum and dad took us to the delights of Scarborough. The bed and breakfast place was conveniently situated over the pub and there was a fish and chip shop just down the road. This could probably be said for every B&B in Scarborough, but at the time, it seemed unique. The "shows," the gardens and Robin Hood's Bay (I'm assured he came out of Sherwood Forest and stripped to his Lincoln green trunks just outside Scarborough) were all the source of enjoyment. Yet the evenings were a source of mystery – would we get served in a pub? No chance! Would we pull the burdz? Very little chance! Would we try and fail? Every chance! Having tried and failed on both 'pubbing' and 'pulling,' we resorted to the picture house. We got into an 'X-rated' picture without a dirty 'Mac' and watched the 'menage-a-trois' unfold – big Steve was baffled but luckily, I had stuck in at French. As the lights went up and we tried to creep out with the other creeps, we spied two smashing young 'lassies,'who would obviously be hot for it. Our trail in pursuit of the smashers went cold after ten minutes and we raced up the road only to get a row for being late.

Some meticulous planning the next year and the dream team (me, Alan Kerr, Stevie (Gillies), big Steve Fullerton, Colin McLaren and Melly) went by 'Golden Rail' to Bournemouth. 'Golden Rail,' now there's nostalgia for you and the modern day equivalent is probably 'Rusty or Broken Rail.' Bournemouth in the 70s was a haven for foreign students and the Bee Hive disco was a real 'honey pot.' Swedish, Norwegian and French language students were all the rage and we all had a measure of success in the language of love – some measures were bigger than others but – what the Hell.

The other side to holidays was that my mum and dad could never really take a holiday – there were all those kids to be looked after. But this changed in the early 1970s, when Marlene was old enough to look after the family when my mum and dad succumbed to the lure of Lloret de Mar, at £39 per person per week as their one and only holiday abroad (excluding Southern Ireland). My mum and dad survived the broken down coach and last gasp effort to board the plane; too much sun and food for which they had no real appetite. It was an adventure and experience with friends, but one they have never repeated, through a combination of choice and necessity. We survived a week 'home alone' with the minor crime count of – one burnt hearth carpet; one burn to Yvonne's back; one broken window; two bloody noses – Bobby 1 – Kenny 1, and a realisation of how much we missed our mum and dad.

As the time drew nearer for the seniors to leave school and we became more 'mature,' we (me, Kerr, McLaren, Stevie Gillies and a few other dubious but artistic characters) decided to give the Prefects' Room a 'makeover' – we were obviously well before our times and 'Changing Rooms,'

Nowadays, the seniors leaving school have a prom and attend in stretch limos, all dolled up to the nines. No such luck (or money) then so the 'makeover' would be our parting gift to the school and the new prefects. Andy Warhol would have been proud, as things had got out of hand. Images, expressions, cartoons and jokes adorned every wall before spray painting became regarded as 'art.' Where beige paint once reigned supreme, a rainbow of colours and rash of jokes appeared. The word got out the guys were painting the Prefects' Room red.. green.. blue.. yellow.. pink.. purple and any other colour they could get their hands on or make.

Sitting happy and in a state of near post-coital contentment (which you could tell from the whiff of smoke in the room), we surveyed our finished work. Genius, sheer, bloody genius!? Then the SAS in the shape of Mr Paton (the Deputy Head) and two of his Stormtroopers bounded in unannounced, uninvited and unwelcome, but also unimpressed. They were at the same time amazed and aghast at the sight which befell them. Paton shook his head in anguish and despair and looked to the heavens (ceiling) for salvation, only to see a huge nude figure winking back at him in all her glory.

Our Prefects badges were duly surrendered and the room was locked until the painters could restore the décor, or even the decorum. It was rumoured that the teachers were given guided tours of the room and at least some of them were impressed by the artwork and others learned a whole new range of words and phrases. The room was restored to its brilliant beige best and refilled with 'beige people' as Billy Connolly would have it.

With seven 'O' levels (six As and one B) and five Highers (four Bs and one C), sealed and delivered by Royal Mail, my ambition was to be a 'drillie.' Jordanhill College offered a Diploma in Physical Education to a very limited number of applicants each year and, at 17, I sought out one of the places. Having been told to return the following year and get an eyesight test, I discovered that time and the glasses helped my myopia, both in terms of sight and future opportunities. Jordanhill would not be the subject of a future attempted entry, as Edinburgh, Glasgow and Strathclyde Universities were all assessed as future places of academic study. The grey matter was exercised as to which of these proud institutions would be my 'alma mater,' and, in the end, after a further year at Loudoun completing Sixth year Studies (English and History), I plumped for Glasgow. It had a good pedigree and more of my mates were going there anyway.

These years of learning was summarised in three bits of paper – passports to learning which spoke a bit for you but portrayed none of the struggle behind their acquisition. Mum and dad were the foundations of my learning, their support fuelled my ambition 'to go on.' Significant contributors to my learning and development at Loudoun were Big Jim McFadzean; Dunky McBean; Wee Eck; and Bill Clark, who in his John Noakes-style grey/green Mini Clubman, in true Blue Peter style, used to shepherd us all over the country in our games for Kilmarnock Hockey Club. Other characters included Rab Ellis and Mr Paton, who were 'real belters' with a wicked sense of timing, i.e. for catching you 'at it.' Back then, as now, the perennial problem for teachers was how to gain the respect of pupils without losing authority and academic achievement. Teachers then, as now, and not surprisingly, seemed to be an educational extension of their own personalities. The dull and grey people taught in dull and grey and those with a zest for life reflected this in their lessons.

Hockey, with the support of Bill Clark and the PE team, really took off at Loudoun from being a girls' game to a fast and skilful male pursuit. Casper, big Fully, Stevie Gillies, Kenny Hunter, Kerr, Kenny Mann, Melly and myself were all part of the once thriving Kilmarnock Hockey Club, which played in the national leagues up until the late seventies. Hockey was also a sociable sport, so we began drinking 'a little' to be sociable and the more we played, the more sociable we became. Selection for South West Scotland U18 followed but the full Scotland jersey and cap eluded the two or three of us in the Regional team. Sociality can have its price!

Leaving Loudoun was funny, sad and totally unheralded; no fanfare, no celebration – just out there and no going back. The comfort of the local red brick was about to be exchanged for the queries in the quadrangle at Glasgow University. As far as Loudoun Academy was concerned, I was history and a new chapter was about to begin at the Uni.

The Western SMT bus drew into Anderson Street Bus Station in September 1975 (I think it had left Darvel sometime in August!). Stevie Gillies and myself, luggage in hand, jump off to climb up the north face of Blythswood Street and seek out Dalrymple Hall of Residence on Belhaven Terrace, just off Great Western Road. The Botanical Gardens, Westerlands Sports grounds, the BBC at Queen Margaret Drive, Byres Road, the Grosvenor Hotel, Studio 1, Queen Margaret Union and Glasgow University Union, were all within staggering distance of 'the Hall.'

Initially, the lure of home and long-standing friends was pretty strong, but new friendships were soon established and activities and relationships were formed, which meant returning home each weekend became less and less a feature. Friends at home became fewer and 'more distant.' Memories that tethered old friendships together were set loose in the face of new friendships, which thrived on being flung together from the four corners of Ayrshire and beyond.

With 'brass in pocket' – in the form of the maximum grant available – Uni life would be sweet. The maximum grant with maximum deductions for Hall fees, books, meals outwith the hall, clothes etc, meant minimum spending money and ongoing reliance and support from mum and dad.

'Freshers' Week' at Uni is the week before the formal commencement of one's studies, during which all the new first year intakes get pissed and get the piss taken out of them. Stevie and myself missed 'Freshers' Week' but caught up with our fellow Freshers at the Hall (at that time and all-male establishment). The 'Hall' contained a large contingent of Ayrshire men and 'Tuechters' (mainly from Dornoch, Brora, Golspie and Helmsdale) in about equal measure and this largely set the tone of the activities in the Hall. The main characters soon emerged – Big Al (the goalie – better than Andy Goram but a 'ginger' or 'fair-headed ginger'). Horm and wee Jimmy (Horm's brother) from Stewarton; Jimmy Auld; Jim the boxer from Irvine (no change there then); John McHale; John Fife; Jim McCaffrey; Sid; Horrible Joe, Paul, Steve, Charlie Mitchell, John and Willie Young (the well-known masons in the black, otherwise referred to as football referees), and The Doc (Doctor Alan Scotney) was the Hall Warden who had a penchant for fine wines and malts, which he shared in gay abandon with the 'Hall Committee' and anyone else who might be in dire need of a wee refreshment!)

Glasgow had moved on from it's 'no mean city' days and was entering 'cultural puberty,' but for all that, you could still get a 'good doin' for nothing – the cry in Glasgow's case was, "*Whit wis that fur?*" Answer: *"Don't be fuckin cheeky or I'll gie ye whit fur*!" Five years residence in Glasgow produced one good' tanning' (not of the Tommy Sheridan variety) and two near misses.

Scene 1, Take 1 - Wearing a full-length denim coat and looking like a dick-head, whilst walking through Glasgow via the University Union early in the morning is a recipe for being set upon – and so it happened early doors in Glasgow. Me and Melly set against five hoodlums in search of a 'donation' to help them through the night. We didn't quite manage to talk them into giving us money but persuaded them we were as skint as they were and narrowly avoided a kicking on a sympathy vote.

Ingredients for a party success include plenty of booze, women, spacious accommodation, some food and decent music. Scene 2, Take 1 - At John Dempster's flat, we had the lot – it would be a good night. Things to avoid even at a good party in Glasgow – letting gatecrashers in; wearing a green shirt, and having the temerity to ask a 'big yin' to 'cool it,' a la Henry Kissinger. The party gear was jeans and my bright green Kilmarnock Hockey Club top; the party gatecrasher was a 'big bruiser' but seemed a nice guy in the very dimly lit lounge. The kitchen was the stock area for the booze and was brightly lit, and true to form, there's always a 'party in the kitchen.' *"Hey you." "Who me?" "Yeah you, fuck face – were you wearing that green fuckin' rag when I was talking to you?" "Aye, how? Do you think I've got a wardrobe to make a quick change at parties?"* Gulp, my mistake trying wit and charm. *"Ya cheeky wee bastard, whit are ye wearin' that fur?" "It's just a shirt – what's the problem?"* Gulp, mistake number two, as 'love mum/dad' and 'love Rangers' tattoos become evident. Beat hasty retreat to dimly lit lounge area and melt back in with the crowd. All quiet?! Back through to the kitchen for a beer, oh no, the big bigot's having a go at Melly and the party host, who politely asked, *"Who invited you anyway?"* The big bigot struggles with a name and starts to turn nasty. *"I'll do the pair of you."* Enter yours truly – *"Cool it, big man, nae hassle?"* and a bottle meant for me cracks open Johns' head as I duck and he steps forward. The big man holds the top of the broken bottle and seems to attempt the New Zealand 'haka' to ward off anyone crazy enough to approach him or try and prevent him leaving – he drops his weapon and flees. The police and ambulance attend, just another Saturday night scene in Glasgow and the 'big bigot' retreats to his lair.

Ingredients of almost certain party failure are too few (good-looking) women; too many guys; some more guys without a carry-out, and some mean guys with a carry-out, who don't feel much like sharing it voluntarily.

Scene 3, take 1 – another victory at the 5-asides and a few beers downed and big Broon knows where there's a party he can get us into along Great Western Road – no problem. Broon, John Fyfe, Big Al, Jim McCaffrey, Horrible Joe and yours truly – minus carry-out, gain entry to the 'party.' It was dire, even before 'Dire Straights' became famous – essential ingredients were all missing and it had all the ingredients for some 'stag rutting' - there was going to be trouble. We 'sneaked' a can each and when rumbled, claimed it as our own – the scene was set – out of the blue corner emerged a tough guy from Ayrshire and it wasn't me. Faced with 'flight or fight,' I chose fight, but only after the tough guy and two of his mates had set about me. A punch and two boots to my head were shrugged off as Fyfe came to the rescue and dived on the back of one of the assailants. The hearth of the open coal fire seemed like a good place to get rid of the other two assailants and, whilst 'shite doesn't burn,' it fairly melts with the heat.

Calm was restored and we strolled back to Dalrymple. My face felt like a £100 bill had been accrued in the dentist's chair, as my lips, jaws, and gradually my eyes, all swelled up and numbed. *"You're not looking too smart, Kenny; is it sore?"* says the concerned Jim. *"I'm o.... and f.....f....but.........,"* I replied.

Early morning light brought the realisation that I would not have looked out of place at the Panda's party in the zoo. The foot mark on my forehead indicated the assailant was a size 10, and was unlikely to be a fan of hush puppies. I missed three days of lectures and tutorials as I couldn't face the outside world with a face which had all hallmarks and heelmarks of amateur cosmetic surgery. Paul the vet (he may have been a doctor) gave me some cream to take away the swelling and remove the multi-coloured bruising from my head and face.

As luck would have it, my 'kickin' coincided with the end of my relationship with a 'big blonde' (at least 5'6") from the Scottish History class, who was less than impressed by my juvenile joustings. In my three-day recuperation at the Hall, the bitch had taken up with a tall, aristocratic, artistic arsehole and dumped me. Scottish History is littered with such personal feuds and treachery!

The natural progression was from street fighting to the 'noble art' and Queensbury Rules. Boxing training was the hardest and most gruelling physical training I have been involved in. After six months of pugilist purgatory, my big nose, big ears and big teeth finally hit home to me – I already had all the attributes of a beaten boxer, so why not cut out the middle man and stop boxing?

Westerlands Sports Ground was the place to be for the sporty types at Uni. Now it's the place to be for those who can afford the houses, subsequently built there. Probably nearing the peak of my physical fitness, I joined a group of sprinters for training, under an up and coming coach called Frank Dick. 200 metre sets were recorded at under twenty-five seconds, with increasing rest periods, as the repetition increased. No-one in this group could reach the speed, elegance and stamina of the tall, dark-haired figure who finished the session as strong as he had started, whilst all others trailed in his wake – sharp by name and Sharp by nature, Cameron Sharp was a flying machine and in a league of his own. Yet he had no peacock strut or disdainful glance for his toiling competitors. He knew he was miles better than us even in a 200-metre race, but he didn't rub it in. His sights and training were set on winning European and Commonwealth medals, rather than University championships.

That one memorable training session taught me I'd never be a sprinter and so instead, I became a javelin thrower!? If I had little to support even an amateur career in the boxing ring, or running, then I had even less to support my aspirations in the javelin – I was almost 5ft 7 ½ ins short and then weighed 10 ½ stones. The training sessions at Westerlands ended and getting a javelin home to Darvel to continue my training was no mean feat. The first leg of the journey was completed when Mark Brodie's dad dropped me off at Brodie's Wee Thack in Kilmarnock (now the Brass and Granite). Looking like an extra from *Zulu*, I sauntered through Kilmarnock to the bus station, where the great debate ensued as to the javelin's eligibility to travel; the appropriate fare for the javelin, if it was eligible to travel? *"Right son, let's go"* and the silver spear was slotted along the length of the parcel shelf on the single decker at no cost – common sense prevailed. Third place at the Uni championships ended my javelin-throwing career.

Hampden Park, Glasgow, was the scene for the Scottish Junior Cup Final on 24 April 1976. Proud as punch I paid my 50p admission to the terraces and joined the Darvel contingent of the 20,161 spectators. I was there – I was there to watch 'Bo'ness beat brave little Darvel' 3-0. Darvel Juniors Social Club was a heaving mass of blue and white as the commiserations extended into the early hours of the morning as the reality of defeat dawned.

Hamilton College Football Park was the scene for the final of the 1977 McEnhill Cup Final between Hamilton College and Dalrymple Hall. There was no entry fee and we were watched by about 80 students and the obligatory 'dug.'

A determined Dalrymple Hall lifted the cup and in the 'Rock' off Byers Road, it was filled with whisky, vodka, lager Guinness and laughter. We won the cup! In 1978, we endeavoured to repeat the feat and came up against the oddly-named NECROS, who turned out to be more deadly in front of goal than Dalrymple. We lost the cup!

In 1977/8, the Glasgow Colleges Football Association (whose President was the aptly-named Tommy Docherty) proclaimed:-

"The McEnhill Cup Final involved the intriguing clash between NECROS, the new league champions in their first season in the First Division, and Dalrymple, the McEnhill Cup holders. NECROS First Division experience counted in the end and the Second Division team had to settle for second place in the competition which they have come to think of (with some justification) as their own."

Football trials at Jordanhill College, Glasgow, for the Glasgow College Select to play a Dutch team turned from the ecstasy of selection to the agony of realising torn knee ligaments meant the Dutch dream was over before it really began.

Social life at Uni was a mixture of feast and famine, interspersed with exams. At the start of the term, money seemed to be no object and exams seemed a long way off. It was time to live a little and the circle of 'bon viveurs' was large. As grants turned to debt and exams clouded the horizon, only the intelligent rich or the doomed to failure could maintain the social pace.

In the late 1970s, the pace of life seemed to quicken and change became the order of the day. Still, some things don't seem to change, as twenty-five years after the 'Green Goddesses' took to the streets in 1977, history has repeated itself with a second period of strike action by the Fire Brigades Union members. Back in January 1978, the Studio One bar off Byres Road, at the tip adjoining Great Western Road and the Grosvenor Hotel, was a favourite watering hole of the lads. In the early part of the first strike, it became a hole with water in it, as the valiant army firefighters failed to douse the initial flames and the fire took hold in the Grosvenor Hotel before being finally put out.

The world was further 'shaken up' after Elvis died on 16 August 1977.

However, 1978 also became a 'quiz question' year, as three popes died that year – John Paul I after only thirty-three days in office.

As ever, it was a case of 'out with the old and in with the new' as the first test-tube baby was born in Oldham General Hospital in 1978.

The University Union (male dominated) and the Queen Margaret Union (female orientated) were the haunts of many a famous or infamous act. John Martyn went close to electrocuting himself on stage at the QMU and that was the highlight of the night. Hedgehog Pie was well remembered – if only for their name but Be Bop Deluxe at the GUU were magic, in a haze of sweet-smelling smoke; but funnily enough, their album was less impressive when listened to in a smoke-free environment! The GUU was also the early husting ground for young Charles Kennedy, current leader of the Liberal Democrats.

Punk music also spat onto the stage as safety pins and black bin bags became 'oh so pretty.' If music has to go 'underground,' and reinvent itself every now and then, punk should have stayed there, or more accurately, most punks should have stayed there!

Taking a trip down memory lane can be refreshing, but with Glasgow's Asian influence, especially in the West End, we were encouraged to take a trip down 'Curry Alley;' – Gibson Street. The Kohinoor, the Taj Mahal all seduced students with the prospect of a hot, spicy, cheap meal and a late drink. Be it a bhoona, madras or vindaloo, no self-respecting student staying in the West End of Glasgow could avoid the curry houses.

The 'modus operandi' was to go out for a few pints (six to eight was advisable if you were a 'vindaloo virgin'); fail to 'get off' with anyone and drown your sorrows a bit more, then descend upon the curry house of your choice or, more accurately, the one you could afford.

The 'Koh' was the scene for Kerr's 21st birthday celebrations (now a celebrated lawyer in Kilmarnock!) It was a low-key affair – me and him! A few pints and an invitation to have a curry on him, I presumed. In the back of the 'Koh' the lamb bhoona was scoffed and a few pints more downed, when Kerr declares, *"How much have you got? I don't think I can cover this – we'll do a runner."* *"Hold on, let's check; get the bill and then make a move,"* I whispered, in a tone Quasi Modo could have heard above the bells. The bill is duly obtained and two pound notes quickly turn into four, through a strategic ripping and placing of change, we "covered" the bill. No sooner had the money been 'double counted' and the birthday boy was out of the back room and gaining freedom at the main door. I followed and we laughed as the great escape had been brilliantly executed, without the aid of a motorbike. Ten yards from the Koh, the laughing stopped, as two waiters and a cook challenged our arithmetic and invited us to return to the Koh. A brief exchange of karate moves devoid of any contact and we legged it – we'd saved two pounds and been on the run two minutes after leaving the Koh, surely a record! Curries at the Koh were off the menu for a time after that.

Studying, or lack of studying, like restaurant waiters, eventually catches up with you. The book mileage and library silence pain barrier has to be gone through for the vast bulk of students. My Modern History and Scottish History Joint Highers Degree was exchanged for Political Economy (Economics) and Modern History, as the reality of two years of study began to bite – do you want to be history teacher? Answer – no. Then why the hell are you continuing with two history options? Answer – Political Economy (Economics). There were no problems with an ordinary degree and I could secure that in the normal three years, but the switch to Economics, part way through, meant a five-year (honours) course. Five years on top of 'O' levels and Highers meant my mum and dad had an extra burden for seven years beyond the norm of leaving school at sixteen, and with no return in sight. It was never questioned, never queried and always supported.

Members of the aristocracy in the 18th century were renowned for embarking on the 'Grand Tour' to seek enlightenment at first hand. Not to be outdone, Melly (Gordon Melrose) and myself embarked on our own 'Tour de France' – we would hitchhike round France in search of 'je ne sais quois.'

A lift to and overnight stay at Melly's sister and brother-in-law's house in Hinkley (the centre of England) got us off to a free and flying start. Sixty fags secured a lift to Portsmouth and we were St Malo bound on the evening ferry. We were 'cool' as everyone scurried on board, no hassle, there was space for everyone. The reality was that good space was at a premium and on a first come, first served basis. We endured the crossing on deck, sprawled between wooden chairs with the sky and newspapers for blankets – boy we were 'cool.'

We got our bearings and stretched our legs out through the quaintly quaint St Malo until we were on the open French autoroutes, thumbing a lift anywhere, from anyone. The North of France was beautiful, with no appearance of affluence or industry. It was a relief from the West of Scotland, both in terms of the rural setting and the weather. Lifts in the North of France came fairly readily, even to two foreign blokes with big rucksacks. The French people there were open, communicative and generous. From St Malo, the happy wanderers went via Rheims and Nantes to St Jean de Monts. In our 'desire' to get somewhere, we went through Rheims and Nantes like an invading (or retreating) army and paid scant attention to their architecture or attractions. We reached our first destination at sundown and gazed along a long, sandy beach. This was a pleasure beach without the Blackpool distractions. This would do for us - if we could find somewhere to pitch the tent. Neither of us were boy scouts, so pitching the tent in a small wooded area, about a mile from the beach, in darkness, was a major achievement.

Early the next day, my French studies at Uni paid off, as we bought wine, cheese, bread and fruit and made our way to the beach, which had the night before seemed full of 'evening promise.' St Jean de Monts was a million miles from Darvel, and even further from Galston – by midday, the beach and cafes were filling up with French fillies. We set up our al fresco picnic halfway along the beach, near to the freshwater shower area. The shower drew some unexpected benefits, as the 'jeune filles' retired from the beach for lunch. It was the first beach I had been on, where the girls went topless and the water from the shower was obviously very cold – our picnic by the shower lasted much longer than our food and drink! As night fell, we enjoyed a beer and some smattered French conversation with the 'locals,' from all over France, until the topic came round to where we were staying. Shit, the tent and our rucksacks were still in the woods, hopefully! A swift return and check and all was well, life was good in St Jean de Monts.

St Jean de Monts was pure relaxation, but after three days, the wanderlust was on us and we hit the road again. We hitched it to a campsite at La Rochelle, with its 'twin turrets' at the harbour entrance. After two days of taking in the sights and forking out on campsite fees, we moved on, to Bordeaux. Bordeaux was a world of difference from St Jean de Monts and La Rochelle and the Youth Hostel was a riot of nationalities, all trying to speak and impress each other, all at once. The linen and our bunks were secured and we enjoyed a chicken and chips set meal, with a bottle of Bordeaux. A brightly-lit shop drew our attention and we floated into it like moths to a light bulb. It was a 'sweetie shop,' or at least, an adult sweetie shop and we fluttered round it, bumping into customers as our attention was drawn to an array of gismos and gadgets. It was the first sex shop I'd ever been in. Some of the rubber, leather and silk gear was so far out I could only imagine that the nuns in France were wearing the equivalent of Anne Summers party gear. Scotland, or so it seemed to us, was a mere backwater when it came to sex shops. We stayed long enough to satisfy our curiosity, but not long enough to let anyone think we were 'queer' – anyway, none of us wore earrings. 'Queer as folk' certainly took on a new meaning after our saunter through the sex shop.

Lifts were getting harder and harder to secure as we moved south and although the cars on the road seemed to be bigger and more expensive, the drivers were decidedly discerning when it came to picking up two male hitch hikers with their rucksacks. The old trick of one hitching at the road and the other out of immediate sight worked a treat (after eight hours!) and we arrived at Cassis after skirting through the menacing Marseilles and an overnight stay in Sete. With no obvious place to pitch a tent in Cassis, we followed the wooden cross AJ signs in search of the Youth Hostel. The wide dirt road became a narrow, rocky track and then a goat path and, after forty minutes, we saw the Youth Hostel in the distance, and looked back to what must be some of the best views in France – rockscapes, caves and trees, dropping back to the blue Mediterranean sea – artists could have a field day, so to speak.

We were parched and in my best attempt at French, I asked where we could get a drink of water. *"Over there, second door on the right, straight through and first door on the left."* Melly sat on a small wall, catching his breath, as I followed the directions given. I sipped water from a drinking fountain as I realised I was in a shower unit – a shower unit from which the most beautiful girl emerged 'starkers.' Ca va, I gasped and continued to drink and drink and drink. Ca va bien, indeed. 'Starkers' is a particularly Scottish word, but it doesn't do credit to this French masterpiece. In my mind's eye and memory, she was a 36-24-36 brunette, shaking rivulets of water from her frame, before the towel was grasped and patted to her body. I recall she was 'an evenly roasted chicken' with none of the usual 'white bits' to break her overall tan and this just added to the sleek continuity of her natural body curves.

I emerged in the sunlight to a burst of laughter, which even Melly joined in – it had been a set-up. In our three days at Cassis, I only ever saw my vision of loveliness once – it turned out she was the hostel manager's wife and he was a big guy, so it was a case of dream on and move on.

Strasbourg, now the home of the European Parliament, was our next real stop. It had real character and was really expensive, even then. We curtailed our cultural tours and made off in search of a lift.

We were dropped off on the outskirts of Saarbruken, which is on the French-German border and as darkness fell, we found a right quiet, grassy spot, with some shrubbery all round. It felt as if we have hardly slept at all, when the nice quiet spot became noisier and noisier. Curiosity got the better of me. I ambled off in a state of undress, through the shrubbery to discover we have pitched the tent on a huge roundabout! Still, it was the ideal place to recommence our hitch hiking!

We had started our 'grand tour' with around £80 and needed about £20 to get a Transalpino train ticket from Paris, ferry crossing to Dover, and train to London, where Melly's brother would put us up for a night. After fifteen days, Youth Hostels and campsites were out of our league. With not even a "roundabout" to pitch the tent on, we made ourselves comfortable in a bus shelter on the outskirts of Saarbruken. After the initial roar of motor bikes and cars died down, we got off to sleep. The bus shelter was of the old metal style, all the way to the ground, with no gaps for cold air and only one entrance to the right of where I was sleeping. A light padding noise, interrupted by slooshing sounds on the front of the shelter, awoke me. The padding and the slooshing worked round behind me and up and down the shelter – this was weird. My first thoughts were a dog, but it soon became evident that there was at least one person involved in the activity – whatever it was, I kicked Melly awake and in my best sign language, alerted him to the potential intruder(s). By now, I was standing up with a glass bottle ready to defend myself, from whatever was out there, as it was now evident it was working its way round the shelter and was now intent on exploring the bus shelter with evil in mind!?

A tall figure moved to enter the shelter with one weapon in each hand and I rose to the challenge; *"Whit the fuck do you think you're doing?"* – my command of French had temporarily left me. The guy, with a bucket and brush, blurted in French we should leave the bus shelter. A quick *"Get tae fuck or I'll stick your brush up your 'derrière'"* persuaded him to leave us to our beauty sleep. A quick look with the torch revealed he had been 'decorating' the bus shelter with illegal, political posters. After that, I was convinced that "Bill stickers should be prosecuted."

A French civil engineer, visiting his relatives in Saarbruken, took us all the way to Paris and even dropped us off at the Gard du Nord, from where we could get a train to Calais and then the ferry to Dover. We arrived too late to purchase our Transalpino ticket and to secure our only remaining money for the tickets, we 'rented' a big locker to hold both rucksacks. With only a few francs in hand, we would have a crepe (pancake) and a coffee and stroll through 'gay Paree,' before sleeping in the Gard du Nord. About midnight, the station security guards pleasantly opened the doors for us to explore the city. In the café bar, I worked out we couldn't have a crepe, only coffee. This was duly ordered and we sat down, only to be faced with a bill we could not pay – with a great hullabaloo, the coffee was removed and we were told in no uncertain terms to get out. So much for French hospitality, we thought, before a bold French knight came to our rescue, bought us a beer, and explained he would put us up for the night – no problem. Halfway up the stairs to his flat, the concierge – the equivalent of the worst Blackpool landlady you can think of – said, and I quote, *"Where the fuck do you think you are going with those two twats?"* A quick sorry from the not-so-bold knight, and it was good night to the 'two twats.'

Making our way back to the Gard du Nord was an uneasy trip at 1.30am. Men in black – not Will Smith – seemed to emerge, first one to the right, then two to the left, and one behind. We were stick-out tourists and these guys looked like serious French-Algerian henchmen in full length black leather coats. The threat seemed real, and I alerted Melly, and our walk across the square quickened, so it appeared did that of the four potential assailants. The threat increased as the square began to taper off and the exit point was the likely attack point. We were worried, big time. From behind rang out *La Marseillaise* and eight French Paratroopers in full gear jumped up in our direction. *"Get fell in, Melly – stick with these guys, wherever they're going."* So we joined the 'Foreign Legion' for about two hours and the men in black leather coats merged into the darkness like some black shadows of the Gestapo in days gone by.

The rendezvous point for the Paratroopers was the Gard du Nord – a wee touch of luck at last. The station security personnel, who so politely and obligingly let us out of the station, would not allow re-entry at around 2.30am – not even armed with eight French Paratroopers. The Paras hunkered down for the remainder of the night at the entrance to the railway station and Melly and me followed suit. Snuggled together with our new-found Para friends, we had survived all that Paris could throw at us. In adversity, this was our Arc du Triumph.

An incessant tapping of metal to stone and a tap on the shoulder from the Para next to me and I realised Paris had more to throw at us. Dressed in red, real synthetic leather, stood the oldest pro from the oldest profession in the world. She gesticulated and beckoned and as each eye opened, blinked in disbelief, and closed, she moved along the 'Maginot' line. If Chris de Burgh had seen this old dear, then 'Lady in Red' would never have seen the light of day! There were no takers, but the Paras were now moved to action. A quick reconnoitre had spied an open window, which was reachable via drainpipes, up two outbuildings. One Para, two Paras, made it up and in, and just as I was thinking, I don't fancy this much, the first Para opened an emergency exit and the troops flooded in. In the warmth of the station, we relaxed and reflected on what might have been.

Transalpino came up trumps the next day, and the journey to London went off without a hitch. A phone call from Melly to his brother and we were on the right bus to go and stay with him overnight. The suggestion to get a fish supper was politely declined - the offer to pay for it was readily accepted. A cholesterol special after seventeen days on bread, cheese, fruit and wine wouldn't kill us. We hitch hiked separately and uneventfully to Scotland. We had done it and to complete our education, it was back to Uni.

If France had been a bit of a culture shock, then returning to Uni was shocking. Studying and people became more intense. For some, the Peter Pan or genial gypsy world continued; for others, finals and fiancés beckoned. The sight of the super six (me, Big Al, JY (John Young), Willie Young, Charlie Mitchell and Gus) in Shotts on a Friday afternoon at 4pm was too much for most of the locals. Dressed in our best "Saturday Night Fever" suits, with flares to sweep the streets, we swept into town in search of the Co-op Hall. Tommy Buggy, a 'ginger' and chemistry graduate, was marrying a Brazilian. Shotts Bon Accord 1, Brazil 0, an unlikely result, we thought, as we strolled through Shotts with our pre evening invitation fish suppers. *"Aye son, up the street, sandstone building on the left, up the stairs, ye canny miss it,"* and we were welcomed to a wedding which was a cross between a ceilidh and a samba - a real "Ceilamba."

The Latinos were easily recognisable from the pale-faced Buggy entourage. In the calm of the early evening, the Brazilian family sang a beautiful "lullaby of Rio" and in return, not to be outdone by 'those foreigners,' we gave a late-night rendition of 'Flower of Scotland.' Shotts Bon Accord - aye right!

In my best (only) grey suit, with wide jacket lapels and extravagant flared trousers, and full of the drink, I fancied my chances. Tommy's bride had a sister and she was gorgeous. *"Aye son, go for it"* was the cry as I tried my best dancing steps (two forward, two back) and command of the French language on the heavenly sister of the bride. No luck with the dancing, no luck with the French; *"Do you speak English,"* she enquired? *"Not very well, but I'll give it a go - I'm Kenny Rodgers, but I don't sing and you are beautiful."* The patter went downhill from there, but there was a bit of a spark and an offer of staying at Tommy's sisters, before the demon drink kicked in. *"No, I had to see the lads home."* - what a prick! A Brazilian belle on my lap, and I blew it! In your dreams, son, in your dreams!

We crammed into Gus's car and he drove back to Glasgow, as *Supertramp* blared out of the car stereo. We stopped on the way for last orders but drink and dreams had got the better of me. I was left sleeping in the car. It was a seminal moment and sign of the times; all around, people were graduating in their education and life, as engagement was followed by marriage.

On the immediate family front, things seemed normal with no big upheavals from my perspective. It was a time when I was really, in a sense, not a full part of the family. Events happened but I had no real conception on the thinking and feelings of my brothers and sisters to these events, as my contact with them had become less over my period of study at University.

I also had no real conception of how close I could have been to losing my eldest brother, Jim, who had contracted meningitis. A lumbar puncture and hospital treatment had saved his life.

By the end of the 70s, Lilian had moved to Sandford and she and Duncan had four kids. Jim and Jessie had two kids;

Marlene and Frank stayed in Galston and Lorraine was their first and only offspring. Elaine and Alister had 'Kevin the infant.' Yvonne had a job in Curtaincraft; David worked for Mappin and Webb, the jewellers in Kilmarnock, and Colin made pallets in a woodworker's yard in Newmilns. Avril and Graham were the last two at school/Loudoun Academy. Like our forefathers, there was nothing exotic, nothing absolutely unique in terms of our individual lives and careers.

A new era was about to dawn and a new (or old) political creed had been spawned. The Tories came to power - the film that followed was a 'PG' - 'personal greed.' As far as Scotland was concerned, the Tory leader, Margaret Thatcher was MT (empty) and the PT (poll tax) was unacceptable. Nevertheless, we and the nation endured eighteen years of 'Tory rule.' 'Francis of Assisi' managed to simultaneously join and split the nation(s) in one fell swoop of the archangel Thatcher.

Irrespective of political loyalties, the late 1970s changed my world and my family for ever. Being a best man at a wedding can be a nerve-racking experience and all the more so if you are on a 'semi-blind' date at the same time. Within a week or so of Stevie (Gillies) and Yvonne's (Milroy) wedding, I found myself without a partner. My sister Yvonne came to the rescue - Nancy McCulloch, who worked with Yvonne, would accompany me as best man at the wedding. We had precious little time before or even during the wedding to speak, as we were seated at separate tables in the Hunting Lodge in Kilmarnock. The 'semi-blind' date stemmed from the fact we had both been at Loudoun Academy, but Nancy was two years younger than me. The wedding went well but ended not with a dance, but with everyone retreating to their own individual house parties. Without a car, we left Stevie's mum and dad's party in full swing and set off for our buses home. It had been an eventful, uneventful day. There was no immediate spark or suggestion of romance, but enough of an attraction and interest to have 'full-sighted' date.

Mavis (Patricia) and Harry were Nancy's mum and dad and, as the "Cinderella," she had three "ugly sisters" - Trisha, Jeanette and Marion. In truth, the three would be a catch for any aspiring suitor, and the only Cinderella in Hurlford was the Cinderella Pub (now the Poacher's Rest).

In marriage terms, four daughters were a nightmare for Nancy's mum and dad, as they would have to pay for all their weddings to follow. On Armistice Day in 1977, a truce was struck and Trisha, Nancy's eldest sister, exchanged her vows with John Collins, as a long Loudoun Academy association came to fruition after years of 'winching.' Nancy was the lone bridesmaid.

The descendants of the Rodgers and McCullochs were pretty similar.

The McCulloch's generally came from smaller families (not entirely surprising, when compared to the Rodgers, although Harry was the youngest of ten), with about four or five 'a-side.' On the paternal side were the McCulloch's and the Quinns, and Marion, Nancy's youngest sister, was named after her grandmother, Marion Quinn. On the maternal side were the Moodie's in the form of Alexander Moodie (Papa Sanny) and the Hamiltons. Nancy got the double whammy in name terms from her grandmother, Agnes Hogg Hamilton, while Trisha got the double benefit from being named Patricia Caroline, with Jeanette bringing up the Moodie line in her middle name.

Whilst the McCulloch family and descendants occupations were by no means exotic, there were some clear differences from the Rodgers. Papa Sanny was a 'locomotive driver' and there were public house keepers, police sergeant, stonemason, inspector of the poor, titles which were a bit more grand than the Rodgers. However, there was also a fair sprinkling of farmers, labourers, general servant, domestic, ploughman etc in the ancestry. In the main, the family hailed from Ayrshire, but with a strain from Caithness. Backtracking to the early

1800s reveals that the McCullochs originated in Ireland, with all but the Moodie roots being traced there.

Stone Cottage in Alloway is but a stone's throw from Burns Cottage and this is from where Nancy's great-grandmother sold ice-cream to the tourists who visited Burns Cottage. Whilst not quite sitting on a 'gold mine,' the move to live with train driver Sanny certainly represented a 'crossing of the tracks' by moving to Barlieth in Hurlford.

After a week or two of 'going through the motions,' in the aftermath of the wedding, there was a realisation that we did 'fancy' each other and we should 'go steady.'

If we were going steady, life for my dad wasn't - he had a major heart attack and sitting with him in Ballochmyle Hospital, he was a 'pale imitation' of himself but even then, his sense of humour never left him - having no slippers, he fashioned a pair from the disposable urinals. Discharged from hospital after about ten days, he was steadily rehabilitated at work and I again helped out when I could - cutting grass here and digging a grave there.

Nancy worked full-time within the thriving lace manufacturing business in Darvel and with my money from the summer jobs, we could just about afford a four-day holiday in the "Jewel of the Irish Sea," the Isle of Man. Memories of the Summerland fire had not completely cooled, but Jeanette and Janet McCann had secured jobs in a local hotel and we set off for a surprise visit, and our first holiday together. This holiday coincided with my first attempt to grow a beard and as I stepped onto the pier at Douglas, I looked like 'Shaggy' out of the 'Scooby Doo' cartoon.

We surprised Jeanette and Janet at the scene of TT Races, offshore dealings and the Casino night club helped us to express our freedom and our commitment to each other. The Isle of Man represented a poor man's hedonistic haven, as the yearnings of yesterday and the trials of tomorrow were set aside for living for today. It was an outward expression of our relaxed, cool and comfortable discovery of each other. We didn't strut, but felt secure and relaxed in each other's company. Friends began to perceive something more than friendship was at stake. Questions dipped and raised like a thermometer, as the question in our heads reverberated - *"Is he/she the one for me?"*

The strength of personal awareness and affection grew until on the top of the double-decker bus to Darvel, I declared,

"I love you, would you like to get engaged?"

It was not pre-prepared and there were no flowers or romantic music, but my offer was accepted. A Christmas engagement was too predictable, and 1st January was a much better time for a traditional Scottish celebration. So it was that on 'Hogmanay' 1979, we 'first-footed,' 'second-footed' all the houses in Darvel with our relatives and friends, to show them 'the rings' after the 'bells.'

It was a frosty morning as we emerged from our 6th house of happiness. We tread warily down the stairs and avoided the treacherous pavements for the safety and sure-footedness of the main road. The 'carry-oot' consisted of a bottle of Dry Martini and a full bottle of Black Rum, and a few cans of Tennents lager. Hand in hand, we gingerly walked to the next Hogmanay haven, when ---- I was down like a Saturday coupon! As glass went to tarmac, I was back up like a shot - *"Don't worry"* says Nancy, "*it will be the Dry Martini*" - no such luck and no Black Heart Rum for me, as the carry-oot bag, complete with the broken bottle, was deposited in the nearest bin. The event and embellished story, aligned to our engagement, got the sympathy vote and a good few drinks in compensation. People in equal measure were surprised and delighted for us. The declaration of our love made things easier and more relaxed in a social sense, but I had yet to graduate and secure a real job.

School and summer jobs had been in pretty plentiful supply in the 1970s. August on the Lanfine Estate, outside Darvel, was a time for the aristocracy to come and bag a few birds, in other words, shoot some grouse. Grouse beating, at

£2 a day, was a good way to earn some money during the summer holidays. There was even a chance you would be walking the moors next to Robina, Lord and Lady Rotherwick's daughter. Lanfine Estate was owned by the Lord and Lady during the seventies, and the young Robina was a class act who everyone tried to follow and chat up, especially the older beaters. There was no danger of me pulling the lady, but there was distinct danger of being shot by some of the arrogant aristocrats, who had over indulged during the lunch-time break. The shooting butts resembled elevated First World War trenches and the shooters, with their Purdys and over and under shot guns, blasted both pheasant and peasant, as they flew or walked towards them

It was much safer to pick tomatoes during the summer and for three years, I tended tomato plants in their rows of three each side of the glasshouses, which seemed to run for about one hundred yards. Potato picking in September/October was also relatively safe at the Ireland's Bradley Farm, overlooking the tiny schoolhouse in which Sir Alexander Fleming's early education was nurtured, and at the Hamilton's Allanton Farm in the shadow of Loudounhill.

Whilst at Uni, any income earned during the summer holidays was tax free, and so a job that offered longer hours and more money was sought. Mitchell & Struthers, Sportsground Contractors of Kilmarnock, took me on. The job was ideal; the money was reasonable, it involved working outside, grass cutting, fencing and general groundwork, all over the South West and Central Scotland. It was a chance to earn some money and become more worldly-wise in the company of real workers.

Renovating gardens in Govan in the shadow of Ibrox Stadium, the home of Glasgow Rangers FC, was both daunting and delightful. Women actually did hang out of their windows, two stories up, and exchange conversation (and insults) with their neighbours, and throw their kids a 'jeely piece' out of the window. For a country boy who had gone to town, the city was a real eye-opener. At 3pm midweek, three kids shuffled through a back court - the eldest, about seven, pushes a pram, whilst the second youngest, about five, carries an infant, about 12-24 months. Weird, I think, why is the baby not being wheeled about in the pram? Maybe there's another baby in the pram? As I try to peer in, the eldest troll advises - *"Fuck off mister."* The baby is obviously lighter than the lead in the pram, which is being taken to the scrappy to convert into hard cash.

The money we earned as students was great and often I would leave Nancy's mum and dad's house to do overtime on a Sunday after a Saturday night out. Money draws greed and envy and when the real workers discovered we could earn as much if not more than them our basic wages were cut to £25 per week. Of the twelve or so students employed, only Hughie Williamson and myself were outraged enough to seek a meeting with management. We demanded, and got, a meeting with the MD, Ian Mitchell, and after a hard day's graft, we put our case to him. Either the force of our argument, or the fact that we were grubby urchins messing up his newly refurbished offices, won the day. In my first experience of potential industrial action, we secured a £10 'rise.' This was still lower than the basic rate for 'real workers,' but true to the MD's word, the increase was paid to all the students and, with overtime, we still made good, tax-free money, with which I could at last pay some 'dig money' to my mum and dad.

Newmilns Vesevius 1974 Ayrshire Cup winning team, Backrow 'The Committee'

Middle row left to right: Drew Taylor (manager/coach), yours truly; John Guild, Rab Struthers, Bobby McNaught; Jackie Ferrie, Billy Fulton, Tony Wright, John McCreadie, John Sommerville (manager/coach). *Front row left to right:* George Fraser, Ian Allison, Ian McWatters, John Spence, Willie McMillan, Jimmy Finnie, Benny Ferrie and James McAllister.

Top: Myself in Torquay in the 1970s
Bottom: Nancy and I, 1980

Our Wedding

Top: 'The McCullochs' – (From left to right) Harry, Marion, Trisha, (myself), Nancy, Papa Sanny, Mavis and Jeanette
Bottom: 'The Rodgers' – (From left to right) Yvonne, Elaine, Avril, (Myself), Nancy, Mum, Dad, Lilian, Marlene, Davy, Bobby, Graham and Colin (Jim was ill).

CHAPTER THREE

"Times, and nappies, they are a changing"

Returning to Uni was traumatic, as an old order was re-engaged, and a new order was about to begin. But first, there was a question of completing my honours degree. Before graduating, I gained my first major title – not in sports or the honours list, but as President of Dalrymple Hall. I had been the dark-horse candidate but my nomination speech, advocating "education, education and education" as my top three priorities, was well received, and well before it's time. However, even better received was my commitment to a mixed hockey team (some person in their wisdom had decreed that females could be residents of the Hall), video nights four times per term, and a Burns Night, complete with pipes and haggis-slayers. I lived up to my election promise as the hockey team was formed and was unbeaten in its Saturday morning outings, even against Queen Margaret Hall, complete with their three Indian and Pakistani exponents of the game, and the video nights, even if of dubious quality (The Texas Chain Saw Massacre and Blazing Saddles were big hits), were delivered.

The Burns Night was 'scary' – Jimmy Auld from Stewarton would address the haggis. Ronnie McGregor would deliver the toast to the lassies, and as the "piece of resistance" I would remember the Immortal Memory. Tickets were sold and 'dignitaries' were invited. It was a sell out. The Hall was genuinely mixed, in terms of sex and ethnic origin and the dining hall was a riot of reds, yellows and greens, representing the African contingent; bright blues and whites for the Eastern entrants, and tartans for the Tuechters and Ayrshire entourage. The top table was formed as the Doc introduced us to the 'high-hied yins,' who obviously had not encountered a Burns Supper of this ilk – in fairness, they acquitted themselves well and did a fair bit of damage to the free wine and spirits at the top table.

A Burns Night without a piper is like a Juliet without a Romeo; a Morecambe without a Wise; a Stevie Wonder without a piano; an artist without an easel. At any rate, it was serious stuff when it was announced that the piper discovered he had a broken nose. "Fuck me!" What will it take for him to play, short of a nose job? A half bottle tucked away in his Bearskin and our man did us proud. The drink flowed and the haggis flew – down people's throats. Everyone was up for it. Jimmy delivered the address to the haggis as if the postcode was missing and he slashed at the haggis as if to find it in its entrails. Ronnie brought all his charm and wit to woo the lassies – their reply would have made your ears prick – at least I think that's what she said. The Black Heart Rum gave me real heart as I delivered the 'Immortal Memory.' It would be good to think that in my Ayrshire accent, my delivery of the immortal memory was responsible for the warm reception, but in truth, it was the sense of occasion as a first, and the sense of the Bard's immortal truth, captured in "To a Mouse" , "To a Louse," and "For A' That & A' That."

To a Mouse

On turning her up in her nest, with the plough, November 1785

We, sleekit, cowran, tim'rous beastie,
O, what a panic's in thy breastie!
Thou need na start awa sae hasty,
Wi' bickering brattle!
I wad be laith to rin an' chase thee,
Wi' murd'ring pattle!
I'm truly sorry Man's dominion
Has broken Nature's social union,

An' justifies that ill opinion,
Which makes thee startle,
At me, thy poor, earth-born companion,
An' fellow-mortal!
I doubt na, whyles, but thou may thieve;
What then? poor beastie, thou maun live!
A daimen-icker in a thrave
'S a sma' request:
I'll get a blessing wi' the lave,
An' never miss't!
Thy wee-bit housie, too, in ruin!
It's silly wa's the win's are strewin!
An' naething, now, to big a new ane,
O' foggage green!
An' bleak December's winds ensuin,
Baith snell an' keen!
Thou saw the fields laid bare an' wast,
An' weary Winter comin fast,
An' cozie here, beneath the blast,
Thou thought to dwell,
Till crash! the cruel coulter past
Out thro' thy cell.
That wee-bit heap o' leaves an' stibble,
Has cost thee monie a weary nibble!
Now thou's turn'd out, for a' thy trouble,
But house or hald.
To thole the Winter's sleety dribble,
An' cranreuch cauld!
But Mousie, thou art no thy-lane,
In proving foresight may be vain:
The best laid schemes o' Mice and Men,
Gang aft agley,
An' lea'e us nought but grief an' pain,
For promis'd joy!
Still, thou art blest, compar'd wi' me!
The present only toucheth thee:

But Och! I backward cast my e'e,
On prospects drear!
An' forward, tho' I canna see
I guess an' fear!"

To a louse

On seeing one on a lady's bonnet at church

Ha! whare ye gaun, ye crowlan ferlie!
Your impudence protects you sairly:
I canna say but ye strunt rarely,
Owre gawze and lace;
Tho' faith, I fear ye dine but sparely,
On sic a place.
Ye ugly, creepan, blastet wonner,
Detested, sunn'd by saunt an' sinner,
How daur ye set your fit upon her,
Sae fine a Lady!
Gae somewhere else and seek you dinner
On some poor body.
Swith, in some beggar's haffet squattle;
There ye may creep, and sprawl, and sprattle,
Wi' ither kindred, jumping cattle,
In shoals and nations;
Whare horn nor bane ne'er daur unsettle,
Your thick plantations.
Now haud you there, ye're out o' sight,
Below the fatt'rels, snug and tight,
Na faith ye yet! ye'll no be right,
Till ye've got on it,
The very tapmost, towrin height
O' Miss's bonnet.
My sooth! right bauld ye set your nose out,
As plump an' gray as onie grozet:
O for some rank, mercurial rozet,
Or fell, red smeddum,
I'd gie you sic a hearty dose o't,
Wad dress your droddum!

I wad na been surpriz'd to spy
You on an auld wife's flainen toy;
Or aiblins some bit duddie boy
On's wylecoat;
But Miss's fine Lunardi, fye!
How daur you do't?[2]

O Jenny dinna toss your head,
An' set your beauties a' abread!
Ye little ken what cursed speed
The blastie's makin!
Thae winks and finger-ends, I dread,
Are notice takin!
Oh wad some Pow'r the giftie gie us
To see oursels as others see us!
It wad frae monie a blunder free us
An' foolish notion;
What airs in dress an' gait wad lea'e us,
And ev'n Devotion!

For A' That and A' That

Is there, for honest poverty,
That hangs his head, and a' that?
The coward-slave, we pass him by,
We dare be poor for a' that!
For a' that, and a' that;
Our toils obscure, and a' that;
The rank is but the guinea's stamp;
The man's the gowd for a' that.

---

[2] This is, by readers *gentle* and readers *simple*, acknowledged to be one of the most perfect little gems that ever human genius produced. One of its couplets has passed into proverb:- "The best laid schemes o' Mice an' Men, gang aft agley." Extract from 'The Kilmarnock Edition of the Poetical Works of Robert Burns' – special presentation edition – The Scottish "Daily Express" Glasgow 1939.

What tho' on hamely fare we dine,
Wear hodden-gray, and a' that;
Gie fools their silks, and knaves their wine.
A man's a man for a' that.
For a' that, and ' that,
Their tinsel show, and a' that;
That honest man, tho' e'er sae poor,
Is King ' men for a' that.
Ye see yon birkie, ca'd a lord,
Wha struts, and stares, and a' that;
Tho' hundreds worship at his word,
He's but a coof for a' that:
For a' that, and a' that,
His riband, star, and a' that,
The man of independent mind,
He looks and laughs at a' that.[3]

Extract from 'The Kilmarnock Edition of the Poetical Works of Robert Burns' – Special Presentation Edition – The Scottish 'Daily Express,' Glasgow, 1939

A prince can mak a belted knight,
A marquis, duke, and a' that;
But an honest man's aboon his might,
Guid faith he mauna fa' that!
For a' that, and a' that,
Their dignities, and a' that,

---

[3] Footnote 2: Burns could make of very humble subjects such as the *Dogs*, the *Pet-Yowe*, the *Mouse*, and the *Auld Mare*: here we have him descending for a theme, still lower in the scale of animal life. Lowly, even repulsive as the subject is, however, he has done it ample justice, and makes it point a moral if it does not adorn his page.

The pith o' sense, and pride ' worth,
Are higher rank than a' that.
Then let us pray that come it may,
As come it will for a' that,
That sense and worth, o'er a' the earth,
May bear the gree, and a' that,
For a' that and a' that,
It's coming yet, for a' that,
That man to man the warld o'er
Shall brithers be for a' that.

For Burns the ploughman and near-pauper, reward and real recognition came with his untimely death. From observation, on the simple Mouse and Louse, powerful and emotional truths emerge:-

"The best laid plans of mice and men
Gang aft agley."

"Oh wad some Pow'r the giftie gie us,
To see oursels as others see us."

For the culturally-deficient (like myself) it's hard to relate and equate Burns to the famous American author, John Updike, who translates the 1785 verse into a 21st century version – *"Entitled to a well connected Mouse (upon reading of the genetic closeness of mice and men."* Burns is unique and universal so Updike's work is either a 'Tour de Force' or a 'Tour de Farce' – you chose?!

Burns was obviously a man before his time as an array of gurus, consultants and Human Resource professionals exclaim the virtues of 360° feedback through which individuals can obtain an all-round view of how others view their behaviours and actions from their perspective. Burns was way ahead of the game, but typically his insight and foresight proved in vain for him. 'For a' that and a' that,' Burns knew that honesty, integrity, common sense and respect were the true stamps of worth in his fellow human beings. Undying and universal truths which didn't make him a prophet in his homeland but which elevated the ploughman to Poet – the National Bard.

The lines delivered slowly, like Braveheart Wallace on the field of battle, were received over-enthusiastically by some who didn't understand a word, but understood the occasion. The Burns Night spilled out to the next morning and the scoreboard next day read – Burns Night 300, Morning Lectures 0. True to Burns's tradition, in any language it had been an unqualified success. New and qualified however, was the name of the game; the passport to the world of work!

The more intense the studying was required, the more intense I became. With a view to the future and as a bit of an outlet, I took driving lessons in the vague hope that when I gained my first job, I would have a driving licence to enable me to drive the company car!! At £8.25 a time, BSM at Anniesland were not cheap but, even after 22 lessons and a prescription of Valium from the Uni doctor, I failed my first test. I had come within six inches of an articulated lorry turning right at traffic lights, as I attempted to drive straight through. I could hardly see the traffic lights, never mind the indicator on the lorry, which was way over the level of the Triumph Dolomite I was steering.

Having failed my driving test, I passed my finals. Not being naturally clever, a 2-1 (Second Class, Level One) honours degree was my own aim, but it was a Desmond Tutu (2-2) for me. Still, after what seemed like an eternal succession of exams, from '0' levels onwards, this was like climbing Mount Everest, or at least Ben Nevis.

The allotted date for graduation was Independence Day (4th July) 1980, but through a combination of bad planning and bad luck, I ended up on my own. My dad had had another heart attack and was not fit enough to attend, but my mum was bursting with pride and Nancy would have gladly have been there, but it was a working day and we had no transport to get there and back. The graduation photos were good, but could not really make up for Mum, Dad and Nancy not being there. The moment and the occasion was gone, never to be recreated!?

Job application had followed job application, as the CV was circulated in the expectation of gaining some recognition for five years of study. Final interviews with Fords and the SSEB (Electricity Board) for graduate trainee positions in Personnel Management failed to get me on the first rung of the career ladder, and self doubt and recrimination crept in. I wasn't good enough; why had I bothered, there had been plenty of jobs in the mid 1970s, and I had wasted all this time and effort? Mum and dad dipped deeper into their pockets as, in the absence of work, I found a place on the Post Graduate Diploma in Personnel Management at Strathclyde University. What was another year in education, it would be worthwhile.

Another year at Uni meant reliance on grant-funding (this effectively amounted to £9 per week to get by on). As usual financial and moral support was provided from mum and dad, Nancy and the family. *"Has your boy not got a job yet? I thought he was clever,"* was the type of comment that got me down, but not my mum or dad, not a word of it.

The Western SMT bus from Darvel to Kilmarnock, Kilmarnock to Glasgow, underground from Bridge Street to Buchanan Street, and a walk to the Strathclyde Uni buildings became the order of the day, every weekday, and every weekday, my mum got up before me and made my breakfast. It was becoming too much and to the rescue came Jim McCaffrey, who knew some people who were looking for someone to share a flat – and the rent – with. A meeting of my potential flatmates was hastily convened. The Great George Street, top-floor flat (off Byres Road) was better placed for Glasgow University, but it was a hop, skip and a jump to the Byres Road (Hillhead) underground station and a world of a difference from a two-hour plus bus journey. The flat itself was spacious, with a bright green shag-pile carpet, which had been fashionable once – and once only! It now had the appearance of a huge, dead cat, with the shag well and truly knocked out of it. My potential flatmates were all Vets (vetinary students) – maybe the carpet was made of dead cats after all! I had no problem with Vets, but they were all female. I expected Nancy to be a bit wary, but pragmatic as ever, she had no problems with it and I joined the Great George Street Gang and slept in a sleeping bag until a bed could be procured for me in my single room.

After deductions for rent, gas and electricity, I had the princely sum of £9.00 a week to cover everything else – travel, books, clothes and food. It was lucky that denim (however faded) never went out of fashion, and even if it did, I never noticed. Cornflakes, beansprouts, cabbage, beans, bread, smash potatoes, pizza, sardines and pork and liver became the main constituents of my diet.

Next to medicine, the veterinary degree is regarded as one of the hardest to get into and one of the hardest to pass. All five vets enjoyed a laugh and a drink but when the time for studying came round, they were focussed on their own personal ambitions and intent, and all succeeded in their 'finals.'

My diploma year fellow students were a mixed but likeable bunch and included pals, poseurs and pot-takers. The exams were completed and after a celebrity dinner, the Diploma team adjourned to the Strathclyde University Union Disco, to share memories, friendship and potential success in our exams. The evening was relaxed and cool, until wee Robert declared to big Frank and myself, *"That guy's jist punched me in the face and I've hurt my hand."* The inevitable question followed: *"Whit did he dae that fur?"* *"Nothing,"* was the reply and I was off. *"Where is he?"* *"Over there, white shirt, by the big guy on the left."* I followed Robert's directions to the letter and confronted the assailant – *"Don't know what you're talking about, now piss off before I…."* I got my retaliation in first, as Robert staggered over, surveyed the guy on the ground and says, *"That's no him, it's him,"* pointing to a six-foot bear of a guy. What the hell, to the strains of David Bowie's "Life on Mars," all hell broke out on earth, as tables, chairs and glasses took to the air in an unreal and surreal fashion. The fatal combination of booze, birds and music had struck again. Later, Robert contemplated perhaps he was at fault in trying to pick up the 'big guy's' girl, as we emerged from casualty in the early hours of the morning, with confirmation he had broken his thumb.

The parcel said, *"Do Not Bend"* as my Diploma was delivered through the post in September 1981 – what a contrast to the formality of the occasion of graduation in Bute Hall at Glasgow University the previous year. The mail also delivered responses to applications for jobs and they were many and varied but most, although polite in tone, were labelled by me as GTFs (get tae fuck). This would have been a good name for a band but was definitely not good for morale, but we would persevere.

Back on the home and family front, the marital focus was on Bobby, Yvonne and myself.

Bobby had met Linda at the 'Covies' (Covenanters Hotel in Newmilns – now somewhat symbolically a sheltered housing complex) and spent many a weekend at Sanquhar, where Linda stayed. Sanquhar is home to the oldest Post Office in Britain, but it appears it was not the home of any 'first class males' as the girls of the town seemed to take flight and find their fiances elsewhere. Their wedding was in Sanquhar and my dad, following another heart scare, had secured the doctor's permission to attend. It was a long day for dad, who had never seen so many of the family living it up on the bus home, while he felt like death.

In the meantime, Yvonne and Jimmy (he of the Mark 1 J registration Capri) were going steady and Nancy and I joined them on the heady days of 18th and 21st birthday parties, engagements and weddings, as life and love develop around and among us. Scarborough was 'revisited' and as Mr Rodgers and Nancy, we joined Jimmy and Yvonne and Tom and Ellen plus kids on our summer holidays. Mr Collins, married Jimmy and Yvonne on his home patch, Darvel Central Church, in August 1980.

Nancy and I set the 26th of September 1981 as the date for our wedding – we set if before realising Jim and Jessie had been married five years previously on exactly the same date. We were not (and are not) churchgoers and there would be no change in our approach to the wedding. The Community Centre in Hurlford was the venue (their first-ever ceremony on the premises), and the perennial pastor, Mr I Collins, conducted the service. It was a close family and friends wedding and even then, we mustered over 100 guests in attendance. My brother, Davy would be the best man and *Jeanette, Avril and Marion* were the bridesmaids.

Marion's photos as an 11-year old Gala Queen, Hurlford's first, adorned the hall's walls in an uncanny link to both the past and the future.

It wasn't really a nervy day as we had had our ups and downs before I had secured a job as a Graduate Trainee with the South of Scotland Electricity Board (SSEB). This had taken the real pressure out of our relationship and ensured a more relaxed approach to the wedding celebrations. "Pay off" and "Stag night" celebrations had been enjoyed and this was it – a lifetime commitment and the biggest decision we would ever make in our lives. It was unequivocally the right decision.

The day was a fairly typical end of September day in Scotland, a bit windy, occasional showers with bright interludes. The weather forecast pretty much summed up the wedding but the bright interludes were larger and more enjoyable. True to form at a good Scottish wedding, as the bride and groom, we were reluctant to leave a good party in full swing. Still, it was our honeymoon and we really had to go.

We had to go to 4 Kirkland Road in Darvel, as our honeymoon retreat and home for the next few years. We had rented a one-bedroomed flat in Darvel and in the absence of winning the pools, this was as far as we got for our honeymoon. It wasn't something that bothered us; there was no envy and no regrets. There was also no peace, as in the early hours of the morning, the drunken guests on return from the wedding serenaded us after they found out we had honeymooned at home.

After three days honeymooning at home (not quite a la John and Yoko), we decided it would be safe to go out. Mr and Mrs Rodgers set off down the street, hand in hand, to get the messages and give everyone the message we were man and wife. Together, we faced the world, or at least, Darvel. Nancy's mum and dad, true to Scottish tradition, had paid for the wedding, and my mum and dad had given us £500 as a wedding gift and, practical as ever, we had spurned the honeymoon abroad for a fridge freezer.

Nancy returned to work and I began work with SSEB on the 12th October 1981. Still without a driving licence, never mind a car, it was back to a bus to Kilmarnock and the connecting bus to Glasgow and a walk to Cathcart House on the south-side of Glasgow, pretty near to Hampden Park, the scene of the 1973 successful encounter with Czechoslovakia and a few more since. Within a couple of weeks, this nightmare journey ended, as I secured a lift with Gordon and Danny, fellow workers at Cathcart House.

Our joint incomes as a Graduate Trainee and a Wire Cutter/Machinist within the textile manufacturing industry were not great, but we could still afford to go to the 'pictures.' "The Champ," starring Jon Voigt and Ricky Schroder was one of the first and saddest films we saw. It was pretty run of the mill throughout, but the ending had me choking and in typical Scottish male fashion, holding back the emotion and tears, which desperately wanted to break free. *"Wake up, Champ, get up, wake up"* resonates in my head and have been my forlorn plea at two particular hospital bedsides since then.

As my training progressed, my salary increased and we became both more personally and financially secure. We took our landlord to a rent tribunal and his failure to respond or attend resulted in the rent being halved. At this rate, we could actually afford a holiday abroad and so eight of us struck out for Benalmadena near Marbella/Torremelinos on the Costa del Sol. The Maite Apartments were not plush but Puerto Banus seemed like a haven for bashful Brits in need of some sun and seclusion. Rolls Royces, expensive yachts and cruisers, male hands with gold rings which shone like knuckle dusters, and knuckle dusters which shone like rings. Puerto Banus was a place to be seen and watch another world and model girls go by.

The 'team' took to the Aqua Park outside of Torremelinos and without a drink in sight, climbed up the 200 steps to 'do a kamikaze.' Open gratings on the stairs left little to the imagination – we were up a helluva height and there was no going back down the stairs once you reached the top. *"Lie back, cross your legs at the ankles, cross your arms in front of your chest and ease yourself forward – whatever you do, don't sit up as you ease forward."* Whoosh and oh shit – exhilarating, frightening, but repeatable – for some. Ronnie King though, had had enough, as he declared, *"Big Mags, I think I've shit myself."* I don't think any of us would have 'done the Kamikaze' if they had told us there had been two fatalities in the previous years!

Our first holiday abroad had lived up to expectations and only the journey home remained. The flight from Malaga to Gatwick, rail journey to Euston Station and the connecting bus to Kilmarnock in Scotland. It was tight and delays with the flight left us to ponder what next, as we sat on our cases in Euston Station. Nothing else for it, we would sleep in the station and catch the first bus home in the morning. No problem – until I peer at my case and discover I've changed my name to Joe Wade – hell, I wish I'd picked a better name or better still, I wish I had picked up my own case at Gatwick. Perhaps Joe has my case, I think, as I phone the number on the address label. No such luck. Joe confirms, in a tone which indicates the insurance money was a better prospect than the return of his case full of 'manky' washing. At 2am, I return

Joe's case to Gatwick, in the vague hope my case is still there. Explaining the position to airport security, I am escorted to an area with ten or twelve unclaimed cases and low and behold, Mr and Mrs Rodgers strike it lucky. Joe's case is exchanged for ours and I make to leave the area. *"Where are you going son?" "I'm just leaving. "You're not leaving without going through customs." "But there's no-one there." "It doesn't matter."* So I pick green for go and I'm out of there and back to Euston in time to rejoin the team and get the 6.30am Stagecoach to Scotland. Thanks be to Brian Souter.

Eighteen months of graduate training and I'm ready for the real world of work in SSEB. Applying more in hope than expectation, I obtained my first post and Training & Welfare Officer at Cockenzie Power Station. The job offers a considerable rise in salary – only trouble is, it is in the 'far east' – in Prestonpans, just outside Edinburgh – a house move is in the offing

Sam Downie, Driving Instructor, was the sign on top of the Ford Fiesta as I tried to enter the passenger seat. *"No,"* Sam says, *"it's actually better if you sit in the driver's seat to learn to drive."* The guy has obviously never heard of me and hasn't a clue that I can't drive. *"Don't despair, I'll get you there,"* should have been his motto, as I fail my test for the second time, by trying to drive down the right way of a one-way street, when everyone else is driving up the wrong way. I knew before the words were on the examiner's lips, that I'd just bagged a brace of failed tests.

In consolation on the way back, Sam suggests I join him in a marathon – *"Fuck me, I'm no having another 26 lessons." "No, no, how would you like to run a marathon?"* I think – well at this fucking rate I've no chance of driving it, so what the hell? The Irvine Valley is to Holland what Dolly Parton is to Twiggy – there's some big hills out there! The training commences and ten or twelve miles, four nights a week is in the bank. My colleagues at work support the Edward Appeal, which is for a wee boy in Newmilns with cystic fibrosis. The training goes to plan and we're up to eighty miles a week - my driving lessons don't cover this mileage.

I sit with the same examiner who had failed me last time round and as he questions me on the Highway Code, I think, you must remember me, because I remember you, but I've done a helluva lot better since the last time. *"Mr Rodgers, I'm pleased to say you've passed your test!"* I resist the temptation to kiss the guy but Sam is ecstatic, or so it appears. Two weeks later, Sam takes a heart attack – I think it was his! Seriously, he offers me his sponsor money if I complete the marathon for me and him – I think, I'll never do fifty-two miles, but Sam reassures me that twenty-six miles will be enough and proceeds to give me directions on the marathon route – once a driving instructor, always a driving instructor!

Jim Richmond becomes my training companion and a one-off, twenty-two mile run (Darvel via Dungavel and return) with one bottle of water in just over three hours, gives me confidence I can complete. Dungavel (near Strathaven) was then an open prison, some twenty years on it's gates are closed as it controversially becomes a detention centre for refugees seeking sanctuary in Scotland.

A two-tone brown and cream Ford Fiesta 1.1l has been secured at Newmains auction, courtesy of Alistair (my brother-in-law). It's an S reg and I'm well chuffed as the car has a low mileage and two careful owners. What a load of shite -–the car must have smoked 120 cigarettes a day, as every winter's morning, it coughed it's guts out. Like a mad John Cleese, I took to giving it a damn good thrashing and returning indoors and then returning five minutes later for the brown bullet to spring into action.

Jim and myself reached the half-way point of the marathon (thirteen miles) in some one hour, forty minutes. We were going well, until we hit Bellahouston Park and I'm sure the Pope in his Pope Mobile would have passed me – I'd hit the wall. The advice to 'take plenty of fluid' had backfired on me, as the freezing water out of what seemed like the fifty-gallon 'oil drums' chilled my stomach. After stopping at the toilet at around twenty miles, I think, *"I don't remember drinking red cola?!"* - I decided to finish the job. People all through Glasgow were fantastic – you could have a drink, a sugar barley sweetie, tea on the back lawn or join the barbecue – like Japanese prisoners of war or Scots football fans in Argentina I think most of the runners have now returned from the first Glasgow marathon, but I could be proved wrong.

Three hours and some fifty minutes, and the journey was done, as I was greeted by Jeanette and Fiona (Nancy was at home, ill) and some tinfoil in which to baste myself later? Events of the day were relayed gleefully as I explained how I have very nearly run out of steam. Steam was the operative word, as it spewed from the bonnet of the wee car – it would have to go!! Never mind, the 'Edward Appeal' benefited to the tune of over £150.

Musselburgh (the 'Honest toun') is home to a racecourse, the pub once owned by Willie Ormond – that great Scotland national football manager; and the Brunton Theatre, and soon it was to be home to us. Six weeks in a hotel adjacent to the racecourse, a period of 'digs' in Tranent with Mrs McGowan, the wife of an ex-miner, were followed by the purchase of a one-bedroomed, terraced house at 17 Monktonhall Terrace, Musselburgh. At £22,500, we could have bought a three-bedroomed house in Darvel for that. Both sets of mums and dads became worried and protective, as we set out to be really on our own.

The house was really a 'manse' in style and décor, as it had once been the home of a minister. The potential of the house was realised as we decorated during the summer and built a new fireplace and fitted new carpets in every room. After two months of bare floorboards and sleeping on an airbed, it was sheer luxury to walk bare-foot on the new carpets and to sleep in our first new bed.

Help with the decorating had arrived in the shape of Marion, Davy (her boyfriend) and Jeanette. Davy was a gem, his character fitted his skin and he was very comfortable in it. He had no pretensions, he knew who he was and lived life as it was. He was big (even fat), bold, funny and straight, but had a gentleness and sensitivity which belied his size and outward confidence. He was also a bloody good football player and a 'teddy bear.'

Marion, by contrast, was petite (under five feet tall), quietly exuberant (bubbly), dedicated to caring for others, and 'incident-prone.' Kirklandside Hospital was her first challenge as to whether she could stick it as a 'carer' at the tender age of sixteen. Bed pans, bed sores and bed linen were all taken in her stride. Personal hygiene was next and the false teeth were collected for cleaning and return to the 'gumsy' owners. No problem with the collection, but recognising who they belonged to in one big bag was a problem!! Hairdressing problems could also be solved, as the weekly visit by the hairdresser was curtailed due to illness. Wee Marion lifts the despair; no problem, a wash and the hair rollers in would set the old folks up fine. Curls turned to drooping ringlets as the awful truth dawned – she'd put the curlers in the wrong way round. Still, the old dears felt better for the hair wash and in the mirror they were the image of their mind's eye.

Help also arrived in the shape of Nancy's dad , Harry and big Robbie , the joiner – their mission to complete a partition in the house to create another bedroom. We're short of plaster – board so I walk down to the wood merchants and fly back up the hill , wind assisted whilst carrying an eight by four sheet of plasterboard. The jobs done and Harry and Robbie its time for them to get plastered themselves. We hit the Ship and then the bar once owned by Willie Ormand . Harry gets pretty merry early on and its easy to see why and how his best days are behind him , and he's only about 50 . He is in fact like George Best today – haggard , drawn , wasting his talent and his liver , but Harry will have to make do with one liver. For now he's happy , argumentative and even arrogant with alcohol and he shares jokes with new found friends who stand Harry as he stands them a drink.

In our early twenties, life was for the living, and even the death of an older family relative did not dampen youthful spirit for long. At six feet four, and barely in his twenties, Danny McCann was a strapping big lad. At Chapel Hall discos, he would delight in saying, *"Hey big man, want to buy some raffle tickets?"* and he was talking to wee Kenny. He had a great sense of fun, fairness and football, but cancer, as in the case of countless others, did not respect his youth, geniality or genuineness. His face and body grew a shadow of their former selves; he strived to be the same Danny, but the 'tammy' on his bald chemotherapy head could not hide his and others fears. A period of hope called remission was short-lived as the revolutionary cancer treatment he was piloting produced hope for others but no miracle for him. He died on 19 November 1982, three months after his 21st birthday.

We'd never been to a funeral of someone so young and close enough to regard as a real friend. It was also the first catholic funeral I attended and the first time I have ever been in a chapel. The atmosphere was not an atmosphere, it was pure emotion. The priest slowly swings the thurible over Danny's coffin and incense does nothing that it is supposed to do : it does not help balance and clear the mind ; it does not purify the air ; it does not increase faith - it stinks – the whole fuckin thing stinks - Danny's DEAD.! A 'celebration of life' in song and prayer and it was all too much for me. Past memories, Danny's family and the sight of the coffin culminated in a dam of tears being released like sluice gates – I had to get out of the chapel and, releasing my hand from Nancy's, I headed for the door before I made a 'fool' of myself. Out on the steps and in the fresh air, I was joined by other 'emotional fools' and we just nodded to each other, tears streaming down our faces in respect and reverence of "Big Danny." These tears and cries were not 'normal' (especially in

Scottish men) but they were the most natural outpouring of grief and anguish and all the more painful for that.

Even in death, bigotry and sectarianism raised it's head; *"That's one less papish bastard to worry about"* were the words reported back to me. The unbelievable was confirmed as being the undeniable. Ignore or confront was the question – confront when ready was the answer. Weeks passed before the day of reckoning, and even then, the bigot hadn't the guts to admit his words or real feelings. He was a typical coward; a 'big man' in the right company but a small-minded, squealing bigot when put to the challenge.

Bigots come in many shapes and sizes but only two colours – green and blue – one extreme is as bad as the other. Neither had a monopoly on religious hate and fervour but when combined, both should remember that blue and green make yellow.'Old Firm' clashes (Celtic vs Rangers football matches) allow '90 minute bigots' to release their religious fervour and return to 'normality' as the heat and hate of the matches subdues. The whole social strata is reflected in this 90 minute bigotry – the poor ; the rich; blue collar workers ; white collar workers ; the intelligent and the not so intelligent. They are all caught up in the history and histrionics of the game.

Bigotry it seems is bigger than patriotism as the majority of Celtic and Rangers fans cannot bring themselves to bear supporting the other team in their respective quests for success in the European field.

"In death there is life" is a sentiment both priests and ministers seem to share and essentially, 'life goes on' – not the same, but 'poorer for the passing' but richer for the relationship. So it was that Joanne came on the scene as the first and only of Nancy's nieces. Fiona and Ian had also got married and it was time for Tenerife. A walk down the Tenerife Main Street at 1am and we thought we were in the 'Caves of Drach,' but no, this was 'Veronicas,' a heaving, sweaty mass of flesh queuing and spewing for drink. Even in our early twenties, this was our one and only visit. The mission was accomplished when we found a good Sol Hotel with a great pool, free sunbeds and entertainment all day and night – we were in and to round it off, free dinner tickets were provided by a fellow Scot, whose son preferred to eat out on 'burgers.' Ah well, "no loss what a friend gets." Away from our own apartment we were residents at the Sol and even gave 'our room numbers' when we won prizes as part of the evening entertainment.

The major obstacle to getting up Mount Tiede (apart from the smell of sulphur) was the cable car. It swayed like a scene from a James Bond movie but it and Mount Tiede were conquered.

From Mount Tiede we were back to the magic of Musselburgh and work at Cockenzie Power Station. In a bright July morning, the wee Fiesta, resplendent with new nearside headlamp, headed merrily from Tranent to the Power Station. A sweeping left hander past the Coal Plant and left onto the main road and I'd be set for a good early start. No such luck, as the coal dust, diesel and slight smirr of rain combine to pull me off the road onto the verge and through a small planting. The driver's door creaked open onto lush green grass. Through the undergrowth, I struggle to ensure the headlamp was still intact – yes, somebody up there likes me – and my car. No – as I peer back and discover, the underbelly of the car has been torn away by stones and tree stumps, and the passenger door has been 'panned in.' The car was no longer the star and for £850, I had secured a 'write off.' Never mind, we'd only paid £1,150 for it two years ago.

Amongst the managers at Cockenzie, Saabs seemed to be all the rage, so I took great delight in parking my borrowed racing bike between the two 'flying machines.' Wearing a suit and carrying a briefcase, whilst steering/riding a racing bike is not too difficult on the flat, or even going downhill, but it's hellish going up the hill to Tranent. It kept me fit and raised my "street cred" with the guys at the Station to the extent I was invited to the football team trials. The guys had nothing to lose; if I was crap, they could kick the shit out of a manager; if I was any good, then I might get a game. Cockenzie vs Glasgow North Service Centre and we're playing well but can't get an opener, until up pops yours truly and fires a shot in from about twenty yards. I'm giving it 'laldy' and waiting for the initial celebrations to begin – they never really did – short of two pats on the back and two glares, which clearly stated, "I am a lucky wee shite." The pub is a great leveller – we'd won 2-0 and to a man, the guys came forward and congratulated me on a great goal – but the sense was almost "you're in the football team today, but the management team tomorrow." It was 'distance' closed back then by personal friendship and good working relationships, enhanced by a drink or two at a social night out ten pin bowling and the likes.

Social and personal 'distance' was not something easily closed for the coach of our local amateur team, Prestonpans. The miners' strike had marked out the 'scabs' and divided a community. Big John Martin, the Airdrie FC goalkeeper, supported and coached our team but hadn't supported the strike and people then never let him forget it.

Physical or geographic distance was also something that had never really been put between the family. Lillian and Duncan lived in Sandford, all of twelve miles away; Bobby and Linda in Dumfries, about sixty miles away; and Marlene and Frank about four miles away in Galston – that is, until they decided to go on an African safari – 'permanently.'

In 1982, the opportunities for welders like Frank were greater in Jo'burg and a whole new life beckoned for Marlene, Frank and a precocious 12-year old Lorraine. Recognition of this opportunity 'out of Galston' didn't hold back the maternal/paternal fears and tears as we gathered in Glasgow Central to say 'goodbye.' One by one (and we had mustered a fair contingent of the family), handshakes, hugs and kisses were exchanged and we were left at the platform, waving to shadows which might never return from the 'dark continent.'

Marlene, Frank and Lorraine work hard and settle in Standerton and adapt to a new style of life with a fair gathering of 'ex-pats' to visit and share a 'bria' (BBQ) over a weekend. Marlene is more faithful in writing than us and one of her 1985 exchanges reads:

"Hi there Kenny & Nancy,

Have you had any luck in selling you house?? It's a bit of a hassle waiting for someone to like it and put an offer in for it. But I do hope by now you have had some luck. We are really pleased that Kenny got promotion, its good that he is proving himself. Kenny you will be started your new job now so I hope it is all going well with you.

The weather is still warm and we have had plenty of rain usually late afternoon or evening. So our grass is growing like wildfire. We have settled in fine here and its great having a proper garden.

We really got a shock when we got a letter from mum about Alistair's accident. But we keep hoping that things will work out all right for Alistair. Elaine must be taking it very hard as it's a strain trying to put a face on.

Lorraine got her braces out on Sat 2nd March so she is pleased as punch. Her teeth are lovely, nice and straight and white. I was supposed to be starting squash again after Xmas but would you believe we haven't started yet, keep putting it off.

About 9 months ago, don't know if you will remember or if I even said. But Lorraine got a cyst cut out of her cheek; well the damn thing grew back in as we had to take her up to a specialist up in Pretoria. So he cut if out again on the 6th March so she has still got the dressings on. She has to get the stitches out 12th March. So we are hoping it is done correctly this time. For seemingly with a cyst if you leave the slightest piece of lining it will just grow back in. Well at last Frank is getting plenty of overtime and kept very busy so that pleases him. So now we are going to save like hell and get some money in the bank.

We bought 2 tyres for the car and would you believe the bloody exhaust has a hole in it now. So that will be the next thing. I got a R50 fine about 2 maybe 3 months ago. Went down to Secunda with

Lorraine and we had quite a bit of shopping so I told Lorraine to wait and I would get the car, so when I came round I drove in where the buses stop, picked Lorraine and shopping up, drove out and the bloody police were sitting; they had stopped a man who had done the same as me, went in a no entry sign. So he writes out the fine, asks me to sign it. I looks, saw R50 and said he must be joking, so he says 'Lady, I could fine you R100,' so I said okay, I'll take the R50, the B★★★★★d. Well, think that's all for so take care.

All our love, Marlene, Frank and Lorraine. xxx"

As if to say, "Well you've had it pretty good for a while; let's test you out a bit further; let's see what you're made of," life dealt an immediate crashing blow to Alistair and Elaine. The car crash was serious but dragged from the wreckage, Alistair would survive, that was not in doubt. How he would survive was in doubt, as confirmation came he was paralysed from the chest down.

The why Alistair? why Elaine? why us? questions were asked often but never answered, but Alistair and Elaine showed 'how.' With immense support from Elaine, Alistair literally took his life in his hands and developed skills and mobility that necessity demands, but nobody wants to have to master. The challenge is confronted, like the crash into the tree – head on. A one-bedroom flat with a two-year old Kevin growing up and demanding more of his mum and dad means a house move. A semi-detached house with lots of potential is bought and the potential is fully realised as Elaine, Alistair and Kevin turn it into a home designed to meet their needs. The wheel chair is mastered; as an ex-garage mechanic the car is re-engineered and fly-fishing is re-invented on a folding chair strapped to a rowing boat on the Lake O' Mentieth – the only lake in Scotland, and painting "draws" Al closer to his latent talent. Independent, inspirational and included were Al's attributes and those which 'able-bodied' people would do well to aspire to. All this was only achievable through exceptional courage and application and support, without selfish pity or condescension, and after considerable nursing care in

Phillipshill Hospital in East Kilbride, and the Victoria Infirmary in Glasgow.

After almost two years working/waiting, like corporation buses, three opportunities for promotion came along for me at the same time. I had offers of a promoted post at Cockenzie, a new one at the nuclear power station at Torness, and a return to Glasgow in Industrial Relations & Policy. The lure and lucre of the west proved too strong and our house in Musselburgh was sold at a £6,000 profit. The terraced house sold quickly but a purchase in the old home town didn't coincide with the sale. Lodging at 4 Kirkland Road, Darvel, was back on the cards, but this time, in ground left with Jeanette. The arrangement was to be that we would pay Jeanette's mortgage and she would return to stay with Mavis and Harry until we bought a new house. Mavis in particular had missed Jeanette, but had also gained another lodger in Davy, Marion's boyfriend. The happy family was recreated, with the exception of Harry. With four daughters, Harry found it harder and harder to be a man's man in a woman's household, and had been taking refuge in a bottle for some time. He was a man's man when it came to allotting housekeeping to Mavis from his wages as a Machine Operator with the Glacier Metal in Kilmarnock. He 'cheated on' his wife and family in a financial and emotional sense and it was becoming obvious to them all – he was losing it and them in a world where alcohol made him feel comfortable, and everyone else uncomfortable. 'Man to Man ' talks with John and myself seemed to help for a while and then he would be off the rails and 'on the drink'. It was a demon everyone wanted him to conquer but events and circumstances conspired against Harry and sided with the demon.

Still, as long as Mavis had her daughters, she was strong enough to deal with her own job and Harry's shortcomings. Trisha and Nancy had left the nest and Jeanette returning temporarily only served to highlight Harry's hopeless fate. A return to her home to stay with us (after less than a fortnight!)

was the only way to avoid some heavy personal clashes and confrontations, which Harry and for that matter, Mavis, were not ready for, as neither accepted reality – one drowned herself in her daughters and grandchildren, and the other just continued to drown himself in alcohol and self-delusion.

45 Anderson Drive in Darvel became our home after we has been 'gazumped' in the purchase of 38 Anderson Drive. In Scotland, it is relatively uncommon for an offer to be accepted on a house and then 'dropped' or withdrawn at the last minute, but our unhappiness with the situation was more than compensated by our move to our 'new' house. Settling back into the old home town provided better opportunities to catch up with old friends and relatives. Alexander Moodie (Papa Sanny) was one such relative. An ex-train driver who had amassed a wealth of railway experience and a range of general knowledge which would not have been disgraced on "Mastermind." Sunday afternoon visits were too quick but not before he had rattled through two chapters of an encyclopaedic mind. Long-term memory was no problem and the 1902 on the birth certificate was always quoted to account for short-term memory loss. Sanny's birth in 1902 had something to do with his physical frailty but it was his loss of mental prowess that was most obvious and disturbing. Mavis's efforts to cope with one 'invalid' was bad enough but as Sanny's dependency increased in proportion to his staggering memory loss, the burden became too much for any one person to bear. Family, neighbours and friends would help, but this was Mavis's dad, Nancy's grandad and he deserved the best effort and treatment to make his life worth living. A brilliant and vibrant mind offers no escape from Alzheimer's and so it was with Sanny. In his early stay in hospital, Sanny recognised this dreadful irony. In his last days, he didn't even recognise the hospital. Before then, he knew his fate and said his farewells well before he lapsed into a state of old-age infancy.

Degeneration and regeneration were walking hand in hand, as Sanny's life was eclipsing in June 1988, culture dawned on Glasgow. "See Glesca, see culture?" and the Glasgow Garden Festival had sprung to life, as Sanny died at Crosshouse Hospital where wee Marion now worked, having 'served her time' with the elderly residents at Kirklandside Hospital. Having agreed to pick Trisha up at the Glasgow Garden Festival, I arrived in plenty of time to get back to Sanny's funeral. Carefully planned arrangements went out of the window as Trisha's coach had been re-routed to park on the other side of the Clyde from our rendezvous point. Frantic phoning came to nought, until the involvement of the police secured Trisha for the journey to the funeral. It was all too late – Sanny had had his send off by the time we arrived in Kilmarnock, but we joined the funeral party at the Foxbar and shared memories of Papa Sanny, before Alzheimer's destroyed his.

Nancy was twenty-seven and I was nearly thirty in 1986 – we would try and start a family – it wasn't just any family we wanted to start, but one of our own. A summer holiday in Gran Canaria was to be our last child-free holiday abroad for a wee while as Nancy's pregnancy was confirmed. From being a relaxing preparation for the new birth, the holiday in Gran Canaria became a real trial as unexplained and undetermined bleeding appeared to be heading for a miscarriage in the early weeks of the pregnancy. Countless couples had probably experienced the same or worse run up to a birth than us, but there is no substitute in terms of emotional involvement from 'being there.'

As Nancy's pregnancy developed, so too did the textile workers' dispute with their employers. As inevitable as a birth was on the cards, so too was an industrial dispute. The pickets and braziers were out. It had taken a long time in coming but it would take a shorter time in going – the days of lace and textile manufacturing in Darvel were surely numbered. It was another case of having to be there and do it.

'Being there' was an easy question for me to answer about the birth of our first child – the answer was simple – if Nancy wanted me to be there, I would be – but preferably with a seat in the balcony rather than the stalls. Maybe, just maybe, our first son would be born on Epiphany 1987 (thirty years after me) but warm and protected in Nancy's womb, he chose to stay beyond his estimated time and was getting close to the time when 'jump leads' would have to be applied before he decided today's the day, I'm out of here. An early morning dash to Irvine Central Hospital got me there in plenty of time. Nancy was 'comfortable' – I don't quite know how this could have been, as an eight pound baby was trying to make his way into the world with no conception of the pain this was undoubtedly causing. Holding Nancy's hand and encouraging her 'at the top end,' the pains of labour became all too evident as sweat and pain etched across a normally faultless face. It was hard labour and pethadene was required to ease the pain and the birth, which was announced by our son being shot out at force down the blue, shiny mat for the midwife to catch, cradle and check, before quickly settling with it's mum and me – it's a boy at 10.12 am on Tuesday, 22 January 1987.

The occasion is too painful yet joyful for tears, as I phoned round the family and tell them the good news. Grandparents first and then as I can get the family in. Having been the bearer of good tidings and with Nancy and the baby asleep, I sit with my bar lunch in the Redburn Hotel just opposite the maternity hospital. The scampi and chips suddenly appear to be in danger of getting soggy, as tears inexplicably start to trickle and eventually roll down my face. I peer to the bar to see if anyone has noticed me and decide who cares? I'm here, I'm proud – I'm a DAD! I actually want to proclaim this now but settle for tears being replaced by smiles and laughter. The bar staff were used to being next to the maternity hospital and smiled knowingly, as I gladly paid the bill for the soggiest meal I'd ever had.

A couple of days at Irvine Central and two more at the Kilmarnock Maternity Home, and then we are handed complete responsibility for our first son. His room is prepared, his cot is prepared, his nappies and clothes are all prepared. Are we prepared? No chance – this is a baby with a mind of its own which preys on your own mind. The carrycot becomes his bed next to ours and to avoid every parent's nightmare, he is checked every two hours (or more) 'to see if he's breathing.' He is breathing all right – only problem is he wants 'to be up and about' when we need to sleep. Gary's, or more accurately, Kenneth Gary's nocturnal activities and desire to prove breast-fed is best are hard for first-time parents to come to terms with, but it helps us lose weight and to be able to fall asleep at the drop of a nappy!

Ten months into the 'survival course' we decide a break in Majorca would be 'nice.' Arenal in October was great. The Mallorcans took to Gary, or 'Gari' as if he was one of their own and for the first time, he slept when he should and took his bottle.

As Gary progressed from carrycot to cot and breast to bottle, Nancy could go back to work in the afternoons/evenings. Mavis could help out and this would keep her busy and help her from wondering and worrying about Harry. Harry, in his own mind and world is still going strong; he's got plenty of friends, helps his family and he's got a good job – what's the problem?!?

As Nancy starts back to work, we share the work and I come home to feed, bath and bed Gary. This often ends up with me sleeping on the floor with one hand on Gary's back through the bars of the cot. Returning from work, Nancy awakens me and we try some adult conversation. The doctors assure us it is cyclical sickness as Gary throws up every day, day in day out for months and carpets and tempers get frayed with unending vomit. Eventually, the day in, day out cycle of sickness stops, after we've renewed the bedroom, living room and hall carpets. A holiday at St Anne's, outside Blackpool, does enough to reassure our faith in human nature, and we'd let nature take its course again – and try to add to the family again.

At this time and at St Anne's, an old association with Leeds (remember Killie v Leeds in 1967) reacquaints itself as we meet and enjoy the company of the Bullers family, from Morley in Leeds. Robert and Gill and family, in the form of Gavin, Shane, Katie and Sofie, combine with us to make a double family holiday.

Their family in a sense is everything that we are not – they're English, artistic and musical, but we share a drink, a laugh, kids' stories and kids playing, and a lasting relationship and friendship is formed.

Rebirth or at least renewal or retirement is on my mum and dads minds as my dad agrees to have a retirement party in the Darvel Juniors Social Club on Friday 19 May 1989. After over forty years' service with 'the Council' the powers that be (Kilmarnock & Loudoun District Council) decided to honour this service with a small presentation to mark this occasion and that of some other 'worthies.' Service and recognition knows no bounds as they present my dad with a 5" x 3" ceramic squirrel – nuts or what?! The expectation had not been out of this world – the reality was certainly within it – it was desultory bordering on demeaning. How many of KLDC's managers and 'high heid yins' picked up the same ceramic squirrel for over forty years service – but these guys were only 'common workers!' Mum and dad were visibly hurt by the totally inept attempt to mark an occasion, which they had looked forward to with 'old-fashioned' pride. True to form, my dad laughed it off, although the squirrel would not take pride of place in the display cabinet – we would find a corner for it and it would be cheap and easy to keep.

Nancy's second pregnancy is coming along just fine and, as 'old-stagers' we are more relaxed and comfortable in the approach to the second birth. Gary is content to know he will have a wee brother or sister soon. May 1989 is hot (unusually hot for Scotland) as we pad up and down the grounds of Irvine Central maternity Hospital. "Nothing" is happening, as I think of leaving for home, only to discover we've got some 'movement.' The nurse is advised that contractions appear to be coming pretty steady now, but the nurse knows best, there's no hurry – *"You haven't got a labour face."* An hour later and I've had a Tory, Liberal Democrat, SNP and back to a Labour face as no-one has been near for an hour, and Nancy definitely knows things have well and truly started. I hotfoot it in search of the midwife, who then casually checks Nancy and declares 'full dilation' and we're off in the wheelchair to the maternity unit delivery suite. The labour is shorter but the delivery is longer, as this baby decides to meander slowly out into the world. There is no explosion of a black haired baby onto the blue mat, only an inexorable entry which tears at Nancy and turns to tears of joy, as the wee fellow is out. He's out, but not using his lungs like Gary; he's a bit blue and a tube is quickly inserted into his mouth and mucus drawn out by the midwife sucking on the vacuum as if she needed petrol to get home that night. The 'gunge' is removed and the wee fellow and us breathe easily. Greg Alexander Rodgers is officially in this world at 12.53am on Wednesday 24th May 1989. He's a contented baby and we're home inside four days to be the new family.

The new and extended family is also extending directly in the McCulloch branch, as the 'live-in lodger' and Marion decide to take up and make a home of their own. Hurlford Kirk is the scene of the wedding as the Reverend Brodie marries Marion and Davy, resplendent in his kilt, on 5 August 1989. We have a great day back at the Parakeet and Harry copes well in his youngest daughter's greatest day. He and Mavis can really dance and this masks ongoing uncertainty and uneasiness, which is never far from the surface. The younger entourage, Joanne, Gavin and Gary all have a ball as, like mini magnets, they draw attention and money in equal measures.

The youngest of the immediate Rodgers' family was also drawing attention to himself, as mum phoned in panic, despair and desperation, to declare, *"You can't go down the street today!"* Expecting the death of my dad, or some near and dear relative, the explanation was offered – Graham smashed the chemist's window last night. In a family of 'no angels,' but no trouble, Graham's breaking of the chemist's window in a fit of emotional and drunken rage was the 'low-light' of our brushes with the law. It was literally a sobering experience for Graham as he's never drunk alcohol since then. Apart from Bobby and me 'being reported' for eating Mrs Clark's daffodils on return from a good night out, there were no assaults, no robberies, no muggings down to a Rodgers. This was no consolation, as mum couldn't face the street. It wasn't as if Graham had smashed the chemist's window to get at some prescription drugs – it was simply the fact he had done something patently and publicly wrong, which would be down to a 'Rodgers.' To mum, everything that had gone before, in terms of 'good' had been undone with the first crack on the window. High standards, in expectation of common-sense behaviour were breached, and so visibly, so mum's reaction was understandable – it was only a window, but it was mum's window on the world, through which the Rodgers' were viewed – the image and reality were now cracked.

As if to repair the crack, I set off down the street – a bit self-conscious, but conscious that the absence of any Rodgers would be tantamount to disgrace and denial. Short-term disgrace it might have been, but there was no denial, least from Graham, as he pled guilty at Kilmarnock Sheriff Court, and was fined £400 plus costs. Being there with Graham, I felt this was harsh for a first offence, to a boy who was genuinely 'good.' The 'object of his emotion' was Elaine (wee Elaine, even wee'er than our sister, Elaine). In an attempt to help Elaine's family taxi business, Graham took on some of the reception/call duties into the early hours of the morning. As a golf course greenkeeper, he was up early anyway and this soon caused friction with his employers, Loudoun Gowf Club (the only Gowf Club in the world, and in the spirit of reconciliation, well worth a visit). It was a short course, then run by short-minded and short-memoried people, who had forgotten why they had recruited Graham as their first YTS trainee greenkeeper and how he had turned out regularly and diligently to prepare the course and greens for early-morning competition starts. Refusal to work overtime on the level and extent previously worked was considered as a breach of contract and dismissal followed.

I take on the case for Graham. A late offer of £400 in settlement of the case was rejected and it was all or nothing at the Industrial Tribunal. I was up for it and we went through the details of likely question, responses and outcomes. All this went for nought, as Gary took ill and was admitted to hospital with suspected pneumonia. We're at the hospital until 2am and leave when he is deemed to be 'ok.' 6am and I'm back up to have an early start and get to the IT in Glasgow in good time. We're there in good time, but there is no good time. Less than four hours sleep kicks in early as I miss a golden opportunity to have the IT delayed, based on the fact that one of the IT (board/members) is declared to be the President of another Golf Club. Damned if you object and damned if you don't. I opt to go ahead and lose.

The report in the Glasgow Herald of course reflected none of the above in its "*Greenkeeper loses appeal over sacking.*"

A Golf Club greenkeeper who was sacked after refusing to work at weekends during the competition season has lost his claim that he was unfairly dismissed.

Mr Graham Rodgers was dismissed from his job at Loudoun Gowf Club, Galston, Ayrshire, last November after twice having refused written requests to give an undertaking that he would work overtime during the 1991 season.

Mr Rodgers, of Muir Drive, Darvel, Ayrshire, maintained he could not be compelled to work overtime as it was not a condition of his contract of employment.

Although he had previously worked at weekends, he claimed this had been on a voluntary basis. At no time had he been told that there would be compulsory overtime to be worked.

Mr Rodgers had started work with the club in 1985 as an employment trainee, eventually being offered a full-time post as an apprentice and qualifying as a full skilled greenkeeper.

An industrial tribunal in Glasgow heard that last summer he told the head greenkeeper he was no longer prepared to do weekend work because of personal circumstances.

When interviewed by club committee members, he explained that he had to work for his girlfriend's father at the weekends due to a family crisis.

In an effort to resolve the matter, the club then wrote to him seeking written confirmation that he would be available and willing to do weekend overtime in 1991. He refused to give such an undertaking.

A second letter from the club, this time making it clear that refusal or inability to give the assurance sought could lead to dismissal, was met with a similar response by the greenkeeper, who was then dismissed.

Rejecting Mr Rodgers claim that his dismissal was unfair, the tribunal said it was satisfied that there was a requirement on golf clubs to carry out work on the greens on the days when competitions took place."

It's the end of Graham's employment with the Gowf Club – not on his ability to perform his duties – he was bloody good at his job – but 'the Committee's' inability to allow a reasonable time for a young boy to get his life together. It was the end of a job, but not the end of the world. It was serious, but not tragic.

Serious but not tragic also applied to Gavin's accident. Like most local authority 'swing parks' in the 1980s and 1990s, the 'swings,' roundabout, rocking horse and 'chute' were all mounted on tarmac, If not concrete bases and surrounds. Hardly the most children-friendly surfaces in the event of the likely fall. The young Gavin had such a fall from the chute, but undeterred he continues as normal. Normal, that is, until his behaviour becomes abnormal – he is listless, has a sore head, and completely uninterested in everything. The doctor declares Gavin to be ok. Unconvinced, Trisha and John observe until they are stirred to action in face of telltale signs which spell 'danger ahead.' The incident escalates to emergency surgery and a young Gavin awakes, with swollen eyes and an eight-inch red ridge and stitches curving round the left side of his head. The red ridge in time will subdue to an unbroken white line but the six-inch permanent scar in his head is infinitely better than a temporary six-foot scar on the ground to mark his grave. Only Trisha and John's insistence that Gavin was 'not right' and the skill of the surgeons at the Southern General saved the serious from becoming the tragic.

Source:- Glasgow Herald, page 7 – Home News, Tuesday 4 June 1991.

Top: My graduation. MA (Hons) Modern History and Economics – 4th July 1980, Glasgow University

Top: Monkton Hall Terrace, Musselburgh – No. 17 is the lower level house with the street lamp next to it.
Bottom left: Davy decorating No.17.
Bottom right: Marion decorating No.17.

Top: Gary and Greg on Holiday in SA Coma, Majorca.
Bottom: Laughing boy Greg.

CHAPTER FOUR

"A Trio of Tragedies"

Personnel Manager, Ayrshire District, became my title, as I move to Kilmarnock as my new employment base with SSEB. Newly rescrubbed and presented, the essentially public service becomes privatised as Scottish Power. A District of just over 300 employees and probably with our 300 relatives, was a great place to be. In the 'economies of scale' Vs 'small is beautiful' debate, the 'small is beautiful' won. Ayrshire is the District to be. The Team gel under John Menzies and Greenholm Street in Kilmarnock becomes the customer service centre for Ayrshire, as we win the first ever Ayrshire Quality Association Award.

Alex Kennedy, Joe Burns, Walter Russell, Les Burns, Jim Johnson, Ken Allan, John Menzies and myself become the first team. The Social & Recreation Club for Ayrshire blossoms, as John and myself do a karaoke cover of "*I've never felt more like singin' the blues,*" and everyone else covers their ears. Seeing was believing, but hearing was painful.

Jobs were also available within Ayrshire District and my brother Colin secured a fixed-term position as a General Duties Assistant (GDA), which, through his own efforts and application, is confirmed as permanent after six months. Marion's Davy meantime decides at (the age of almost twenty-four) he is too old to still be a milk boy and there's not enough money in it to pay the rent. An HGV licence would be useful to secure a job so Davy pays the course and exam fee with money borrowed from Nancy's mum, Mavis, whilst still living with her and passes first time. Some short-term lorry driving work proves this driving about all day and night is not what it's cracked up to be, or at least, not for Davy on short-term contracts with employers who paid only what they could get away with. An 'anonymous' interview with Scottish Power results in Davy also securing a job at Kilmarnock, based on his own merits.

In the midst of all the relative contentment, mum and dad face up to the inevitable – the older they got the more difficult it was for them to continue to live at Hillcrest. Their home since 1959 would become someone else's house. 44 Glen Crescent in downtown Darvel was the address on all the gear, and Davy Clements, brother Davy, Colin and me get all the belongings down to the new house before Christmas 1992. Well into retirement age, this is an absolute wrench, but also an absolute must for mum and dad to be able to get out and about and for us to ensure everything is ok. Physically and mentally shattered from the exertions of the move, the early days at Glen Crescent seem a bit of a trial, but familiarity breeds contentment and a growing realisation that the good days at Hillcrest were 'banked' as carefully as dad's weekly wages had been for over forty years. Grieving for Hillcrest was short-lived and living for Glen Crescent took off.

Normal working day follows normal working day, as the pattern of life begins to be beaten out at a more even rhythm. There are no huge upheavals, things and family are coming together. Small but very significant things happen – these are normal, happy, family things – Gary learns to walk and talk; Gary goes to Nursery School. Greg learns to walk and talk and thinks he should go to Nursery School with Gary. Nancy and I decide that the two Gs are enough family for us and I 'get the snip,' Friday 8 May 1992. After overcoming my mental block and the painful reports from fellow 'snippets' or 'snippees' I am stripped and ready for action – at Ballochmyle Hospital. The action starts and could have ended with a quick shave but the nursing assistant has a keen eye, and a very steady hand, which is more than can be said for me. The action continues with a quick needle jab to the right testicle area and things are looking well —pretty numb – that is, until the doc decides to make the incision, cut the tubes and tie a knot in them. *"Relax, you seem a bit tense,"* was the nurse's observation – too right I was. There are a helluva lot more painful things than a vasectomy; torn ligaments, leg breaks, childbirth etc and after a day or two and three or four baths, "all's swell" becomes "all's well."

Physical pain, in whatever guise, cannot compare with the impact and long-lasting effect of emotional pain and loss. It had been a wee while since life had given us a kick in the teeth to remind us not to take it for granted and to value each and every moment. As if a 'wake-up call' were needed for the family, we were delivered not one but three blows – a kick to the stomach, one to the head, and then, when we were down, another one to the head. A trio of tragedies awaited us and there was not a thing we could do but live through it and in spite of it. It was something Marlene had to go through with Lorraine at a distance, when her Frank was killed in a road traffic accident in South Africa. At least we were at home and could comfort each other.

Like many 'ex-pats' Marlene and Frank had worked hard and made good since his first job as a welder in South Africa. The Scottish work ethic provided a base for progression to management and then to self-employment and a business to run. The lifestyle developed in line and holidays to Swaziland and a new house and the purchase of land followed. Triumph precedes disaster as Frank's pick-up leaves the road on the journey home and he is killed. Throughout the years since the early 1980s, in South Africa Frank had returned on a few occasions, including the death of his mother – but in his death, his brothers, sisters family and friends could not return their respect to him – Marlene and Lorraine had to shoulder this on their own as telephone calls were no substitute for a mother's embrace and family's empathy.

By late March 1993, Davy and Marion were well settled into their new house in Hurlford – it's been redecorated and friends and relatives had all been round to help with the 'house-warming.' Two days of unabated sickness and diarrhoea are originally put down to a carry out meal on the Friday evening, but by Sunday afternoon the suspected food poisoning becomes a suspected obstruction and Davy is admitted to Crosshouse Hospital.

The following extracts from the 26 pages of Ayrshire & Arran nursing notes summarise Davy's medical conditions and treatments.

***5/4/93*, 13.00 hours**

Emergency transfer via 4a at 10.45am, with history of ? food poisoning/nausea vomiting and loose foul smelling stools. Relatives spoken to by Dr Kidd.

15.15 hours – *intubated and ventilated*

21.00 hours – *patient stable but ill*

Nursing care – *all care as tolerated, eyes clean, mouth dry, pressure areas intact. Family in attendance throughout the day – wife staying in Short Stay tonight.*

6/4/93, *Night report – very unstable throughout the night.*

Sweating profusely, salivating ++++++++

Nursing care – bed bathed, incontinent of faecal fluid x 4 overnight.

Condition deteriorated 5am. Blood pressure down, no urinary output, peripherally shutdown. Seen by Dr Wilson, renal physician and Mr Paterson, theatre originally planned but patient not stable enough.

13.30 hours – *stable but ill.*

Seen by Mr Livingston and Dr McKay. Family in attendance.

***6/4/93*, 8.30pm** – *In theatre 5.30pm – 6.45pm for laparotomy ; division of (Mr Livingston and Mr Shetty) adhesions and release of obstructive loop of terminal ileum (?approx 2-3 litres of faecal fluid drained from gut under decompression).*

Air entry fair – harsh and duller to bases. No aspirate from chest.

Given extra fluid during theatre.

Nursing Care – *now on air fluidised Clinitron bed. All care given as conditions allowed. Family spoken to by Dr Pary and have visited.*

7/4/93 – *Inaccurate Swan Ganz reading*

Care – *bathed, shaved, central and arterial sites re-dressed, eye and mouth care, 2-hourly. Eyes remain oedematous. Wife and sister visited, prior to staying overnight in Short Stay.*

1.30pm – *Steady tho' slow improvement maintained.*

Nursing care – *Abdominal wound redressed, wound satisfactory, abdomen less distended. Blood-stained … secretions continue to 'ooze' from nasal passages and mouth when disturbed. Mouth moist, tongue slightly coated. Wife spoken to by Dr Miller.*

7/4/93 – *Generally stable.*

Nursing care – *All care 2° eyes remain oedematous mouth moist saliva and bile from op +++ pressure areas intact. Family in attendance throughout evening.*

8/4/93, am – *Condition fairly stable overnight.*

Nursing – *Bathed this morning. Pressure areas satisfactory. Skin looks quite red, not hot to touch. Eyes remain very sore care given. Abdominal wound cleaned. Suture line left exposed, clean and dry. Light at times, settles well with sedation.*

8/4/93 – *Generally stable but ill.*

Ventilation – *patient making effort (to breathe) but not moving volume.*

8/4/93 – Output – *Nasogastric tube not in correct place as bile leaking from mouth and nose. Repositioned and 1,000 mls bile in suction container (on low suction).*

Nursing care – *Bed bathed. Pressure areas intact. turned hourly. Eyes clean, mouth now clean and moist. No further twitching or seizures. Wife spoken to by Dr Wilson. Family visited this afternoon/evening.*

9/4/93, am – *remains ill. Making very little respitory effort overnight.*

Neuro – *Frequent twitching of trunk and upper limbs overnight. Extending both arms during seizures, tho' flexing arms to pain. Lower limbs flexing to pain – no response. Pupils are unequal – right size 4mm, left size 5mm. Very sluggish reaction to light.*

Nursing care – *bed bathed. Mother phoned this am.*

***9/4/93*, 14.00 hours** - *Remains unwell but stable. CT scan shows cerebral oedema. To be fully ventilated to keep PaCo , 30. CMV FcO^2 increased to 70% post physio, as he desaturated to 86%.*

Neuro – *Left pupil slightly larger than right, reacting very sluggishly. Withdraws from painful stimuli 0800.*

Sedated and paralysed now and for CT scan. Was still "twitching" prior to this.

Nursing care – *Wife and family spoken to by Dr Hildebrand re CT scan, also visited this morning.*

21.00 hours – *Condition still poor but very stable.*

Nursing care – *Wife says she sees "a big improvement in his appearance." Relatives in attendance almost constantly, obviously very upset and asking lots of questions and needing information repeated several times. Neuro obs discontinued as he is sedated and paralysed. Pupils – right size 4 and very sluggish, left size 5 – very difficult to tell if pupils are reacting at all, Abdominal wound redressed. Bed-bathed and shaved.*

10/4/93 – *General condition remains very ill.*

Neuro – *Pupils only size 2. Unable to detect any reaction.*

Care – *Bathed, shaved, pressure areas clean and intact. Eye and mouth care as charted. Visited by family. Relatives staying overnight in Short Stay.*

13.30 hours – *Condition stable tho' chest condition not improving.*

Nursing care – *Pupils small and don't appear to be reacting.*

***10/4/93*, 8pm** – *Condition unchanged.*

Nursing care – *Bed-bathed, turned hourly. Eyes satisfactory now, mouth moist – tongue slightly coated. Light and making insp effort in afternoon, since sedation turned up, now more settled. Pupils remain small, ? reacting. Visited by family.*

***11/4/93*, 6am** – *Condition static*

Nursing care – *Bed-bathed. Mouth dry, eyes as before, all care 2-hourly. Pupils pin-point, difficult to ascertain whether light reactive or not.*

***11/4/93*, 13.30 hours** – *Sedation off from 07.45am, Making respitory effort.*

11/4/93 – Output – *One episode of rectal "bleeding" – query collection from siggy (colon) biopsy, seen by Mr Sugden – just observe meantime.*

Nursing care – *Air fluidised Clinitron, nursed side to side. Eyes still puffy, dirty oral secretions. No response to painful stimuli. wife, sisters and parents visited. Very distressed that he has not woke up and quizzing everyone.* ***Will need to be spoken to re overdoing visiting. Wife is still in residence in Short Stay ward.***

6pm *(Dopamine) increased to 10mls with no effect. Patient not breathing at all. Unofficial brain death tests carried out with no responses. Family spoken to by Dr Miller, very distraught. Condition deteriorating quite rapidly.*

9pm – *Condition very poor but stable at time of report.*

Post rectal bleeding, copious amounts fresh/serous blood before 5pm 300mls–500mls. One episode following 5pm. 300mls in suction line. Pressure area care carried out each time.

Mother and father gone home. Brother has gone home. Wife and other relatives staying in Short Stay.

12/4/93, 6am – *Very slow deterioration overnight. Members of family with David throughout the night.*

Nursing care – *Bed bathed and shaved. All care provided. Support provided for all family members, appear aware of David's imminent demise.*

Neuro – *Pupils fixed, dilated. No response to painful stimuli or otherwise.*

12/4/93 – *Continues to deteriorate.*

Neuro – *Brain stem death tests carried out by Dr White and Dr Young. No response. To be repeated at 9am tomorrow. Family spoken to at length by Dr White and myself.*

Nursing care – *All care given as required. Support given to relatives.*

12/4/93 - *Family present – support given.*

13/4/93, 4.45am – *Ventilation unchanged, as directed. Blood pressure slowly deteriorated further. Heart rate slowly falling, ECG becoming ischaemic, rate below 60, became asystole at 5am, thereafter* *certified dead by Dr Cunningham. David's wife and other members of family present. All supported and comforted as much as possible.*

Without the aid of these medical notes at that time, we try to make sense of it all and to us, it seems by Monday afternoon, Davy is really struggling to breathe, and is put on a ventilator and lapses into unconsciousness, before we all get to see him and are told how serious he is. He has septicaemia.

Davy fights for his life in a silent struggle that is only broken by our pleas to wake up and letting him know how things are going outwith the hospital. Day in, day out, we try and have someone there for him to speak to and wake up to. Life support machines function for Davy as he ceases to function; he's with us in body but doctors decide they need to check if he's still with us in mind, after confirming that he has suffered from 'toxic shock.' This is a rare condition overall and even rarer for a male of Davy's age, 28 years old, but it seems to have emanated from adhesions related to an appendix operation (some six years earlier).

Davy is operated on at Tuesday teatime to remove/repair the obstruction, and things are looking a bit better. By Wednesday evening, Jeanette, Nancy and Trisha are in better spirits as they clean their house a bit, changing the bed etc, in preparation for Davy being released, but Marion has "a bad feeling about all this," which Mavis tells her is because she feeling low and run down – Marion doesn't really believe her. By Thursday, Davy is 'twitching,' which we think is good, he's trying to waken up – Marion thinks differently – the twitching is a bad sign. Attempts at weaning him off ventilator and drugs don't work, so they decide to leave things for 24 hours and try again. Brain scan on Friday – 'Good' Friday' -confirms swelling on brain, causing twitching and they warn that even if he regains consciousness, there may be damage.

The immediate family is gathered to hear and face the results of the brain stem tests. *"There is no brain activity. Davy (your son, husband, brother, brother-in-law) is brain dead."* The result and truth is too hard to take in, as Davy is warm to the touch and he's still Davy – just wake him up, he'll be ok.

After eleven days of illness and a titanic struggle to hold on to life, there was no waking up for Davy. On the evening of 12 April, I said my last goodbye and left Nancy and the immediate family to be with Davy for the inevitable end. That inevitable end came at quarter to five in the morning of 13 April 1993. There were no words, no consolation, no explanation that could make any sense of "Why?"

There was no waking of the dead. After a mammoth struggle to live, Marion went to Davy for him to finally and formally to die. Her less than five-foot, now fragile frame, clung to Davy for a desperate last time. A living nightmare has no sense of reality and no sense of justice and fairness.

REM have a number one hit with "Everybody Hurts," and to us, it became Davy's commemorative song. Nancy, Trisha and Jeanette stay with Marion on an alternating basis to offer sisterly support in what becomes hours, days and weeks of greatest need, once the shock gives way to reality. Davy will never return – his wardrobe, clothes, razor and toothbrush are superfluous and his scent, voice and touch are at best recorded in video or memories of the past, but never again to be present in the future. A double bed with a wee teddy bear is no substitute for the big 'teddy bear' and the pillow becomes a sponge for tears that never seem to cease to flow.

The funeral service is arranged in the same church which had been the scene of Davy and Marion's wedding, in which they declared love and faithfulness, 'till death do us part.' The church and the service overflows to the cemetery in Hurlford. As part of the funeral cortege it is difficult to get to the cemetery and the newly dug grave evokes personal but now painful memories of helping dad at the new cemetery in Darvel. Getting to the graveside we scan the hill above and it appears as a forest of newly sprung mourners standing respectfully between the headstones all around. The forest contains a swathe of Scottish Power Ayrshire employees, who decide en masse they will attend and catch up with work later. Individual people are not really recognisable as cord members are called and we concentrate on putting Davy to rest as gently as possible.

Focusing on the task in hand with cord number six helps to stifle tears that flow all around and are only interrupted by the agonising cry of 'no' as the finality of the farewell/funeral is felt by father, mother, brothers, sisters, sisters and brothers-in-law, friends and other family. Marion holds it together but Don McLean's *'Bye, Bye, American Pie,'* a Davy favourite, is too much to contemplate.

We have photos of Davy but it's funny how it is some of the oddest possessions of Davy's which evoke the sharpest of memories and which are still capable of bringing a smile to our faces.

We have his old racing bike, a silver and now rust frame on tyres, which never seemed thick enough to take his frame.

We have a pair of his brown, steel toe-capped working boots, from his last job with Scottish Power.

We have £6 in a jar, which was his 'skin,' from his previous job as a milk-boy.

We haven't the heart to throw the bits and bobs out and they remain like favourite ornaments which link you to another place and time and which, if lost or broken, would only be a source of further grief and sadness. We have 'treasured memories' of Davy. We have no Davy.

With Marion, there was little we could say as we had lived Davy's death with her. Being there for Marion became a rallying call and Nancy and Jeanette's weekend stays and meals with John and Trisha helped ease Marion through grieving and a return to work to the scene of Davy's death. Nowadays, this would have raised cries and the spectre of post traumatic shock and stress, but wee Marion was made of sterner stuff, which gave her the resilience which could not be discerned from her 'wee lassie' image and figure. Involvement became the key for Marion to 'get over her loss,' but at the same time, it also became the focus to highlight her loss – at parties, meals, nights out, she was in company – on her own – nightmare was reality.

Painfully and slowly, some smiles returned to a cherub face and Marion joined us on holiday in Majorca. The sun, sand and sea have a therapeutic effect but music, in the shape of Don McLean or REM became songs of tears as dry eye looks to dry eye in recognition and blinks away, but fails to hide the tears that flow freely and unashamedly. Marion comes to stay with us on a more regular basis and Nancy, Jeanette and me enjoy a drink with her, before Nancy and Jeanette call it a day and go to bed, sometime in October 1994. I stay with Marion to 'have another wee drink,' and I 'fuss' over her and how she's getting on. The response is, *'I'm no a wee lassie, I'm nearly thirty and I know that I have to move on – you (and other people) can't wrap me in cotton wool – remember, I work in a hospital."* This is after a year on and I think she's right. A new normality is restored to Marion's life a she starts to take charge of her life, as it's evident Marion looks and feels better. The second Christmas since Davy's death was understandably looking a helluva lot better than the first.

Presents were bought for Gary, Greg, mum, dad, Mavis, Harry, Marion, Jeanette, Trisha... and stored away till the Christmas tree could be put up. Works nights out were arranged and Marion would join her long time pal, Pauline and her colleagues for a 30th birthday celebration meal in Ayr, on 17 December 1994.

That relatively late-night/early morning call came calling. Nancy is answering the phone and I instinctively turn down the telly, as the conversation does not ring true – there are too many question and gaps in the conversation – something has happened. Is it mum, dad, Mavis, Harry or some of the kids who've had a fall or an accident?

It's Marion – she's collapsed at a club in Ayr and has been taken to Ayr Hospital. Maybe she's just had too much to drink on a good night out; maybe her drinks have been mixed or spiked; maybe she's had an 'E' or some drugs; maybe, maybe, maybe?! Nancy, Jeanette and Trisha, picking up Mavis and Harry en route, rush to the hospital to be by Marion's bedside and get first-hand medical reports to dispel the 'maybes.' In the early hours of the morning, Nancy confirms the facts – Marion's had a brain haemorrhage and it's touch and go. As early as is reasonable, I take Gary and Greg to my mum and dads to explain the position – as ever, it's no problem, but their eyes tell a story of absolute concern and dismay.

On arrival at the hospital, Nancy updates me on the position and 'progress' to date. Naturally agitated, she explains that they have been waiting for over two hours for the doctor to come back and give the results of 'tests.' We attempt to go into the room to see Marion and the nurse firmly but politely confirms that we can't come in. Another twenty minutes elapse and we 'push' to get in after the nurse has disappeared to attend the next high-dependency casualty.

At either side of Marion, Nancy and I sit and try to take in Marion's calmness – there are no cuts, bruises or bandaging of the head – she is as she's been lately – quietly contented and warm with no sign of pain or anxiety in her life. I touch her cheek and she's warm, I press forward and say, *"Come on Marion, come on, wake up."* We sit for a few minutes and comment on how calm she appears and if only the doctor would come, re-examine her and let us know how she would progress. From no sign of pain or anxiety, there was also no sign of breathing. Like a new-born Gary or Greg in their cots, we move forward to check for breathing – nothing. *"She's not breathing, she's stopped breathing,"* I try to say calmly and quietly, but cannot contain myself, and I rush to get a nurse. *"What's her name"* the nurse asks, and she repeats, *"Marion, Marion, Marion, can you hear me?"* after we confirm her name. She checks for vital signs and says there are some and Marion is still living – after the huge unexplained delay, the family are asked in 'to be there' in what are now said to be Marion's last moments. Within two minutes, Marion is declared dead –

perhaps this is a way to help the realisation and grieving process – at least we were there when Marion died? "*A subarachnoid haemorrhage is quite rare, especially in someone of Marion's age (29)*" – I've heard this type of explanation all too recently and whilst true, it offers no real explanation of 'why?' We have what and how but the 'why' is never, ever answered and never will be. Harry, who's done pretty well to hold it together with a voluntary job at Crosshouse Hospital, sits holding Marion's hand and stares into her face and sings, "A bonnie wee Jeanie McCall," over and over in a tormented state, which eventually he realises he's in, and makes way for other members of the family. A true maternal bond is broken along with the hearts of Nancy, Jeanette and Trisha, Marion's sisters.

Phone calls from hospitals that are the exact opposite of those made for newly born babies have to be made. I phone my mum and dad to tell them the news and see if they will look after Gary and Greg for a wee bit longer. The call starts out on a straight and factual basis and ends in uncontrollable sobbing – this time it's not mum, but me, as she realises, for my sake and that of Gary and Greg, she needs to hold it together, despite all her own maternal instinct saying 'cry' – that would come later.

Ironically or symbolically, "Stay Another Day" by East 17 is high in the 'charts' and it becomes our anthem for Marion. It is written in tribute and remembrance of another tragedy (the death of a brother) and the longing for him to be there – even if for just another day. The song, the anguish and emotions behind it are a painful but all too accurate fit that can still cradle a tear and hurt the heart. It may be naïve, even pretentious, to think and link the words to those that would do justice to a latter-day Burns' lament but they are real, relevant and irresistable in our memory of Marion.

"Stay Another Day"

"Baby if you've got to go away
I don't think I can take the pain

Won't you stay another day
Oh don't leave me alone like this
Don't say it's the final kiss
Won't you stay another day
Don't you know we've come too far now
Just to go and try to throw it all away
Thought I heard you say you love me
That your love was gonna be here to stay
I've only just begun to know you
All I can say is won't you stay just one more day
Baby if you've got to go away
I don't think I can take the pain
Won't you stay another day
Oh don't leave me alone like this
Don't say it's the final kiss
Won't you stay another day
Good times we had return to haunt me
Though it's for you, all I do seems to be wrong
I touch your face while you are sleeping
And hold your hand don't understand what's going on
Baby if you've got to go away
I don't think I can take the pain
Won't you stay another day
Oh don't leave me alone like this
Don't say it's the final kiss
Won't you stay another day"

Even before Marion's death and the exact nature of it, with no nursing or consultant staff available or seemingly in attendance, the family were uncomfortable with the way in which Marion's care had been 'handled.' This became all the more intense with the death and the manner in which the consultant/doctor eventually explained what had happened. Scottish people are very slow in general to complain, especially in situations where essential services are stretched and trying to help, but in this case, the doctor's attitude and approach left Nancy with no option but to write a letter of complaint – it would not bring Marion back, but it might just make the doctor reflect on how he had handled this case and do it more humanely and respectfully the next time round?! The letter was never acknowledged let alone responded to!

Within two years of Davy's death, we were solemnly gathered in the same church where Marion and Davy were married and where Davy's funeral service had taken place. The Reverend Roy was becoming the equivalent to death and funerals as the Reverend Collins was to marriages. *"She never got over Davy,"* was to be heard amongst the muffled cries in the church and at the cemetery, and I guess that's true, but heartache did not kill Marion – headache in the form of a subarachnoid haemorrhage did. We didn't understand it, we had never heard of it before, but then, few of us had heard of 'toxic shock' before. When Davie Cooper, the Rangers and Scotland football star died of the exact same condition, aged thirty-nine, whilst filming a football training video, and just a matter of months after Marion, recognition of what had happened became real – *"Our Marion died of that."* Like many an illness, a brain haemorrhage was no respecter of age, talent, fame or age – it simply struck and left every family the poorer.

At the same 're-opened' grave as Davy had been interred some twenty-one months ago, Marion was now being committed to the deep. The cords were called out – Harry, John, Kenny, Faither Davy, Jim and Craig Clements, John Houston and Hugh Hewitson. Nancy, Trisha and Jeanette were there for her all the way, as we rested Marion alongside and reunited her with her Davy. The sense of loss was felt doubly acute as the injustice and unfairness of Davy at twenty-eight and Marion at twenty-nine, dying was incomprehensible. As we walked from room to room in Davy and Marion's house, it was clear Marion hadn't and never would have thrown out or given away all her memories of Davy, as we come across some of his clothing, records, CDs........... Every move, however slowly and delayed to clear the house for sale, became a trauma in itself. *"Remember we helped decorate this room." "Remember this ornament? Davy loved it, but Marion hated it. "Everything is so neat and tidy." "Remember the Picasso?"*

Art had never been Marion's forte and when Jeanette went to the Isle of Man in 1979, Marion and Nancy had a room of their own for the first time (Marion didn't even go to wave her off at the harbour – she was too busy moving in her gear!) she declared she would like a picture for her room – how much would such a picture cost? Jeanette explained it depended on whether she wanted a Sara Moon or a Picasso. *"How much is a Sara Moon?" "About £5/£10,"* was the reply – a moment's hesitation to check her purse and Marion declares – *"Oh I'd better have a Picasso."* As they say, knowing the price of things is not really important; it's appreciating the value of what you have that counts and Marion had known the value of Davy, her mum and dad, sisters, relatives, friends and her job at Crosshouse Hospital.

Changes in life and death are also reflected by changes at work. In order to keep ahead or at least keep up on a professional basis, I decide to do an MSc in Human Resource Management at Stirling University. The deal is that Scottish Power will pay the course fee and I make up the time for my day release and if I fail, I pay the money back – no pressure? The course is modular with continual assessment of course work, an exam and a dissertation of some 15,000 to 20,000 words, involving a piece of work-based research. The day release is actually a half-day, extending into the evening, every Monday for the three terms. The course work and four assessments are completed and passed. Four down, two to go – I chose research into the increasing role and involvement of line management (Team Leaders) in HR activities, as the theme for my dissertation. My workload is heavy and the dissertation work falls behind and I am granted an extension until the 18th September to complete and submit my work. I contemplate 'chucking it' but know we can't 'afford' that, and I will persevere if I can find a way through it. Nancy finds the way – *"For the next four weekends, your working to complete the dissertation."* It's agreed and I sit in my old office in Kilmarnock for the next four weekends to complete the task. On a few days, Gary and Greg join me and with videos in hand, we set them up in the Conference Room, which has an electronic drop-down 'picture screen' and a video projector. Crisps, sweeties and drinks keep them occupied for up to four hours, with the only interruptions being toilet breaks. The work is completed, typed and submitted by the revised deadline and all that is left now is to await the outcome of the exam and the grading of the dissertation.

With the excitement of school kids or undergraduates, I drive to Stirling for the 'posting' of the exam results. There's backslapping all round as pass after pass is noted – the dissertation grading remains the final hurdle to my MSc qualification. The result finally comes through and whilst not a distinction, it is a solid pass and I'm on my way to a third graduation. Depending on your perspective, I am in good company graduating from Stirling University, as in September 1995, Mel Gibson and a Braveheart contingent attend a special graduation ceremony. However, no disrespect to Mel Gibson, Jackie Stewart, Ian Bannen, Gavin Hastings, Catherine Zeta-Jones et al, I will have the best company at my graduation – Nancy and my mum and dad – no mistakes this time round – this will make up for 1980. My mum is especially delighted and both are relatively fit to attend. Graduation day in February 1996 goes very smoothly and professionally. We meet and talk with fellow 'classmates' and eagerly await the ceremony. From school days onwards, it's a fairly familiar routine – sit in the specified order, await your call, row by row, and then proceed to the stage on the calling of your name, don't run and exit right. It's familiar to me, but absolutely unique to Nancy, mum and dad and that in turn makes it unique for me. The robes and the scroll don't quite sum up a year of effort, but the photo captures the absolute magic of the day in a way that words never will.

Maternal pride in me becomes maternal concern for Mavis (Nancy's mum). She smoked years ago and has the equivalent of a smoker's cough, which is never really diagnosed as anything. A pain in the chest lingers and is not cleared by antibiotics (chest infections and variously angina, Meniere's disease, gas leak are all suggested causes). Mavis is fifty-nine and pretty fit, but after a prolonged period of to-ing and fro-ing to the doctors and consultants, in November 1996 she is confirmed as not being as fit as we all thought – in fact she has cancer.

Looking back, it seems obvious, but then looking forward, nothing was obvious. Complications came at every turn as Mavis (became diabetic in February 1997, as a result of taking the steroids she was prescribed), then came the shattering confirmation that she had multiple lesions (tumours) in the brain, that are too far advanced to treat. At this stage, we begin to curse our luck and every no-use bastard that healthily walked the street; some of those bastards had our share of luck and there was no getting it back, so we got at them. Mavis's condition was terminal with the primary cancer being found in the lung, and the days, weeks, months, years question was answered by *"a few months."* Consultants and counsellors explained what was likely to happen and how it would affect Mavis, who was stoically resigned to her fate – she was stronger than us and more concerned for us than herself – but that's a mum.

Christmas 1996 was videoed in a new light and a huge black shadow - it would be Mavis's last – she knew it, we knew it, but for the kids' sake, no one could say it. It was a good, sad day and the kids got the biggest Christmas presents ever. Jeanette spent a huge amount of time with Mavis and it was emotionally draining, as Mavis became physically slower but so mentally alert, that her physical impairments were aggravated in her mind. Harry took a new focus on life or death, and made a fuss that Mavis didn't need or want. Social workers visited the home in Hurlford and given Mavis's condition, agreed that a stair lift would be vital to assist Mavis's failing movement and mobility. Harry, in a focussed effort to help and care for Mavis, was the first the try out the newly installed stair lift in the first week of February 1997 – Mavis watched in horror as the reality of her crippling fate came home to her.

Having been discharged from hospital on 29 November 1996, the how long question was getting to an acute stage and getting to us. How long became how short as Mavis was readmitted to hospital on 11 February 1997, and I visited Mavis in hospital on 13 February for the last time – Nancy was already there – Mavis was already on a high dosage of morphine when I arrived and when I entered, she appeared to be sleeping. On speaking to Nancy, Mavis opens her eyes and without hesitation, says, *"Hi Kenny, how are you?" "I'm............fine,"* and I'm struggling to cope with this and you ask me how I am? Typical Mavis. We talk a little and Mavis pulls at the needle inserted into a vein in the back of her hand and says, *"This is hellish;"* – that just about summed it up – this was hell and it was painful, even on morphine. The doctor is called and says she can't be feeling pain, as the morphine dosage is just about as high as they can legally give. This is hellish, but some 'adjustments' are made and Mavis seems easier in herself and drifts off, as I say my goodbye, to return home to Gary and Greg, leaving variously, Nancy, Trisha, Jeanette and Harry to see what the morning will bring. There was no miracle, only an ending of one pain, and the beginning of another, as we mourned Mavis's passing on the 14th of February 1997. Born on St Patrick's Day, 1936, married on 'D-Day,' 6th June 1956, so I suppose it was fitting that she died on St Valentine's Day.

Even the Reverend McCulloch's faith seems to be tested by the news of Mavis's death, as we again gather in Hurlford Cemetery (Riccarton), some twenty-five feet from Marion and Davy's grave to bury Mavis. Again, the cords are called out, Harry, John, Kenny – but relatively unusual in Scotland,

Trisha, Nancy and Jeanette proudly take their mother's cords (Bob McEwan and Allan Connell take the remaining two). In a sense, Mavis's death was worse than Davy's and Marion's, as we all knew for longer what was happening, but still remained absolutely helpless, as Mavis coped better than we did. Harry was coping well; he had all too dutifully phoned relatives and friends with the news of Mavis's death and the funeral arrangements, when confirmed. He was the focus of great attention and enormous sympathy and he revelled in it. Nancy, as usual, was quick to see that Harry's expectation of help and assistance from his daughters in his sad plight could and would never be matched by the reality. When the reality dawned on Harry that Mavis's death did not secure him the permanent attention he demanded, he sought this security by reverting to type. The bottle brought a better world and 'new and old friends' were acquired and reacquired, as Harry splashed out in an effort to close his 'attention deficit.' He moved in his new circle of 'friends' and entered a final spiral of descent, in spite of 'get a grip of yourself' conversations with numerous members of the family, but the grip on reality had been loosened and lost years before.

In a sense, I had a pretty narrow focus on these 'tragedies' – the events seem to take on a momentum of their own, like a volcano erupting and being faced by a white hot lava flow, which appears to be removing everything in its wake. Eventually though lava, like emotions, cool and hard reality sets in. There is a new physical and emotional landscape in its place – there is a realisation that what we've just gone through does and did happen to others. Close to home there are many examples – my uncles, Jim, David, John, Tom, and aunts, Annie and Margaret. The wider perspective was that my mum and dad had experienced the same types of anguish and emotions we had endured in a four-year spell or hell and now they also suffered on our behalf, in support and sympathy.

The family soldiered on in the face of adversity, and life had to go on for the sake of the kids. The kids literally became bigger and bigger features in our lives. At four years of age, it was off to Nursery School, then at five, to the wee (primary) school and on to the big school (Loudoun Academy) at around twelve years of age. Along the way, Cubs and Scouts are attended, swimming lessons are a must and for two or three years, they represent the Valley Vikings at roller hockey. In between times, we go fishing for rainbows at the fishery in Lanark; go bike runs; go to the cinema and all the other type of things that normal families do or hope to do. We visit Disneyworld in Florida, which is tremendous, but also energy sapping and involves flights which add or take away two days of your holiday. We try something new – a week's cruising in the Mediterranean and a week in Majorca. The Island Breeze is a four-star floating hotel, casino, cinema, sports complex, ballroom, hairdresser, shopping mall and much more (service is service with a smile but not a plastic smile, but of generous warmth and interest, especially with two relatively young kids, who can still be utterly cherubic and charming). Visits to Malta, Messina, Naples, Corsica and Minorca are relatively short and sharp, but give a great flavour of each and every location. Day trips or half-day trips to Rome, Pisa, Lisbon and Barcelona all offer the opportunity to behold some European wonders of the world – the Vatican; the Leaning Tower of Pisa; the Neu Camp and, surprise, surprise, a little piece of Darvel. The plaque read, 'Barcelona A Sir Alexander Fleming,' above a bust of Sir Alexander Fleming in the public park. It seems that the Union of Matadors in Barcelona were so impressed by properties of penicillin to cure the wounds inflicted by wounded bulls that they paid for the erection of the bust in his memory. There appears, however, to be no such memorial stone funded by the 'raging bulls!'

Lisbon is beautiful , polished and professional and even the street urchins who comes to our table at a local bar puts on a show – playing his flute. He is dressed in raggedy clothes which are clearly too big for his slight frame and only the designer trainers arouse our suspicions . He plays the flute and flutters a few dance steps before offering us a can so that we can offer our appreciation of his playing and his apparent plight.

The scene is played out at every table around the street bars and we realise this is a modern Dickensian sketch. We spy a female Fagin who follows the raggedy boy and is in her twenties going on forty . She does the 'junkie shuffle' as her boy dances and delights to feed her habit. She shuffles from left to right foot almost on the spot and her right hand is run up to the shoulder of her left side and returned to scratch at her left wrist only for her left arm to return the complement to her right arm. She shuffles from right to left foot and moves forward one or two feet. She pulls a packet of cigarettes from her loose fitting jacket pocket, lights it and draws in temporary solace.

The 'junkie shuffle' is repeated till her last three fags have gone up in smoke and her only hope now is the contents of the collecting can. The later day Oliver Twist performs and picks at people's heart strings but only to get to their pockets. The female Fagin beckons for the boy to return to her in desperation , empties the can and curses the tourists generosity or lack of it. The raggedy boy gets to keep a100 pesetas and gets to return to the tables with his flute in fake reality. You name the city and the view will be different but the scene will be the same.

Barcelona has different memories. Pets were not our forte. Goldfish won at the 'shows 'in a plastic bag that dripped until you got your goldfish home to transfer to a glass jar or bowl died after two days of feeding them breadcrumbs. Progression for us was to two exotic tropical fish in a real bowl with coloured stones and an archway to swim under. Greg's exotic goldfish was called fruit salad and Gary's black equivalent blackjack. They were fed on fish food from the pet shop not breadcrumbs . Regular cleaning of the bowl would help prolong the fishes lives, or at least Fruit salad's. Blackjack didn't appear to relish life in the newly cleaned bowl and started doing a Michael Jackson. He couldn't actually moonwalk but gradually but perceptibly he was turning white – maybe washing the bowl in mild disinfectant was not so great an idea after all ?

Blackjack aged prematurely , turned grey then white and then turned over in the bowl. Nancy feared the worse in telling a young Gary that his fish is dead. She breaks the news gently – Blackjack is poorly and a bit off colour – in fact he's deadly white which is a distinctly bad sign for a black fish. Nancy starts to cry as she explains to Gary that Blackjack has died during the night and the youthfully mature Gary states – I know mum , don't worry , he was only a fish.

We've left our latest pet – Thumper – a dwarf lop rabbit at home in the safe keeping of our neighbours – the Lyons- the name should have been a clue to Thumper's fate whom we've had since he was six weeks old and he's now going on six years – our greatest pet feat ever. On board the Island Breeze cruise ship after a beautiful day touring Barcelona the news via the mobile is stunning. Thumper has been attacked and killed by a MONGOOSE. Even in the east of Darvel there were no Mongeese . Brother in law John explains the mongoose had in fact been an escaped ferret or polecat which did the natural thing for ferrets and killed Thumper before John relieved the ferret of half its tail with a spade in an effort to save the ailing Thumper.

Nancy and Jeanette have a good 'greet' – this is more than just a fish, this was the family rabbit . Gary and Greg are sad by the manner of Thumper's death but have really grown out of childish affection to youthful acceptance – that's life and death – miss you Thumper.

Each of these holidays and every one before, however short, is accompanied by a note from Mum and Dad to wish us safe journey, a good holiday and a safe return. Invariable within the note a 'luck penny' is tucked away for us to spend – the 'luck penny' is not a penny, it's always pounds, but even if it had been a penny, it was the genuine concern which was of more and lasting value from parents who were literally generous to a fault.

The latest such note which is tenderly handed over on 20 June 2003 contains £100 and reads ;

' To Nancy , Kenneth , Gary and Greg,

I trust you a will have a safe and enjoyable holiday. A well deserved rest from work. Come home refreshed in health and strength to start all over again.

I trust you all travel in God's safe keeping.

From Mum and Dad.'

The note is written on a small three inch times three inch card with a bluebell flower on the front of it and contained in the lilac envelop is the £100.

I probably have twenty such notes for breaks and holidays before getting married and another fifty or so since.

It's unbelievable to think that this was done for us all and covered birthdays, Christmas , short breaks and longer holidays (mum and dad are not religious ; weddings , christenings and funerals are church occasions , normal Christian life is not). However, religiously they have shown tremendous devotion to both immediate and extended family . The money was what they could or perhaps couldn't afford , the love and devotion was something that you couldn't bank but you could 'bank on .'

Back home, we've taken out season tickets for Kilmarnock Football Club and attend as many home games as possible, as both Gary and Greg take to playing the game with Galston Boys Club, in their respective age groups. Gary is not a natural football player and starts playing in goals, as he is quite tall. Greg is smaller and has more natural ability. Both stick in and do well in their first year with the Club. At an Easter tournament in Blackpool, Gary decides being a goalie doesn't involve you very much and gets a game outfield and there is no turning him back as he is turned into a full-back. Another year on and both pick up the merit trophies in their respective teams and this reflects the fact that both are team players who are full of commitment and effort.

Killie also fare pretty well under Alex Totten and Bobby Williamson and reach the final of the Scottish Cup at Ibrox, on the 24th of May 1997, Greg's 8th birthday. Late in the day, we decide to go and I secure three tickets. The first half is fairly uneventful and even, as both Killie and Falkirk fail to break down each other's defences. As the half-time reflection began, "Happy Birthday to Greg Rodgers" is reflected up on the electronic scoreboard and I quickly point it out to Greg – he's well chuffed and his Aunt Jeanette had made the day, as Killie eventually secure a 1-0 victory.

The Ayrshire District Management Team is reassembled in the Park Suite on 1st May 1999 and it's a 12.30pm start. We're in dangerous territory as Walter Russell is attending and the hospitality flows and flows. 6pm and we adjourn to the Killie Club. Eventually I stagger home about 9pm, having forgotten to phone home. On 'sprachling' through the door, it's evident we have mini family gathering – perhaps it's a party. No such luck but I'm no longer in a party mood, as Nancy confirms her dad died earlier today and I couldn't be contacted. I sober up and offer to 'go and help,' but it's too late for help tonight. The events leading to Harry's death become clearer in the morning and it's confirmed, he's died of a heart attack at home. Nancy, Trisha and Jeanette's years of frustration and worry over Harry turn to genuine tears of sorrow at the death of their Dad. We're back at Mavis's graveside late that week and again some twenty-odd feet from Davy and Marion, Harry joins Mavis.

3a Craigie Road, Hurlford, is now empty – no Marion, no Davy, no Mavis, no Harry – no need to keep the house which had been the home to Nancy, Trisha, Jeanette and Marion from childhood. It's another break with the past.

The future and the year 2000 are hurtling through space towards us. A new Millennium is looming and it's tempting to think –*"Things can only get better."*

Marion's last photo at the party night out on 18th December 1984 (Marion is on the right).

CHAPTER FIVE

Millennium Mayhem and Magic

The new millennium accentuates our thoughts that we are getting older. 40th birthday parties and silver wedding anniversaries are more our 'territory' now. Even if you attend an 18th or 21st birthday or a wedding, there is in your mind a sense of no real change, but then you remember you are there as an uncle or an aunt and not one of the 'gang.' Your youth is going or gone but is also growing round you in the shape of sons, daughters, nieces and nephews.

Nieces and nephews have sprung up all around, as Lillian and Duncan have four children (Shona, Roddie, Alistair and Lorna); Jim and Jessie have Bobby, Claire, Jim and Lillian; Marlene and Mike - Lorraine; Elaine and Alister – Kevin; Bobby and Linda – Paul and Stephen; Yvonne and Jimmy – Jim and Ian; Avril and Andy – Aidan and Vhari. Counting Gary and Greg, mum and dad have eighteen grandchildren. The cycle of family life continues and expands as families become families within and beyond families as thirteen further offspring extend the roots and branches of a living family tree.

I am proud to be Aidan's godfather and the christening is a great day in Middleton, just outside the centre of Manchester. Avril, following teacher training, graduation and a placement at our old school (Darvel Junior Secondary) has secured a good position in a school in the Manchester area. Aidan is a fit and healthy two-year old whose world is opening up before him – he's at a stage in learning where phenomenal progress is made. But just as easily as lights can be switched on, they can also be switched off.

An active and attentive Aidan becomes awkward and alone. Initially, the signs are minimal but are magnified in the comparison with the progress of his peers. Visits to Mum and Dad become harder for them as they realise they can't quite articulate that 'something's not right with Aidan.' Avril and Andy struggle for over twelve months to get a diagnosis and come to terms with it before they can tell Mum and Dad what in their heart of hearts they already knew, as Aidan becomes a statistic in the great MMR debate – he is diagnosed as having autism.

The reports we read confirm that autism in children under eight has increased ten-fold since 1988. British babies now receive six vaccine doses in a unified shot before they are eight weeks old. They will be the recipients of another twenty-two doses before they get to school. Some fifty years ago, the only needle jab was for smallpox. The debate over MMR vaccination or lack of it rages on and is not likely to be settled in the near future. In the meantime, unless unorthodox or 'unapproved' treatment and medicines are attempted, Aidan's future is clear – constant, unrelenting care for a growing child who cannot understand or communicate.

In the midst of all the misery of our tragedies, there was the enjoyment of some silver and golden moments. Mum and dad celebrated their Golden Wedding Anniversary at Seamill Hydro on 31 March 1998. A Golden Wedding Anniversary is an absolute treasure; a joy to behold and yet its also muted in its celebration, as a goodly number of the good people who attended the original wedding are no longer with us. There's emphasis on the marriage, the missing and the memories. Anniversary presents abound but are almost incomprehensible to Mum and Dad, who are simply delighted and dignified in the devotion they have shown to each other and their family. Lillian and Duncan, Jim and Jessie and Elaine and Alister have all celebrated over twenty-five years of marriage.

Perhaps in search of our Irish roots, we venture with mum and dad to Dublin. Dublin is a versatile and vibrant city but as a city, it was too hectic for mum and dad, who would have been more relaxed in the more rural Southern Ireland.

At the other end of the spectrum, Graham and Elaine 'ran away' to Gretna to get married, after years of living with each other. Marlene gets remarried to Mike Gibb. Mike is not a 'Bee Gee,' more a 'wee G' – a wee Geordie, who's proud as punch to marry Marlene on 6 June 1999. Mike, like Marlene, has been married before and following his separation from Alison; the three kids, Jonathan, Julie and Beverley take to the maternal Marlene like an older sister. It's not easy for Mike to work abroad a lot with GEC/Alston and support his new found wife and family but 'things will get better.' Only David and Colin remain unmarried in the family.

'Things can only get better,' if people strive and commit to making them better. Shutting our eyes and minds to take the easy option or dull the pain is not a solution. In Scotland, there was already a sense of 'off with the old and on with the new,' as the new Scottish Parliament had been finally opened in 1999, with Gary in attendance for the big day. Gary is captured on video and the event and potential seems to capture a nation's ambition 'to be a nation again.' After a prorogation of 292 years, we Scots look to the Scottish Parliament as a source of innovation and optimism. In reality, innovation and optimism appear to be to the fore but governmental cronyism and constipation are never far behind. The jury's out as the Scottish Parliament reaches the end of its first term on 27 March 2003. The May 2003 elections produce another 'Lab-Lib' pact as the Labour and Liberal Democrat MPs form a Government

However, the old Millennium is not quite out when the approach of the new Millennium conjures up ideas of renewing the spirit of a Darvel in decay. In marketing terms or estate agent speak, Darvel was the gateway to Ayrshire; the birthplace of Sir Alexander Fleming; a Lace Town, full of country properties at affordable prices and a warm and inviting community. Not all of this was bullshit and in best advertising parlance some of it was actually true, but the warm and inviting embers on the community fire were all but out. A few characters and a few clubs kept up the good fight to put the community back in Darvel – but it was an unequal struggle, against apathy, alcohol and amphetamines. It was also a struggle that virtually every other town in Scotland faces as personal commitment and endeavour replace social conscience and consciousness.

Ironically, it was mostly 'interlopers,' those not born or bred in Darvel, or relatively new to the town who took up the initiative to breath more life into it. The Millennium Association is formed and comprised – Nancy, Trisha and Jeanette (the triple-trouble McCulloch sisters), Bobbi (Trisha's sister-in-law), Alexis, Lorna, the two Maggies, Dugald, Michael and Bobby, the town's SNP Councillor.

The immediate aim was to arrange an event at the town 'Square' to celebrate Hogmanay/New Year in the old-fashioned way – gather at the Square with family and friends, share a drink, have a laugh and enjoy the 'crack.' There could be a whole series of events for young and old alike to help celebrate the new Millennium and rebuild a community spirit which had been sadly lacking for many years. This was a task which the Millennium Association relished and Nancy, Trisha and Jeanette could look forward to help create some happy memories in the future without ever forgetting the tragedies or those happy memories of the past.

From 9pm on Hogmanay 1999 at the Town Square the hum of the diesel generator is silenced by the strum of Maggie McRae and the Tattiehowkers. Some 800 residents brave the elements and gather at the Square to mark the historic occasion, hoping the millennium bug won't bite or byte! Gary and I have our St Andrew's Ambulance Association First Aid certificates so we are Millennium Association Marshals/First-Aiders. The atmosphere is lively but light as whole families take to the streets to form and take some community spirit. The grant from the Lottery Commission (obtained with a lot of help from Maggie McRae) was money well secured and spent. The new Millennium is welcomed in as never before and the people of Darvel begin to see themselves in a new light. "Will we have this next year?" and "What else are you going to do?" are the most asked questions.

Community events, including dances, discos, quiz nights, ceilidhs, talent contest, sponsored walks, river cleans and open air café days followed and a bit of Millennium Magic is created through sheer hard work and effort, with a good measure of planning and team work thrown in.

The Community Council eventually woke up to the fact that the Millennium Association was making a bigger impact in the community than they were.

A Darvel Improvement Group (DIG) is formed to capitalise on the renewed interest in taking the town forward. The Millennium Association is 're-invented' as The Social Committee (and latterly, Entertainment Committee) and a hierarchy of committees is structured. With a hierarchy of committees comes a hierarchy of people – however volunteers and initiative do not generally sit well with hierarchies!? Burns' "For a' that and a' that" should be a salutary reminder of the folly of rank and pretence. The headaches of hierarchies are temporarily out of mind as a Gala Day to remember is held in August 2002.

The event is captured in all its glory by the Valley Advertiser, which reflects on *"Darvel's Glorious Gala Day…*

"What a great day it was! The sun shone, the crowds turned out in their hundreds (if not thousands), the procession was excellent, and the varied programmes of events at the Morton Park entertained young and old alike. Many ex-Darvelites returned to the town from far and wide, friendships were renewed, and there was an infectious atmosphere of enjoyment about the town. The community spirit was almost tangible. After months of organisation by various groups throughout the town it was excellent to see the whole plan fit together, and the bonus was that the weather was excellent also.

The parade assembled at Campbell Street at 12.30pm and Councillor Bobby McDill presented certificates to the floats and individuals taking part, all of which were colourful and imaginative.

As the procession followed its route through the town, led by parade marshall Albert Anderson, the streets of Darvel were thronged with appreciative spectators.

At the Morton Park, Max Flemmich, Chair of Darvel Community Council, welcomed everyone before handing over to Reid Ross, Chair of Darvel Improvement Group, to conduct the programme. Provost Jimmy Boyd of East Ayrshire Council then officially opened the Gala Day and his wife, Mrs Anna Boyd, JP, crowned the Gala Queen, Fallon Spencer (11 years old), who made a confident speech about Darvel and the honour her town had bestowed on her. The Gala Day Princesses who accompanied the Queen were Heather Brown, Rhonna Glynn and Heather King. The Lace Queen tradition of the dresses being made from materiel supplied by local factories was maintained. On this occasion the dresses were fashioned by Joan Rankin from fabric donated by John Aird & Co Ltd.

After the crowning ceremony a varied programme took place in the events arena including an excellent performance by Black Rock Pipe Bank from Troon, historical re-enactment scenes by the Swords of Dalriada group, a children's sports programme, a fiercely contested tug of war competition, and a duck race (with plastic ducks) from Ranaldcoup Road Bridge to the Rab's Pool.

The large marquee in the Park was busy all afternoon selling tea, coffee and snacks, the beer tent ran out of beer, and the various craft stalls, ice cream and chip vans, hot dog stalls literally all had a field day. Ongoing throughout the afternoon were activities like beat the goalie, archery, laser quest, mini quad bikes, bouncy castles and inflatables. Other stalls sold keepsakes, stained glass, handknitting, sweets, greetings cards, jam, candles, plants, bottles baking, pet food and toys. Demonstrations of woodworking, painting, mosaics, spinning and weaving were also popular.

A novel activity demonstrated at the Park was the traditional Darvel sport of quoiting. Quoits are cast iron hoops varying in weight from 2 to 16 pounds, and the experts demonstrating this sport were lobbing the quoits 40 feet onto a square metre of clay.

All people involved in the huge variety of events which made up this highly successful Gala Day deserve the highest praise for their efforts. Particular thanks (must go to Darvel) Community Council and to Darvel Improvement Group, and, above all, credit must be given to the overall Gala co-ordinator, Neil McKenna, whose energy and enthusiasm provided the driving force for this event.

The organising committees would like also to pay tribute to the following sponsors – Scottish Power, East Ayrshire Council, Moonweave Ltd, J H Donald Ltd, ABP Signs, Milligans Electrical, Westsound Radio, Kilmarnock Standard, Lowes Transport, Ged Cunningham, McDonald Transport and Articulate Logistics. Prize donors must be thanked sincerely – Seacat, Scottish Co-op, Kilmarnock FC, Guinness, Clydesdale Bank, Woolworths, Marks & Spencer, Odeon Cinema, Asda, Heather's Florist, Westsound Radio, Moscow Leisure Centre and B & Q Superstore.

A video of the whole Gala Day – procession, coronation, field events – has been made in colour) by Bobby and Margaret Young and will be on sale soon. It captures the enjoyment of the day, and is a 'must' for all lovers of the town, a happy souvenir of a wonderful day."

The emphasis is on the rebirth and regeneration of the community but individual initiatives help a focus on individual people, personalities and reinforce the fact that families help make a community as a family of families. Special fund-raising events are also a great success and sufficient to provide the opportunity for Rachel McColl to visit Disneyland with her mum and dad, before her tragically-short life is wrestled from her by cancer. Graham and Elaine's own personal triumph is also turned to heartbreak, as Elaine's pregnancy ends in the stillbirth of Cara. To Graham and Elaine, the pain of 'losing and never having' is stronger than 'having and lost, ' but it is a 'call' no-one should be asked to make!

Some three years on the efforts of the original Millennium Association volunteers have helped engender a new spirit within the town. The talent shows, tea dances, line dances, discos, Street cafes, ceilidhs and quiz nights have all been successful thanks to the original Millennium Association and the ever helpful Ronnie (Karaoke) King and Sandy and Lilian Mair. The challenge is now for others to pick up the cudgels and the workload. The opportunity is for DIG leading lights to lead the way.

More emphasis is needed on providing facilities for the youth of this town to help capture their imagination and involvement. The planned skatepark would be a welcome addition if the red tape and bureaucracy could be skated over. The town's celebration of its 250th anniversary ends in 2003 and in paying tribute to the past Darvel must now pay attention to the future.

In the meantime, there is tension in the town reflecting an age and culture clash. The roller-bladers and skateboarders attempt their 180°s and grinds at the area surrounding the town's War Memorial. What is lost on those condemning this action is that this is not an act of vandalism or disrespect for the dead but due to a lack of facilities for the youthful living. The dead of the two World Wars on the War Memorial would surely understand and respect that. People should remember that yesterday's different often becomes tomorrow's norm. As Jocko Weyland eloquently tried to explain in *"The Answer is Never,"* in the 1980s:-

"Outside the local grocery I was stopped for skating on the sidewalk. The man wants to know when my type is going to learn our lesson. Skating away I know the answer to his question is never.

-Lowboy (C.R Stecyk 111), 1981"

"Twenty years later I'm still at it. I'm not entirely sure why, though I do have some theories. The primary one is that there is an inexpressible freedom in the act of skating and also in the culture of skateboarding. It has influenced and affected many of the choices I've made in my life, informing almost everything I've done. I'm under the spell of an athletic activity that lies at a unique junction of sport and art. ***There are no coaches, no rules, no one telling you what to do. It is a solitary pursuit that engenders intense camaraderie****. There are no limits to what can be done or imagined except for the ones you impose on yourself, because skating is open-ended and always evolving.*

It can be done anywhere there is concrete, and reconfigures the public spaces of modern architecture, using constructed areas in imaginative ways that become second nature to the skater but are not understood by the nonpractitioner. Skating is a narcotic that offers release and a negation of self that defies analysis. ***Skating is different.****"*

There is so much concrete and wood in the world that riding a skateboard is possible almost anywhere.

Why skating has had such a profound effect on so many people might be because it is a kind of play that defies any practical purpose – that is, it's fun*. At some point in the middle of the twentieth century, the apple cart broke off the front of some anonymous kid's homemade scooter and the skateboard was born. Skating has now progressed from these humble beginnings to Hawk's and Rowley's feats, and along the way, what began as a toy gained tens of millions of adherents, spawned magazines and would change our culture, influencing music, fashion, art and film.*

Concrete has become humanity's natural habitat, and this is what skaters utilize in a way no other group does. Because of this appropriation of the physical world, skating is inherently in conflict with authority*. This taboo aspect fuels a "The more illegal they make it, the more attractive it becomes" mind-set and has spawned skating's trademark rebellious behavior and ethos that other segments of society have increasingly come to emulate over the last twenty-five years will.*

Skateboarding is different , difficult and diverse. Its history goes back over forty years , but unlike the ' twist ' or ' jive' it has not been accepted . It's not fashionable to be a skateboarder or skater, but then again skateboarding is not about fashion , it's more a way of life. Again as Jocko Weyland explains,

being a skater means a life lived differently, in pursuit of something elusive. ***Skateboarding is misunderstood because it is outside the normal scheme of things. The rest of the world often watches, follows and imitates aspects of skating without really getting it****. It is a singular activity with fluctuating and contradictory philosophies, a true subculture that has resisted attempts at going mainstream.* ***Skating***

isn't nice. It's ugly and beautiful at the same time, a physical activity that isn't really a sport but is definitely a way of life.

Skateboarding is about getting towed behind cars, about riding off of picnic tables and ollieing onto them, about the sound of wheels carving on tile and trucks barking on coping. It's slamming onto cement and getting purple hip contusions that stick to your pants for weeks, riding on rain-soaked sidewalks and arguing with old ladies and running from cops. It's breaking your arm and getting your ramp burned down by hostile nonbelievers. It's skating the pools of abandoned houses or riding a good spot in a gang-infested neighborhood. It's boards breaking and wheels falling off when you're doing twenty-five down a hill. It's getting eggs, rocks and bricks thrown at you while doing ollies off a sidewalk bump late at night, or putting Bondo on cracks in rails so they can be slid down. It's inventive and often obscure board graphics, a way of dressing, a way of acting, of being.

This isn't a textbook; it is biased, prejudicial and discriminating, while also trying to be inclusive and wide-ranging. ***It's about the allure of scummy backyard pools and off-limits full pipes, of marble ledges and triple sets of stairs, of practicing an activity that has never really been understood by a public that is unaware of the rich rewards and inexplicable pleasures that start with the simple act of rolling.***"[4]

The Millennium occasions and fuels a sense of renewal, if not rebirth. The family take part in some 'global expansion' of their own. Elaine and Alistair visit George (Alistair's brother) in New Zealand, to experience the sights and sounds of the Southern Hemisphere. The new soldiers, Bobby and Jim, form part of the Royal Highland Fusiliers and have tours of duty in Belfast, Bosnia and Germany. The equipment and weapons of warfare may have changed since wee Jock's day at the Battle of the Somme, but whether it be Belgium, Belfast or Bosnia, it is still about 'man's inhumanity to man.'

---

[4] Footnote: Excerpt from *"The Answer is Never,"* by Jocko Weyland (A Skateboarder's History of the World, 1988)

Joanne, in an effort to help eradicate some suffering, joins the Volu International Workcamps Association of Ghana and adventures to West Africa for five weeks to help build a school. The inoculations and effort are rewarded through the gratitude of a people who eke out an existence, which is a far cry from Joanne's relatively comfortable life at Uni. It's a small but significant step in helping restore 'man's humanity to man.'

On arrival in Accra, the dream of the Volu mission to build a school turns to reality for Joanne and her friend Claire. They will be helping to build a toilet block within the school complex and they both have to sleep in the upper bunk beds as the rats have had the first choice and are fairly settled in the lower one. These are 'big, sleekit and not-so-timorous beasties' and eventually, Joanne and Claire are rehoused to a rat-free dorm, in old Ayomah, a six-hour drive from Accra. In fairly typical African style, this six-hour drive is made in a 'mini-bus.' Passengers and luggage fit to fill a double decker bus double up on each other in cramped contentment and amazement.

At the welcome ceremony, the volunteers are embraced as brothers and sisters who had been lost in other lands and who had now returned home to lend a willing hand. The work was hard and basic but involved 'using your head' on the two-mile journey on foot through the forest to transport sand and water to the 'building site.' The seemingly simple process of balancing a bucket of water on your head and walking with it was a source of great mirth to the locals as Joanne had one 'wet hair day' after another 'wet hair day.' The fruits of Joanne's labours would be 'bananas' and a toilet block but not just any toilet block – there would be eight toilets in each of the two blocks but only four in operation at one time so that the other four, when full, could be shut and the 'end products' could be used as fertiliser!?!

The jovial Joanne endeavours to make friends with the reticent locals but both the work and locals are heavy going and suspicion and unease are hard to bridge. In a material world it was a lack of materials or 'wee Cynthia's shoes' that provided the breakthrough. Cynthia is about twelve years of age, a naturally inquisitive and curious child, who is nonetheless shy and hesitant in the company of white Europeans.

Joanne's eye for detail spies out that Cynthia's shoes, or what passed for shoes, were beyond repair. A quick visit to the local store and a pair of what could only be described as 'flip-flops' are offered to an unbelieving Cynthia. In the material world these were only B*h*S or M&S run-a-rounds, but in the third world, they were precious and practical possessions. The free and unsolicited manner of the giving (Scots are famed for their generosity) produced an unexpected but welcome response. From the day following the giving to the day of leaving, Cynthia's mum brought Joanne and Claire bananas. Bananas were the natural commodity to express their thanks for a small gift – the rarer commodity was Joanne's natural desire to do and give something to someone who had so very little. Warm memories of the unexpected return of personal and practical philanthropy eradicate those of rodents and the human rats who cheat and fail nations. These memories live with Joanne and make her think, *"The whole experience was brilliant, it really makes me realise just how lucky I am and I'll definitely do something like it again."*

Global movement turns out to be two-way, as Lorraine and JD, her South African husband, decide to give living and working in Britain a go. Jan Van Aswegan (JD) was a police officer in South Africa, but not the burly, brutal type depicted in the abuse of blacks in Jo'berg and beyond. He is as cerebral as Lorraine is comical – a couple that would be hard to pair from the individuals they are. JD's interest in computers leads to a job in Nottingham and then Bolton where Lorraine becomes a hairdresser to the stars, or at least some Premiership and First Division English footballers.

On the home front, Galston Boys Club decide to invade Belgium and Holland! The under 12s, 14s and 15s will represent Scotland in Europe at the Easter Football Tournament in Eindhoven. It's a coach trip to the channel at Dover and by tunnel to Calais, before travelling through France and Holland. The long journey is eased by the comfort of the facilities at Molenheide Holiday Village in Belgium. The boys of the under 14s are 'shared out' by 'degree of difficulty' – Andy and Kate draw the short straw or straws in the shape of Big Gary, Gal, Colin, Ali and Midget. Davy and Jane are next 'worse off' with their David, Kris, Duns and Calum. And we have our Gary, Craig Boy, Kenny and Kerr. Robert, Mel and Drew joined Andy and Helen.

The fine weather sets us up for a football finale to remember. A glorious weekend is completed as the under 14s win their age group and the under 12s and 15s are runners up. The experience is brilliantly captured in rhyming form by Alex Milligan, Chief Reporter of the local *Kilmarnock Standard*.

"The Footie Tour"
Bags and cases lie around
The Galston boys are Euro bound
Jim Trainer checks we're all inside
The troops are set for Molenhide
Soon Smithy's in his sleepy haven
And we'd only gone as far as Strathaven
No bottle opener, Jesus Christ
As Lorna breaks the Smirnoff Ice
Soon we're there and in our chalet
A bite to eat and then a swally
The lads were great, the weather well
And boy were there some tales to tell
Organiser Bobby G
Who also doubles as V.P.
Described by some as Super-Gub
The biggest bastard in the club
Poor Vanda, married to our Lex

For one night had to forego sex
The poor guy's dislocated shoulder
Stopped him getting close to hold her
Mrs Paton, my oh my
Thought the pavements rather high
But snake Hips Audrey found a pal
When 'Oo-Ah Baby' shouted Gal
A rose among the sweaty males
Was the Baywatch Babe, physio Gail
Whose healing hands and magic potions
Gave the lads some naughty notions
Chairman Ian went on a hike
And was almost knocked down by a bike
His immediate reaction was to yell
'Have you no got a fucking bell'
Shortlees Carol, no one could phase her
She forgot to pack her razor
Gave the referee a fright
When she wished on him a prickly shite
Nancy Rodgers caused a fuss
As she sat waiting on the bus
Took it out on husband Kenny
'Cause she thought he'd had one too many
Mary Gemmell likes her lager
Too much sometimes makes her stagger
When she hears the punters roar
Mary pipes up 'What's the score'
There's a big one, shouted Kate
It's long, it's thick and stands up straight
Help ma bob, she must be gassed
But no, she's spied a mobile mast
It all went well, the trip was fun
The 12s and 15s almost won
The 14s finished in first place
To put a smile on Andy's face
We're heading home with driver Joe

A thousand miles or so to go
Galston Boys Club, shout it loud
You played it well and did us proud
****

Back on home soil, Greg progresses to second year at Loudoun Academy, whilst Gary sits his Highers in fifth year. Greg is artistic and something of a 'free spirit,' who becomes a 'Mosher' and a real talent on a skateboard, so much so that he uses his initiative and writes off to skateboard companies and suppliers to seek sponsorship for his favourite sport. Gary is more serious and has secured good Standard Grades (6 one's and 2 two's) and has a career in medicine in sight – preferably as a doctor. He 'keeps his hand in,' as we enrol on a nine-week (evening class) course to renew our First Aid certificates at Kilmarnock College. Gary has held his certificate since he was twelve and the exam on 20 November 2002 is a breeze for him, but I struggle a bit.

The first aid exam is conducted in groups of threes and fours, and we are last to go. As we sit and chat away the time 'till our exam, the conversation almost inevitably turns to accidents and death. We talk of a car accident in which two local teenagers have been killed, and we talk of someone's workmate who has died at the age of 45. I'm 45 and there's a rumour one of my friends died during the week. "Do you know the person's name or what he did or where he stayed?" I ask. The response is, "I didn't really know him that well, but he was a clinical psychologist and stayed in Lugar – I think his name was Colin, I think his name was Colin." The echo was still in my head, as I heard myself query – "Colin McLaren?" "Yes, that's him – he's dead!"

It's not the best preparation I've had for a first aid exam, but I don't suppose McLaren planned it that way when he went out to lay some paving stones in his garden at the weekend. The funeral was over before I had received the confirmation of death and a weird feeling of 'that could have been me – I was at school with him – he's my age' – all pervade the thinking. Others dying older or younger have a reason, however inexplicable and unacceptable, but here is one of my peers, just keeling over and dying, as if it's perfectly natural!! It's all a bit disconcerting and distracting to remember a real character with whom you have shared some of the most defining moments in your character and realise he's gone. In his early 20s, he'd gone to Huddersfield Polytechnic, rather than a Scottish University and then 'dropped out' to become a croupier in the casinos in Glasgow, where I met up with him again after a gap of four or five years. He worked in Swaziland and then returned to an executive position with Save the Children, where again in Musselburgh, our paths again crossed. A degree in psychology at a Scottish University followed, our addresses did not follow our career paths. He was a character on whom I had based the fledgling attempts to write a book about apartheid in South Africa. The book was based on a good idea (a white-inspired rebellion to end apartheid), but never quite go off the ground in the face of sound advice from my big sister, Marlene – "Why don't you write a book about something you really know about?" There's a sense of I wish I had kept in touch and of I wish I had written that book – but then there's this book.

Being old (or relatively old) and enjoying the respect and company of the young (or relatively young) is both admirable and achievable – Guy Collins is testimony to that! A weekend in Dublin celebrating a 40th birthday party (Guy was 69) was followed by 'a day at the races' to mark his 70th birthday. The Marx Brothers would not have looked out of place as the entourage descended on the Brig o'Doon House Hotel for drinks and dinner, before descending on the Western House for the Ayr Gold Cup meeting in September 2001. The gentry at the Western House needn't have worried, as 'the boys' did themselves proud. The event was so successful that the 'Turf Accountants' (at least we left from the Turf Hotel in Darvel) again dined at the Brig o'Doon and from there, sprinted to the Western House for the first race on 21 September 2002. There was Guy, sons John and Hugh; son-in-law Derek; the McAllisters (Ian, ex-captain of Ayr United, James and Alex); Jack McKie; big Scoobie, Sanny, Bobby, Morton, wee Jim and another ten or so betting cronies and drinking buddies. The rafters of the Western House are again ringing to the sound of Elvis and the latest tunes of the day. The professional and polite join the punters in song – it's a day to remember – pure dead brilliant!

Another day to remember is 26 September 2002, as we celebrate 21 years of marriage (and Jim and Jessie's 27 years). It's a bit daunting to reflect on 21 years of marriage and Gary nearing sixteen, when he could leave the nest to go to university, work or marry?! Colin, my brother, after some thirty-seven years of staying with my mum and dad, decides to leave their nest and set up on his own. The house in Darvel which he buys and moves to on 1 August 2002 is less than a mile from mum and dad, but in emotional terms, it's a million miles away. Only Davy now stays with mum and dad and it's been a lifetime since there was only one offspring in the house. The lack of the companionship of Colin in the family home is confirmed and reflected in visits to see mum and dad, as mum reflects "I miss him terribly." She is quick to confirm that she missed us all when we left, but Colin was a permanent feature of the home, much as a real fire was once the focal point of a living room.

For Colin, the gaps in his home life take a lot of getting used to and he is drawn between his and the family home that was once his. In the run up to Colin preparing to leave for his new house, in typical fashion mum and dad declare, "There will be a wee something for all of you when we're gone, but Davy has to get the house."

At work the old adage of 'things happen in threes' seemed as if it could be positively coming my way as I am promoted from Employee Relations Manager to Human Resources Manager for ScottishPower's PowerSystems Business. It's a big Business with over 3,000 employees who work to provide a safe and reliable supply of electricity to some 5 million customers in Central and South West Scotland and in Cheshire , Merseyside and North Wales.

One up and another two good things on the way !!

Events did happen in three's ; there was the Fuel Crisis in September 2000; the outbreak of Foot and Mouth and a bout of Industrial Action for the first time in 30 years.

Yes , things happened in threes and if the black plague had been going around I think I would have coped for that as well.

As the Human Resources Manager I was 'lucky enough' to deal with these three emergencies.

The Fuel Crisis which resulted from the lorry drivers' action to prevent the supply of fuel to petrol stations required daily emergency meetings to ensure our essential service could be maintained.

The outbreak of foot and mouth restricted the effective operation of the Business as access to land to either erect or repair electrical apparatus and overhead lines was denied or restricted.

The first bout of Industrial Action in over 30 years during December 2001 and January 2002 involved nearly 2000 industrial trade union members of the AEEU, GMB and T and G.

From a Business perspective the industrial action was treated like a storm and through a 'business as usual' approach, the storm died down and life and business relationships had to be picked back up and improved. Working relationships with the full time trade union officials(Danny ,Jim, Michael and Alan) ,shop stewards and employees had been stretched and strained and were only restored through realisation of respective positions and the renewal of mutual respect.

It was also a situation that had all the potential for family strife. In the blue corner was yours truly as Human Resources Manager (and previously Employee Relations Manager) and in the red corner 'brother Colin,' Craft Attendant and GMB member. At the Gavin Hamilton Sports Centre in Darvel, we would train twice a week together but there was no personal strain or pain; we simply recognised each other's personal positions and got on with it. Like many an industrial dispute, individual views and relationships are subsumed in what becomes the management and trade union collective consciousness or perhaps, more accurately, collective unconsciousness. To mum and dad there was never really a quandary – they continued to support both sons. It was not a matter of equivocation or sitting on the fence; it was a matter of pride in both sons – 'striking never really resolved anything but you have to stand up for what you believe in' – there is in a sense no right or wrong, only steps that have to be retraced, redrawn and renewed. Mum and dad could therefore without contradiction sympathise with me, Nancy and the kids in my loss of a family holiday abroad in October, but they could and did equally sympathise with Colin in his loss of pay over six days of industrial action.

Brothers even in adversity were easier in a sense to deal with than the 'conman.' A Sunday afternoon's visit reveals Mum and Dad have 'switched' to British Gas for their electricity supply. An all too flippant 'well that will put me and Colin out of a job' reveals just how vulnerable elderly people can be. A tea-time salesman comes a' knocking and gets a foot in the door; 'no' is not taken for an answer and all it takes to solve the problem and get rid of the guy is a signature. The duly-signed papers are shown to me and there is no 'cooling off period.' Within five minutes the agreement is deemed to be null and void as British Gas, to their credit, accept the explanation offered. There is no apparent harm or loss but the vulnerability of all elderly people is highlighted, none the least to them.

It's a scene and 'scheme' that will be repeated a thousand times over in a thousand different 'scams.' Trust and respect for the elderly or lack of it is not the preserve of callous youth - a few mature individual and corporate consciences need to be pricked.

“ Off with the old and on with the new ‘is a recurring theme as I take delivery of my new company car. It’s a Mercedes 220 CDI and at about £25 grand it’s weird to think this car costs more than the house we live in when we bought it some seventeen years ago. Is any car more valuable than a house? Is any car worth more than a home ?

At work I learn that my Managing Director (John Menzies of Ayrshire District and Cambuslang Rugby Club fame) is to retire on 31 March 2003 . A fifteen year association is about to be broken and new working relationships formed. Our first acquaintance at Waterloo Street in Glasgow as part of the Glasgow Clyde Area seems fresh in the memory despite numerous changes to District , Regional and Functional structures, as our professional careers cross and re-cross. If the zenith was Ayrshire District then the nadir was the bout of industrial action.

As we celebrate Christmas 2002 and enter the New Year of 2003, it’s a very typical Scottish (and probably worldwide) approach, to reflect on what’s been and what will be? The old adage of “what’s done’s done” comes to the fore.

The pain, suffering and hurt of loves lost are summarised each year in the Kilmarnock Standard Intimations.

This is not the Robert Burns ‘Kilmarnock Edition’ , but for each and every family ‘in memoriam ‘ it evokes painful but proud memories.

We are no different as the 10th anniversary of McCulloch/Clements memoriam reads :-

‘ Remembering today and every day , our Mum , Patricia (Mavis) , Moodie who died on 14th February 1997, also Dad , Harry, died 1st May 1999 ,sister Marion, died 18th December 1994 ,and brother in law Davy , died 13 April 1993.

Always in our thoughts, forever in our hearts.

With love from all the family.’

It’s a memoriam repeated in a thousand versions of the Kilmarnock Standard but there is nothing standard about the personal circumstances, emotions and grieving that accompanies each small note.

Looking back can be instructive, insightful and enjoyable, but whilst memories live in the mind, we cannot live on memories. It's not a case of forgetting, but more remembering and appreciating that things and people change and move on. If there are 'five ages of man,' then Mrs Brownlie represents the character and substance of my mum and dad's parents in the 90-100 years old bracket. Mum and dad, at 79 years of age, really represent the fourth age and, somewhat unbelievable, we, I suppose, represent the third age. In a sense, we represent the 'old' (and not so old), but the remaining two ages lay with the nineteen grandchildren of the family, including Gary and Greg, and indeed, the sixteen great-grandchildren of mum and dad (Rachael, Ross , Rebekha; Rory, Melissa, Aaron, and Bethan ; Alan and Andrew; Teigan, Kyle, Aidan; Jack, Emma , Amanda and Elise.

With so many in the family, birthdays are always looming but 10 March and 20 May are unique – Mum and Dad were 79 – nearly octogenarians. 31 March 2003 is Nancy's birthday (21 again) and Mum and Dad's fifty-fifth wedding anniversary. It's a lifetime of marriage and real parenthood that raises the ordinary to the extraordinary.

Extraordinary courage is also required as the dreaded early morning call from Yvonne, on Friday 11 April 2003, confirms another death in the family – Marlene's Mike has died.

At around 9pm that evening, I summon up the courage to phone Marlene and let her know how sorry we are and that we are thinking of her.

From her house in Rugby, Marlene, in a calm state of numbing shock, explains –

"Mike hadn't been well since about Monday and had flu-like symptoms, a high temperature and a really sore head. He'd been to the doctor mid-week and was advised to continue taking paracetamol during the day and Neurofen at night for his headache. By Friday he wasn't really any better. The visiting

doctor prescribed antibiotics after we had told him how Mike had been and how he felt. I got the antibiotics from the chemist and Mike took one about lunchtime and one about eight hours later. We were late going to bed at about 11.15pm and Mike was still uncomfortable, so I rubbed his back and he was really hot. We didn't really sleep and at about 1.30am, Mike said he couldn't sleep and had to get up; he slipped out of his side of the bed and I got out of my side and put my dressing gown on. I walked through to the living room and Mike was supporting himself at the unit but as I came through, he started to slump to the floor and his hands couldn't hold him up. I caught him under his arms and eased him to the floor. He wasn't breathing – I tried to resuscitate him – his mouth was hard to open – I opened his airways and did two breaths and then started thumping his chest. I phoned for an ambulance and the doctor talked me through the resuscitation and kept asking, 'is he breathing yet?' *– but he wasn't.*

The doorbell rang and I left Mike to let the ambulance men in. They tried resuscitation and then the electric cardiac arrest shock treatment. They put the pads on Mike and the screen showed a straight line and a blip and then a line. They tried again and then said it would be better if I would get dressed. I went to the bedroom to get changed and couldn't get back out while they were working on Mike – I don't know how long I was in there but when I got out, the ambulance man said, "I'm sorry" *– I said* "You're joking," *and he said,* "I'm sorry."

A doctor had to be called to sign the death certificate and the police had to come, as it was a sudden death. The doctor who came was the same one who had seen Mike earlier in the day. He looked at me and looked away and looked at Mike on the floor. He bent over Mike and took a wee while to stand back up and then he wrote out some notes and signed the paperwork and handed it to the police and then he just left. It took the police a wee while to realise what he had written and when they did, all hell broke out with the police contacting the health authorities to make their report. The doctor had written SARS (Severe Acute Respiratory Syndrome) – he couldn't diagnose it when Mike was living but he could when he was dead.

Eventually, the police asked me if I wanted some time alone with Mike as they put him back on the bed – they said he could stay there for up to twelve hours. I spent about an hour with Mike.

Early in the morning, the same doctor came back to see me and gave me a prescription for sleeping tablets and advised me to take them – I said I wouldn't. He said he would leave the prescription anyway and if I didn't use it to tear it up. I said to him then I wasn't happy by the way he had treated Mike – he asked me why? I said because he hadn't admitted Mike to hospital with all the symptoms he had. He couldn't look me in the eye, and just said, "In hindsight….." *and left.*

Lorraine and JD and Denise are here with me – I don't believe it – I must have done something really bad for this to happen twice.

There will be a post mortem on Monday and they said something funny that the results should be available later on Monday but I've read it takes three days to test and get the results.

I'm tired now; I'll have to go and try to get some sleep. Thanks."

There are no histrionics at Mike's funeral, only genuine family tears, fears and magical memories as the curtains at the crematorium open and close to the strains of Mark Knofler's 'Cumberland Man.' It's only been about ten days since Mike had gone to Pennsylvania; now he was gone for good. It's also twelve years since Frank died in South Africa and Lorraine, as then, is there now for her Mum. The family and friends, like almost every family, start to draw together and put a protective and supportive cocoon round Marlene as a poor but genuine substitute for Mike's arms.

There are six suspected cases of SARS reported in the UK on 11 April 2003 – a fact that tells you nothing. There are as yet no reported deaths from SARS in the UK. There are those who would suspect medical 'cock-up' and those who might suggest 'establishment conspiracy' but neither theory nor reality can return what has been lost. Mike would have been fifty-one on D-Day (6 June 2003), and, coincidentally, the day I complete the 'final draft' of this book. The inquest decrees that Mike has died of a lung infection but loo and behold there is no mention of SARS !

Life and death as the opposite ends of the spectrum can really be regarded as 'closest together' and so it is with Graham and Elaine who attend Mike's funeral whilst harbouring fears and hopes of new life. Days after Mike's funeral, Elaine's confirmed pregnancy offers Graham and Elaine opportunity to ease the still-painful memory of Cara's stillbirth. The bitter-sweet taste and rhythm of life beats on – the same in principle but oh so different in person.

On 19th December 2003 there is a real birth as a four pounds fourteen ounces tiny bundle of trepidation brings enormous relief for Elaine and Graham. The wait to bring Mikayla home is over as her weight is sufficient to gain release from hospital and join her mum and dad at home.

Our Galston Boys Club under 17's team have also found a new lease of life in the Scottish Cup and after beating Leven Thistle , Douglas Lads , Strathaven Dynamo , St. Peters (Paisley) and Paisley United a place in the final is theirs if they can beat Port Glasgow in the semi-final at Somerset Park in Ayr.

Port Glasgow are beaten two nil in a fast and furious encounter that sends the pulses racing in Galston and the Valley beyond. Airdrie's Excelsior Stadium is the venue for the final on Sunday 23 May 2004. There is no dream win at the end of the road as Calderwood Blue Star from East Kilbride prove to have a touch more skill in key areas and deservedly win 2-1. However the match report reads what might have been:

' NO EQUALISER CAME' – The Valley boys gave their all in a pulsating Scottish Cup under-17 final held at Airdrie's Excelsior Stadium last Sunday, but just failed to lift the cup.

Their opposition from East Kilbride may just have had the edge on skill but the sheer hard work and effort and commitment of the Galston players should have earned them the right to take the match into extra time.

And had that happened there can be no doubt that they would have gone on to lift the trophy with their opponents struggling to match the Galston's side fitness levels.'

It was a great achievement but the boys were shattered – it should and could have be so much better- but that's football. The boys were shattered but they remembered to congratulate the winners and shake hands with them all and as hard as it hurt we clapped hands when they, not us,lifted the cup. For Bobby Gemmell, Andy Black and myself the feeling of misery and hopelessness was worse than when we played and lost in cup finals ourselves – no amount of shouting , coaxing and coaching could change the result. We know it's all over but it's about to start again with the under 19's next season.!

At work there is also a ' birth ' – it's the birth of a new UK Group – wide Human Resources Function under the direction of the UK HR Director of the Year , Stephen Dunn. Putting in place this function displaces and replaces the best HR Team I had ever formed and worked with in our Business Partner and Shared Service Centre model – like cars the model will have higher performance , better economy and be able to handle all the turns and twists of the UK Businesses. The old team Willie (and his entire shared services team) . Kenny B . Kath., Hilary , Jim F , Irene , Joe , Ian , Linsey , Karen , Pamela , Jim McC , Bill , Lorna , Jim M , Mike , Heather , Dave and the luckless Gavin all have to find their new way in the new HR world but it's now a normal part of working life and change. As in life there are trade, business and work cycles and if and when you fall off you just have to get back on again and keep peddling away.

The Power Systems Executive Team also has some new talent – joining 'Big Davy' the MD and the ' old guard ' (me , Dave , Gordon and Steve) are Dorothy , Janet , Marion , Guy , David W and Paul. The challenge of continuous change at work begins again – never ends.

Scotland fail (again) to qualify for the European football Championships , so we content ourselves watching England and other teams of interest, The ex – Celtic player , Henrik Larsson , is a player of interest, so we sit and watch Sweden vs Bulgaria on Monday 14 June 2004 – Dad though not a Celtic supporter liked Larsson as a player and as a man – no pretensions or poncing – an extremely gifted professional and hard –working team player.

The game flows but there is no scoring when at 8.25pm the phone goes. It's Marlene and in a short , low tone she delivers an un-expected message which has been on the telephone horizon for probably two years , ' Kenny, you better come quick , it's Dad he's collapsed and it's not looking good'. Experiences and emotions flood back and Nancy knows the nature of the call in not the extent even before I relay the message to her. I change out of my shorts into a pair of jeans and grab the mobile and make my way to 44 Glen Crescent.

An ambulance and paramedic car greet my arrival- it's a scene you've passed many a time and now wish you were passing again. I always entered Mum and Dad's house by the back door (the trademan's entrance) but this was blocked by Dad's collapse in the kitchen. You could sense people watching the to'ings and fro'ings of the medics and relatives – you could almost hear them saying in hushed tones - , 'It's Bobby Rodgers'. It's Dad on the kitchen floor , flat out , head towards the cooker and feet towards the dining table; Mum is distraught and tries to explain how Dad had been sick and collapsed and she couldn't get him up on a chair. The medics have two' lines' into Dad ; the evidence of Dad's reliance on warfarin – thinned blood is smattered on the green carpet. There is a pulse on the heart monitor but not strong – it's weak like Dad. Marlene comforts Mum; Jim is by our Dad's side holding his left hand and Dad holds Jim's hand with a firm grip on him but not on life. Davy and Elaine are there and we speak to Dad, loud and clear , ' Come on Dad , we're here for you , come on'. And Jim says the response is a firmer gripping of his hand. The medics work at pace and professionally but breathings a problem so a clear plastic tube is inserted in Dad's throat – his breathing is aided and he seems more restful but is wrestling with life.

When he's stable enough Jim accompanies Dad in the ambulance and the emergency dash to the blue sound of the ' meew – maws ' is on – thrilling as a child but chilling as an adult. I can't keep up with the ambulance as it zips through Darvel , Newmilns , Galston and Hurlford on the way to Crosshouse Hospital – here we go again! Davy and I arrive at accident and Emergency (A&E) – ' Mr. Rodgers, ah …yes, straight through, I'll take you to the room and someone will speak to you.' Jim is already there, 'Dad is going to be lucky to make it'. We all silently think but worse still would be 'making it ' and left paralysed or in a vegetative state with no quality of life and not worth living. No worries on the latter point as a tall female doctor explains, You know your Dad was really bad when he came in, we did all we could but your Dad died.'

It's about 9.20pm – Sweden are going on to beat Bulgaria 5 – 0 and Henrik Larsson grabs a double – Dad liked Henrik Larsson.

Colin , Davy , Graham , myself and Jim look around at each other and there are tears rolling down every eye- there's no wailing or gnashing of teeth but then muffled cries let themselves go as we hug each other. There's an awkward silence that is broken by the medical assistant who offers to let us go and see Dad in a few minutes. We all go but before then the mobile phone will take the small but stunning message , ' Dad's dead' back to all those waiting in Darvel and beyond. I tell Marlene – she tells Mum – for once you can actually feel the anguish and pain Mum feels. Nancy next and the whole circle of tears is complete. We go to Dad – he's fought his last brave struggle he didn't lose – he won over twenty –five years ago when he beat his first heart attack – he reached his goal of being eighty with Mum – he wasn't paralysed, bed – ridden or a brain – dead burden – that's what we all said to each other to rationalise the sudden but not unexpected departure of Dad.

He'd left us but left us in peace after giving birth to eighty years of his life and hundreds and thousands more for the family and the future. He's warm, no real sign of the struggle in the kitchen, in the ambulance and finally in A and E. We all touch him and have our own private thoughts and discussions but we all say ' THANKS DAD'.

We return to the 'Rodgers Room ' , a drunk rattles around outside oblivious to reason or respect . Mum , Marlene , Elaine and Yvonne (wee Elaine , Jimmy and Leslie) all arrive. Lilian is in Sandford , Bobby in Dumfries and Avril in Middleton but they all know by now our Dad is gone.

The Police arrive – it's 'normal' for a sudden death and Jim , as eldest son , goes with them to explain events and provide details of Dad. The medical assistant is great, he gives us some forms / booklets and coffee and with the coffee , conversation rather than crying returns.

'Dad's target was really to get to eighty', he would have hated to be an invalid, ' he told me and Jim that if he was ever on a life – support machine to switch it off, he didn't actually think or mind if it was illegal; ' He always said the way he wanted to go was out fishing and having a wee dram by the water's edge and then lights out'.

It's all true and even if he didn't get all he wanted he got the bits that mattered – no slow, mind-numbing decay – a relatively quick death.

Mum, Marlene, Elaine , Yvonne , Jimmy and wee Elaine arrive and go to see Dad in the hospital room at the mortuary. Almost 60 years of being together is together no more and the physical pain of having eleven children bears no comparison to the love of losing Robert (Dad) . Everybody has a final word with Dad in the hospital and the night wears on and we leave to gather again on Tuesday morning. I drive Jim back home and agree to help him with 'the arrangements'. 'The arrangements ' – two impersonal words that suddenly turn hugely personal and involve all the family. Tuesday 15 of June is a bugger of a day – Dad's gone but did he hear us calling on him; did he know we were there for him, for Mum? The arrangements aren't really that hard to make after big Jimmy pulls us together to action – ' you might want to phone an appointment to collect the death certificate and phone the undertaker ,'he sympathetically guides us to a conclusion to reach an end for Dad. Jim and I pick up the death certificate at 3.48pm – it gives Dad's personal details and reads,

Time of death Monday 14 June 2004 at 9.13pm.

Cause of death 1. Heart attack / Heart disease.

2. Old age.

'Old age 'indeed – that was a bloody achievement to reach eighty ; there's many a man and woman who would be happy to die of ' old age ' – eighty was a ' good age ' without the sentence of senility. Infancy is for the very young – old age infancy , being constantly cared for , changed and spoon – fed would have been a living hell for Dad – leave this infancy stuff to the kids . Eighty was a good age for Dad.

For nearly thirty years Dad had worked at the Darvel Cemeteries (old and new) and for much of that time Jimmy Dykes and George Collins (the undertakers) had been ' customers ' of Dad at the cemeteries with their funeral cars and cortege. Today, George Collins would visit to make arrangements for Dad as a 'customer'. We agreed Dad would be buried in a lair on the top plot behind the house that was our home for some thirty years. It's where we had run, skipped and played hide and seek in summer and played in Mrs. Smith's (the waiting room) in winter and we all recalled those times and Dad playing us to sleep to the skirl of the bagpipes - Mull of Kintyre and even Z-cars!!

George took the details down carefully and waited patiently as we made out the words for our 'notification of death'. It eventually read:

RODGERS.

Suddenly at Crosshouse Hospital on the 14th June 2004 Robert (Bobby) in his 81st year of Darvel. Dearly beloved husband of Lilian Allan , much loved dad , father in law , papa and great grand-father to all the family. Forever in our hearts.

It could have been a five pager if we'd listed out the whole family from Lilian , Jim , Marlene , Elaine , Bobby , me , Davy , Colin , Avril and Graham and the sixteen grandchildren and nineteen great grand-children. After the arrangements were made, I drove up to the new cemetery, a journey I have made on literally thousands of occasions as a young boy , youth , with just Nancy and then later with Nancy , Gary and Greg, but this was unique. I was going to see the best resting place for Dad. I stood at the top plot – the cemetery was a bloody disgrace. Dad would have kept it a hundred times better than this – there was barely a level plot to be seen, the grass was mangled not cut , the edges were mashed and yet the view over the valley was stunning – this would do for our Dad and only two lairs away from Graham and Elaine's little Cara.

Flowers too beautiful for this sad occasion start to arrive and are followed by a spray of sympathy cards that eventually reach over a hundred. Friends and relatives write words on the cards that are easier to write than to read for Mum – all are absolutely genuine and simultaneously soothe and strike at the senses and sense of loss.

The coffin's picked and the lair is ready for a Friday burial, Friday 18 June 2004; 11.45am for the house, 12 noon at the Church and 12.45pm at the cemetery. The minister (Dr. Robertson) comes to see us and learns a little about Dad , he's relatively new to Darvel but is sympathetic and attentive and offers up a prayer in the house for Dad.

Dad would have wanted a Piper – we all come to the same final and fitting conclusion. Jim Richmond, near neighbour, ex-marathon running partner and friend of Bobby and family is a bonnie Piper. With a tear in his eye he agrees to get time off work and pipe the best his heavy heart will allow – at the entrance gate it will be ' Colin's Cattle ' ; ' the Rowan Tree ' at the graveside – Mum liked Rowan Tree and ' When the Battle's Over' as a final farewell.

Everyone's gone to see Dad in his suit at George's place in Newmilns – everyone but Avril as she won't be up until Thursday evening – and me. Everyone including Mum says she's glad she went – Dad was good – a slight wink in his eye and a glint of a smile on his face. The family have placed their final momentos in the coffin with and for Dad. Graham, a teddy bear for Cara and a hip flask which is inscribed 'with Graham's thoughts '. Colin some money , a lottery ticket (or a copy of the real one) with the numbers 1 (number one Dad) , 5 (May , his birth month) ,14 (date of death) , 20 (date of birth) , 24 (year of birth) and 40 (2x 40 = 80 , his age) and an un-scratched scratch card – Dad liked the lottery and a gamble. Marlene, Elaine and Yvonne left momentos but not memories. I've not gone to see Dad at George's. I want to remember him warm – it's a bit daft but that's what's in my head but in my heart I need to go.

I go on Thursday evening myself before Avril, Andy , Jimmy , Yvonne and Elaine arrive. I see Dad and he looks good and warm but I won't touch him - that's the compromise. I say 'Thanks Dad ', again and 'don't worry ,we'll look after Mum ', and I leave a 2 ½ " diameter bronze medal of a fisher catching a trout.

Friday 18 June is another bugger of a day or at least it starts that way – it rains. It rains until the funeral cars arrive and then it clears. The Church is busy for ' Bobby ' when we arrive and old family faces not seen frequently enough nod in sympathy and appreciation.

We sing 'The Lord's my Shepherd '(Psalm 23) and 'Amazing Grace'. They are sung proudly but not too loudly as snuffled cries are only partly stifled by song. We pray – is it ever too late to pray ? The Minister recounts Dad's and the family's life and Mum, softly but audible to the front pews corrects him , ' We were married on 31 March 1948 not 13 March ' – Nancy's birthday is the 31 March. We follow Dad's coffin to the car, only a few people are really recognisable as we walk up the aisle. Heads sorrowfully bowed when they really should be proudly and heavenly high. Eddie Wilson is recognisable , with a face of tears that reflect years of friendship and a loss sorely felt ; he's immaculate (as usual) and as usual , he's with Georgina , almost inseparable – our hands touch as I walk by. We all get into the cars and rays of sunshine replace the showers of rain. It appears as if half the town and more are gathered at the Central Church at the Square – The Millennium Party seems a millennium away.

The cortege meanders its way out of town past the old Manse, where Mr. Collins used to stay. The road narrows and steepens till 'Hillcrest'.

'Hillcrest, Manse Brae ', the cemetery is in sight and we enter through the rusty green double gates to the strains of ' Colin's Cattle '. The sounds and strains of Jim on the bagpipes almost symbolises being Scottish – we hull and puff and we strive to be better and there is this end product and pride of a noise which is not beautiful to the ear but hauntingly hair-raising – it is no different today, it is a noise for spirits to be lifted and drunk by and it is a noise to lift the spirits. We all get out at the top of the cemetery on the widest road and on the road to the farms above Hillcrest , people are streaming back down the hill , not to be late for Bobby – we delay going to the graveside so that they'll arrive on time even if they are late for the late Bobby Rodgers. The grave has been dug by a mechanical digger which has left its mark on the tarmac ; it's mark on the grass is a gouged out square hole. I almost wish I had dug the grave myself, neat and evened out and squared off at the shoulders and the feet.

We've decided that all the immediate family will take a cord ; Mum and Jim , number one ; Lilian and Graham , number two ; Marlene and Bobby , number three ; Elaine and me , number four ; Yvonne and Davy , number five and Avril and Colin , number six – Mum actually stays at the foot of the graveside – the head of the grave is three steps too far for her today. From the strains of the pipes it's now the strain of the cords, as we gently lower Dad's coffin – it's deadly still and quiet , the air is as breathless as Dad and yet , as we lower , a small windmill two lairs away starts a ratchet turn and turns some more as if mimicking each lowering we make. We all look up and laugh in our eyes, if not in our hearts – DAD ! As we drop the cords the windmill stops, as if to say ' I'm safely down now '. The minister starts his oration as we all join hands in a circle of sisters and brothers in arms around the grave – a car alarm breaks the solemnity and the minister tries to raise his voice above the level of the car alarm. Others at the graveside are thinking the same and smiles break grim faces as if to say, 'Typical Bobby'.

Friends and family step gingerly forward to pay their last respects and the coffin is offered an array of parting tributes. Flowers, coins, Bobby and Jim's cap badges, the soldiers' ultimate tribute and words soft on the ear but hard on the heart. Rhoda, Dad's eldest sister, a bit frail but bright as a button, simply and sisterly says , 'Bye Robert'.

The flowers too beautiful for a grave arrive – a double heart from Mum , single hearts , 'papa' in flowers , pillows , sprays , heathers and thistles all provide a blanket of warmth over a six foot hole.. Jim Richmond literally blows his heart out in the last lament. We adjourn to the Masonic Hall for something to eat and drink – it's full, full of respect and the warmth of friendly faces gloomed by the day and glistened by the sun – it starts to rain a little, nature's tears for the man. We meet and re-meet relatives, aunts, uncles , nieces , nephews , cousins and half cousins we half know.

Rhoda , William and Peter are Dad's only remaining sister and brothers – Peter has not made it to the funeral. None of Mum's brothers and sisters remain. Eighty was a good age for Dad.

The Hardy's, the Wilson's, the Kerr's, The Crozier's , the Allan's and the remaining Rodgers are there. William Kerr the coconut man from Gan is there – he was a frequent visitor to Mum and Dad and he'll be sixty soon and he's crying and laughing at the same time and each family member and friend regale each other with a story of Dad. We decided we'd tell our story in memory of Dad and we all added bits till it became a complete memory , a story or series of stories worth telling and worthy of the man. I spoke for about ten minutes, backed up by Jim , Bobby , Davy , Colin and Graham in case I broke down. For ten minutes, Dad was in the Hall, as everybody hung on mental pictures of days before death. The stories were worthy and humorous and include:

Two old women stand at the bus stop opposite the terminus and see Dad coming along towards them on his way to the old cemetery and they ask, ' Are you the young man who's going to bury us ? And Dad says, 'naw , I only bury the deid yins'.

Another sunny day he meets Trisha Collins along the water lip (the path by the river Irvine) and as he's carrying a fishing rod she decides to ask him if it is a good day for fishing – ' Naw hen, I'm no fishing , I just huv'ny got a dug'.

At weddings and anniversaries he would say to Mum, 'I want a £100 for that pocket and £100 for that pocket ', and he would get it , and he was never happy until he had spent it on his family and friends.

Even when he was ill he still had a very sharp wit and sense of humour as the local nurse found out.

The nurse arrives at the house to do an annual assessment on Dad and they get to the subject of mobility and if he can get up the stairs okay. Dad jokingly says , ' I've got a chair lift now ' and the nurse says , ' That must be great help ' to which Dad responds , ' Aye it would be if I could remember to use it '.

However Dad was not always right.

One early evening he returned home from work after one or two pints and says to Graham ,' tell your Mum to get the pot on there's three rabbits out there in the field. Graham , you come with me and pick them up when I shoot them '. So they creep to the railings outside and Dad fires off two shots and Graham cries out ,' did you get them did you get them 'as Dad walks over , kicks over some dirt and mutters , ' BLOODY MOLEHOLES'!

At last the bugger of a day grew better and people laughed their faces dry – that's how Dad would have wanted it and everybody having a drink on him – so they did. As Dad would have said, 'Why all the long faces, you would think someone had died! Day drew to night lightly and friendships and families renewed, people began to drift away from death to return to 'normal' life at their homes. The younger ones and some of the not so young ones , Bobby , young Jim , Yvonne's Jim and Iain , Kevin , Davy , Colin are intent on drowning a few sorrows – so they do and only occasionally one of them breaks down as the drink heightens the sense of grief and loss but it's been a good day – Dad would have enjoyed himself.

Big families, small families and the family of mankind are all touched by the hand of death at some time, but this was our moment, our day, our Dad.

Before the end of the day Graham's been back at the cemetery; he's arranged the blanket of flowers that's just not a patch-work quilt thrown on a bed, it's an ordered tapestry of tiered floral tributes.

Funny, weird things happened at the cemetery and after that, our minds were teased with a sense and signs of the uncanny and inexplicable.

Mum's washing machine packed in and came back to life the same week. Our laptop , some six months ago had been diagnosed by a ' Computer Clinic ' in Kilmarnock as ' terminally ill ' – the hard drive worked but the TFT screen was irreparable and would have to be replaced with a new one. I'd been loath to pay an estimated bill for £350 and Gary and Greg connected the laptop's hard drive to our IBM screen and this did the trick. The other trick was that on Tuesday or Wednesday after Dad died the TFT screen sprung into life as if brand new – what had Gary done different - absolutely nothing ! Dad was not into computers, he preferred outdoor pursuits or at least he did before. There is probably some explanation, but none that we can fathom. Big Jimmy wins £250 on the horses – now that's beyond explanation! Jessie wins £250 on the Irish Lottery – Dad liked the lottery, especially the Irish one. Coincidences probably , but they kinda make you think and maybe believe , believe that there is something out there , some place that will be at home with Dad's humour, humility and humanity and somewhere where he'll be able to fish , play darts , have a hauf and a laugh and play the bagpipes again.!

It's hard not to but we dwell too much in the past that has been lived; the moment is gone never to be re-created; saviour it and move on. Moving on doesn't mean you don't remember or you don't care or care less with time , it means respect and having the courage to face hard days , bad days and make more good days than bad days for you and yours.

Saturday 19 June is a good day- we're off (me, Gary, John Hamilton and Alastair Smith to pick up the Scottish Youth Football Association) SYFA) and Dunfermline Building Society 's Team of the Year Award'.

Ian Caldwell and wee Jack Elliot bring club captain Kriss Paterson up and we all attend the SYFA AGM and presentation of awards.

If we didn't quite deserve to win the Scottish Cup we deserved this award- for Galston Boys Club , for the supporters , the sponsors and the under 17 boys themselves . The trophy sits proudly in our cabinet in the living room and for a couple of weeks it is flanked by sympathy cards but upwards and onwards the cards are packed physically away but the reward remains – no one can take that away.

Summer is a new season and sparks new and changing life. Gary has attended his 'prom' all dressed up to the nines or more accurately ' all kilted out'. We dwell too much in the past. Our photos of Gary come back from the developer and there it is the last photo of Dad alive. He's smiling with Mum and Gary in his kilt between them. Round every corner of your mind and walk of life you bump into your past but it is a past with renewed and refreshed people and experiences.

Renewed and refreshed is what we really need now. We have the opportunity to be renewed and refreshed at the Loudoun Academy Prize Giving.

The Programme reads:
Loudoun Academy
Prize Giving Ceremony
In the Assembly Hall
7.00pm Tuesday 22 June 2004.
PROGRAMME.

- *Fly me to the moon – Jazz Band – musical introduction.*
- *Chair's remarks – Mrs E. McLean – Deputy Head Teacher.*
- *There are worse things I could do – Adrianna Crotch – vocal soloist.*
- *Head Teacher address – Mr, B. R. Johnston.*
- *Rock and Roll Party Queen – Andrew Sloan and Alistair Bell – vocal duet.*
- *Presentation of Prizes – Mrs, Gemmell – Head Teacher , Fenwick Primary School.*
- *Vote of Thanks – Gary Rodgers – Head Boy.*
- *Closing Remarks.*
- *Dancing in the Street – Jazz Band – Musical Conclusion.*

Gary receives a prize for first in biology and the Vesuvius prise for sport – thirty years ago I received that award and was school sports champion but as they say 'the older you get the faster you were'. Gary speaks well and the audience laugh in all the right places and times. There is a further following in footsteps as Gary will commence his degree in Biomedical Sciences at Glasgow University in September 2004 and then do a degree in medicine to become a doctor. Mum always thought I'd be a doctor but I'm too squeamish and struggle to give blood every year.

Our holiday cruising round the Med is another opportunity to get refreshed and we take in Palma , Palermo (Sicily) , Naples , Ajaccio (Corsica) , Marseilles , Barcelona back to Palma and out again to Civitavecchia (the port for Rome) , La Spezia (Italy) , Villefranche (France) and Palamos (Spain) before flying back from Palma.

I remember Sete from 1978and even after twenty six years it looks pretty much the same along the canals. The significance of the gondola – like boats becomes clear as I read, 'From the stands set up along the quays of the Canal Royal during the Saint Louis festival you can have a close up view of a spectacular combat known as the ' Joutes ' (water – jousting). The winners deserve their memorable nicknames. Follow the men in white, the knights of eternal August and follow the fishermen too in their Saint Pierre procession. In Sete there's always people in search of beauty, singing poets, groups of painters and sculptors….' All we were in search of was a taxi to take us back to the port where the Thompson Spirit awaited.

Pompeii was a world away. Monte Carlo is a different world as Gary and I visit the Casino and shelter from an impromptu and unfashionable shower that soaks the fashionably rich and poor alike.

Marseilles is much better than I remember and has a skate-park where Greg unpacks his skateboard and skates in freedom and as an expression of himself. The 'parallel ' in Barcelona is not a skate-park but film crews capture the young and not so young skaters and boarders in the afternoon sun.

As usual before we went on holiday, Mum has a luck penny for us to pick up – a £100 and a note which singularly brings home the fact that Dad has gone.

' To Nancy , Kenneth , Gary and Greg.

I trust you have a safe and enjoyable holiday. Travel in God's safe keeping. Come home refreshed in health and strength. Thank you for all your help. With lots of love from Mum'

It has been said that:

'When you lose your parents you lose your past.

When you lose your child you lose your future '

But

When you lose a husband, a wife, a brother, sister or close friend

You lose your sense of justice, reason and what's right.

Often there is no justification; no acceptable reason ; no respect for God and no sense of ever being right or being made right in the future.

It is in most people a temporary loss, permanently held and only tempered by reason, respect, memories and time.

The cycle of life irrevocably turns.

It turns for Lilian and Duncan and their sons and daughters, Shona , Roddy, Lorna and Alisdair and their sons and daughters.

It turns for Jim and Jessie and their Claire, Lilian, Bobby and Jim (the soldier sons) and their young families.

It turns for Marlene , now back in Darvel , and for Lorraine and JD in Bolton.

It turns for Elaine, Alistair and Kevin.

It turns for Bobby, Linda and their Paul and Stephen in Dumfries where Rabbie Burns died.

It turns for me, Nancy, Gary and Greg; Gary going to University and Greg skateboarding towards his Standard Grade exams.

It turns for Yvonne and Jimmy and their Jim and Iain in their new jobs making their way in the world.

It turns for Davy at home with Mum – without the love of her life but still with a life of love to give and get.

It turns for Colin and Leslie sharing homes and their lives.

It turns for Avril, Andy and their Aidan and Vhari in Middleton on the edge of Manchester.

It turns for Graham and Elaine and the oh so precious Mikayla – the youngest born of the youngest born.

The cycle of life turns for everyone in the sure and certain knowledge that, 'Everybody has to Cry Sometime'.

UNIVERSITY OF STIRLING

Special Supplement

Published jointly by the PUBLIC RELATIONS OFFICE and the GRADUATES' ASSOCIATION

A SOUVENIR OF A SPECIAL WEEK
for those who were there and those who were not

September 1995

▼ *The Director and film star MEL GIBSON makes his way from the MacRobert Arts Centre to Logic Lecture Theatre with colleagues*

▲ *Locals KIRSTY YOUNG of TV fame and KENNY LOGAN, the Scotland rugby player*

▲ *BLYTHE DUFF, star of STV's 'Taggart'*

University of Stirling special supplement, September 1995, covering *Braveheart* with Mel Gibson and graduates.

University of Stirling, February 1996. Mum, Dad, Nancy and myself at graduation on receipt of MSc in Human Resource Management.

Top: Gary, Greg and Friend at Loudoun Castle.
Bottom: Gary and Greg – ready for Loudoun Academy.

Top: Nancy and Jeanette leaning at the Leaning Tower of Pisa.
Bottom: 'Four coins in the Trevie Fountain' – Gary, Greg, Nancy and Jeanette make a wish.

Top: The 'Goldengate' Bridge in Lisbon – Gary, Nancy, Greg and Jeanette.
Bottom: Killie win the Scottish Cup in 1996.

The skateboarders at Perth

Top: Skateboarders – Greg is bottom right, No. 73.
Bottom: The 'new soldiers' – Jim and Bobby Rodgers with a proud dad Jim.

The victorious Galston Boys Club Under 12s, Under 14s and Under 15s football teams in Belgium.

Top: Gary and Greg with their merit trophies.
Bottom: Gary going to the prom with Ariana and Natalie.

Top: A happy Mum and Dad at Jim Richmond's 21st birthday party, 2004.
Bottom: The last photo of Dad – Dad, Gary and Mum, 10th June 2004.

Galston Scottish Cup Finalist, 2004

Back Row: Kenny Rodgers (coach), Gary Rodgers, Stuart Melville, Kris Paterson (captain), Gary Denim, Craig Parker, John Hamilton, Colin Dunlop, Robert Gemmell, Bobby Gemmell (team manager).
Front Row: Matthew Richardson, Kenny Erskine, Craig McCaffrey, Alastair Smith, Drew Kirkland, Antony Gallagher, Andy Taylor, Craig Dunsmuir, Jamie Philipson.

Mikayla aged 8 months; 'the youngest born of the youngest born'.

PART TWO

Introduction

Part 1 of this book was originally the whole book in its entirety but of course life and the trials and tribulations of the family did not end there, indeed for many the journey had hardly begun.

In film-terms Part 2 would be more 'Three Funerals and a Wedding' than 'Three Weddings and a Funeral' but it is not about 'doom and gloom'. It is about life and changes in life and to life which ultimately affect individuals, families, wider communities and ultimately society.

It is about a relatively few small things in the 'grand scheme of things' but small things which have a ripple effect that touches many.

In Part 2:-

Life goes on from 2004 to the beginning of 2013 – it repeats itself but not in the same 'ground-hog day' fashion.

New local heros bring out the best in people to help other people.

New careers are carved out and old careers re-carved out as renewal follows redundancy.

A young life is saved by two young 'unsung heros'.

Sporting success and unexpected victories are recorded in 'tales of the unexpected'!

Unfairness and alleged bullying are challenged in a 'David and Goliath' struggle.

The Town of Darvel faces up to its 'lace industry past' and to a 'festival future'.

Part 2 of 'Everybody has to Cry Sometime' reflects nearly nine years of good luck , bad luck and the fortunes of the family as one generation approached its end and the new generation embarked on the first stage of life to come.

The cycle of life irrevocably turns in the sure and certain knowledge that,

'Everybody has to Cry Sometime'.

Chapter Six

'Getting on with it'

There is a saying that there are only two certainties in life, 'Death and Taxes'. Although tax can be avoided or evaded, especially it seems by the rich and famous, everybody has to pay the 'duty of death'.

There is however another near certainty after death and that is 'life goes on', if not unfortunately for you, then for other people.

Traumatic events hit you and knock you down but it is normality or the new normality of your personal loss that picks you up and you pick up – eventually.

The alternative is to stagnate in a stupor of mourning and attempting to live in a past that has gone.

Even although a nearest and dearest family member has gone there are others to take care of and to take care of you.

After Dad died there was no real option for us but 'to get on with it'.

It was a bit weird really as we all went through the 'grieving process' but at different rates. Looking back you could recognise the classical stages of this process we all entered and emerged from at different times.

For many of us there was no real 'Denial' stage and no real 'Anger' stage as we all knew that Dad could have died of a heart attack over 30 years ago. Equally there was no real 'Bargaining' stage as Dad had reached 80 and it wasn't as if he was in his twenties and some of the older members of the family could then have queried ,'why wasn't it me instead of Robert'?

The whole issue of Dad's death was 'Depressing' but none of us were really depressed and all of this meant we could genuinely see Dad's life as something to celebrate – quite simply we had been lucky to have him for so long.

But Mum had had him as her best friend and husband for so long that it was clear she went through all the stages of the grieving process and arrived at 'Acceptance' later than the rest of the family.

But no matter what , she did get on with it.

For me and Nancy 'getting on with it' mainly revolved around Gary and Greg.

We had always been closely involved in their interests and activities from Cubs to Scouts; the Irvine Valley Swimming Club lessons and Championships; the Valley Vikings Roller Hockey Club and Galston Boys Club football teams but they were both becoming more independent.

In many ways it was harder to keep involved especially when Gary started his B.Sc. Degree in Bio-medical Sciences at Glasgow University as the first stage in his plan to become a Doctor. The Doctor Mum thought I might be but sciences were not my strong point and when Gary wanted to watch a live 'blood and guts' operation on TV I hid behind my newspaper with only the occasional ' keek ' to check Gary was still watching the live operation , and he was !

Greg although still at Loudoun Academy had 'independent' tastes and had taken up skate-boarding a few years before when it became more attractive than football to him. He was a really good footballer but in truth he was a better skateboarder and that was what he really enjoyed and was interested in.

His music was hard rock and hard on our ears but it was his taste, his music, his choice.

He came home from the 'Download at Donnington' with a black eye which he explained he had got from jumping into the ' mosh pit'.

I was struggling to come to terms with what a 'download 'was never mind what a ' mosh ' was but Greg downloaded his music and just ' moshed away' as ' Moshers' do or did ?

Gary like me , only 29 years later , went to study at Glasgow University and went to stay in a Hall of Residence in his first year at the ' Yooni ' in 2004. Unlike me he had two cars packed with his stuff to be delivered to his room at the Murano Village in Glasgow. I had had 2 bags.

Mum kept a keen interest in all of her grand-children and events like these helped put a new focus on and in her life – albeit a life without her Robert. Her grieving process was running its course.

It sounds odd to describe such a traumatic event as a process but it made sense and helped you understand your own feelings and emotions.

'Normal' events helped form and forge the new normality of life after Dad.

Events like Gary passing his driving test; Greg attending a heavy Rock Concert at the Corn Exchange in Edinburgh ; going on holiday to Majorca; attending a Parents Evening with Greg , getting a new Company Car and attending engagement parties and weddings ; me going through yet another Human Resources Functional Review at my work with ScottishPower and Nancy working away at the Lanfine Factory as the lace industry in Darvel was losing the last of its looms.

All these 'normal' events got us through the rest of the year – even Christmas and New Year.

There were joyous occasions like the wedding of Alisdair McTavish and Ashley with Mum proudly in attendance with us but on her own.

All of this got Mum through to another birthday on 10 March 2005 when she was 81; eighty – one and still going strong at the head of the family. Strong enough to face and 'pass' the next challenge that was the first anniversary of Dad's death.

And so it was that time marched on and life did return to its 'new normality'. Mum brighter as the months went on but still not at her brightest.

The first anniversary of Dad's death passed slowly but irrevocably and we all took the next steps to a brighter future and got on with it.

Underneath a sadder surface we all had to remember that Mum was still the Mum we had before Dad died,

'She still cared so much for the family that it hurt. She would like to take any pain and hurt suffered by her children and shoulder them. She would have your cold , flu , your broken bones , your tears and grief and what do you get in return ?

A real Mum without comparison.'

One thing was for sure that she never stopped her caring for the whole family.

There were still hand – written notes in envelopes with 'Luck Pennies' when we went on holiday.

She never forgot a birthday or anniversary.

We were all just getting on with it and it seemed Mum was coping

During traumatic times it can be easy to get fully immersed in the immediate aftermath and walk about with your head down not really wanting to face other people. But often it is the example of other people and how they have coped with tragedy from which you can draw the most inspiration and motivation to move positively on.

Darvel's Steven and Lynn McColl were and are one such inspirational couple.

They have been instrumental in raising thousands of pounds for charities since their daughter, Rachel died of cancer, aged three.

Their next fundraiser in August 2004 was 'Stars in Your Eyes'– the Darvel Charity version.

For this event to succeed some of the old cronies aided and abetted by their younger buddies had to bring it all together – the date , the venue , the publicity , the tickets , the programme , the sponsors, the bar, the compere and last but not least the acts.

It was all brought together by a relatively small group including Nancy and I. We even had the cheek to hold auditions and the good sense to hold a rehearsal so that it would be all right on the night.

The Compere would be the inimitable Ronnie King.

The original Stars for the cream of Karaoke included singers from across the globe – America, Ireland and the UK. With our local Stars all expense was spared as they travelled from as far away as Kilmarnock – all of nearly ten miles.

Tom Aitken was Dean Martin sponsored by AA Motors.

James (The Voice) McAllister complete with black Fedora hat was Frank Sinatra sponsored by Galston Boys Club 1848.

Marnie Smith was Whitney Houston sponsored by The Railway Inn.

Drew Kirk (aka Big Scooby) was Elvis sponsored by QTS – he was resplendent in the high – collared white suit and tight flared trousers and a pair of Gary's size 12 shoes painted with white emulsion especially for the occasion.

The white suit was a necessary and allowable expense for a big finale but size 12 white shoes were not for hire. So there was Drew in Gary's shoes 'overcome by emulsion' and that was before he started to sing.

Scott Hamilton was Ronan Keating sponsored by The Railway Inn.

Maureen Young was Cher sponsored by Glacier.

Gordon McRoberts was Bobby Darin sponsored by Direct Mortgage.

Gordon's wife Lisa was Christina Aguilera also sponsored by Direct Mortgage.

Ronnie King was Elton John sponsored by Leisure Curtains, Fenwick Buildings and Billy Duncan.

Catriona Collins was Madonna sponsored by Nancy and me.

Robert Ingram was Bryan Adams sponsored by GMB, East Ayrshire.

Last but not least Peter McCubbin was Meatloaf sponsored by Loudoun Hill Contracts.

The singers were all great but the funds raised for The Rachel McColl Fund were even better.

Steven (a local 'postie') and his wife Lynn continue every year with their charity fundraisers. ' Stars in Your Eyes' was not a one off for them but part of their way of making things better for other families facing up to the challenge of their lifetime.

It is a remarkable commitment from which many charities and people benefit.

Steven and Lynn are new 'local heroes who don't look for hero status.

They just get on with it as Mum and most of the previous generations did before them.

Chapter Seven

Holding On… to Heartache

"The cycle of life irrevocably turns. It turns for Mum – without the love of her life but still with a life of love to give and get ".

In the days, weeks and months that followed Dad's death we all tried to be there for Mum. 'Getting on with it 'and trying to help establish a 'new normality' for Mum.

Visiting at first more often than we perhaps did before and fussing more.

We tried to ensure Mum had company but we knew that the company she really longed for was the company she had lost.

We each had a sense of our own personal loss but hard as we tried we could not really completely close the void in Mum's life and nor would she have expected us to.

Time they say is a great healer and so it was to us that the rawness of emotions that had appeared like a knife cut across your face subsided with time.

The cuts left by raw emotions were stitched with everyday living – working and taking care of the kids.

In further time the stitches that bound the raw emotions were removed and all that was left of the open wound was a thin red scar line on your face that became a normal part of your normal everyday life.

Ultimately others would hardly be able to see the scar of a death in the family but you still felt it every day but it hurt a bit less and remained a permanent memory of your loss.

You never had the physical scar but the mental scar never leaves you.

Time, work and family commitments also forced us back into a routine.

Life goes on and went on as we all learned or were learning to get on with it.

Friday 9 September 2005 started the same humdrum way as the previous work days and looked like ending that way – me late home again.

I had been at work since before 8am. I was the Head of Human Resources for ScottishPower's Energy Networks Business. Within the Business there were over 3,000 employees, mainly craftsmen and engineers who were literally responsible for "keeping the lights on 24 / 7".

My main business of the day was a Resources Review with the Executive Team. We completed the eight and a half hour review of our manpower and skills plans to help identify any skill shortages and also career and development plans for current and future leaders in all the Departments of the Business.

The day had gone reasonably well but there were other pressing problems to help resolve.

Big David Rutherford was the Director of the Business and he was planning a Business restructure as part of ScottishPower's response to a takeover bid by German energy giants E.ON.

With the outcomes and the actions agreed from Resources Review I turned my attention to support big Davy in thinking through the type of revised Business structure the Company now required. Call it what you will, 'down-sizing ' or ' right-sizing' at the heart of the restructure was the need to cut costs.

We discussed and agreed a new Business structure which would deliver the necessary cost savings and still have the capability to deliver the Business goals and customer service targets safely and securely.

I was drawing up the proposed organisational charts in Davy's office when I got a call on my mobile and decided to take the call.

It was about 6 o'clock.

Marlene, Davy and Colin were at Mum's house and Marlene told me Mum wasn't too well and had pains in her right arm and was a bit dizzy. They had called the Doctor and she was on her way.

It didn't sound too serious and Mum had had a number of ailments over the last few months but being of the 'old school 'she did not want to bother the Doctor or take any pills.

I decided to stay at work and complete the organisational charts for big Davy and told Marlene I would pop in on the way home in around an hour or so but I would also call them back to see what the Doctor had said.

I was a bit concerned about Mum but also concerned that I needed to complete the work for big Davy as he needed the charts for an Executive Meeting early the next morning.

I convinced myself Mum would be OK, the Doctor was on her way, she would be in good hands and the others were there.

The completed charts were left for big Davy and I telephoned home or at least Mum's home before I left the office.

Marlene confirmed the Doctor was there examining Mum but she thought Mum was worse than before and needed help to go to the toilet , she had numbness in her arm and leg and was having difficulty in speaking.

We both agreed that the obvious conclusion was that Mum was having a stroke.

The Doctor's conclusion was that Mum had had,

'a transient ischaemic attack (TIA) - ' a ' mini –stroke' ,

and in a matter of fact style indicated that it should pass.

Her view was that having checked Mum out,

'apart from her age she was doing pretty well and the TIA should pass shortly but you should keep an eye on her and in the event her condition worsens you should call a doctor',

and with that advice she was preparing to leave.

None of the family was happy with this.

Dad had had TIAs and we all thought this was different as everything cried out Mum was having a major stroke and if Mum could have cried out she would have told the Doctor that was the case.

We needed to get Mum to the hospital for a thorough check and the Doctor finally relented in the face of family pressure and the fact that Mum could not move her left leg properly to support herself or walk , her left arm was numb and she could no longer tell anyone how she felt.

Her silence was deafening – it was a major stroke not a mini-stroke.

An ambulance had been called but precious time had been lost and had delayed Mum's admission to hospital.

'Mum's going to Ward 4 D at Crosshouse Hospital' was what Marlene told me – I wrote it down on one of my Business cards – Business which had paralysed me whilst Mum had been having a stroke.

We all attended the hospital that night, that night of 9 September 2005 and like any other caring family feared the worst and hoped for the best.

Mum was initially quiet and acknowledged we were there.

The name label that was Doctor MacMillan spoke to us in a quiet but very clear voice,

" your mother has had a major stroke but I think you already know that. We won't know the full extent of the damage until we make a fuller examination and assessment of her condition. However I think I need to warn you that even at this stage we know this has been a major stroke and it is highly improbable that your mother will ever get back the degree of mobility she has had. We'll update you on progress over the next few days. She is in no immediate danger.

I would also advise you to read the leaflets and literature on stroke conditions , there are a few at the Ward reception which you can take away with you to help you understand a bit more about this condition'.

Before she could ask us if we had any questions she was 'buzzed' and politely excused herself to call on her next stroke victim and their poor family.

There was nothing more we could do or learn that evening but hope for the best.

I read the Leaflet and researched the history of treatment for stroke victims – it did not make for good reading.

It was a fact of life, death and disability that stroke patients were not originally classed as a medical emergency so there had been no flashing lights for Mum's journey to hospital. No gathering of children who would have been thrilled to see the blue flashing lights and hear the 'mee maws' of the ambulance siren.

Strokes were Scotland's third biggest killer after cancer and heart disease. Strokes were Scotland's biggest single cause of disability and Mum had entered the stroke statistics.

I read that the reason that strokes were so far / high up on the Scottish 'killer list' was because there had been and was a scarcity of trained and focussed groups of staff in this area of work / medicine.

The facts were that stroke patients tended to be old aged – over 65 years of age and so the more natural and traditional approach had been for stroke victims to be looked after by geriatricians.

Only around 23% of stroke patients at that time were actually under age 65.

They were therefore mostly geriatrics and were treated as geriatrics - but strokes involved an interruption to the blood flow to the brain or an actual blood vessel bursting like a dam in the brain.

This was really an area of work for neurologists but for the relatively few neurologists in Scotland geriatric stroke victims were not their main or focussed area of work.

This work with geriatrics was not exciting break – through work and the outcomes both for the patient and financially for the neurologist were generally poor.

Mum and other stroke victims required vital services – access to MRI or CAT scans within 48 hours to determine the type and extent of the stroke and which part of the brain was affected but this in turn required radiologists and radiologists were also in short supply.

These were the basic facts that could form the spiral of descent from patient ability to disability.

The actual stroke statistics were equally perturbing – almost one third of stroke patients died within the first ten days ; another third were likely to make a recovery within a month and the final third were likely to be left disabled and in need of rehabilitation.

Dead – Discharged – Disabled: these were the options.

The older you were and the more severe the stroke the more likely it was that you would be in the 'ten day'third' !

Mum was 81 years of age but we didn't yet really know how severe the stroke had been and how she would emerge from the effects of the stroke but the dead, discharged, disabled options were clear.

The Rodgers set up camp at Ward 4D or it must have seemed that way to the nursing staff. We covered the weekdays 2 to 4pm and 7 to 9pm and at weekends the longer day-time visiting hours but the same 7 to 9pm slot at night.

By day 2 Mum's own personal position was fairly clear – she was not in any immediate danger in the Hospital but most definitely did not want to be there.

She simply wanted to be home.

The Doctors at Crosshouse never did say Mum was fit enough to come home directly from the Hospital. Instead after a few days the journey home for Mum involved a transfer from Ward 4 D at Crosshouse Hospital to Pavilion 10 at Ayrshire Central Hospital.

The Consultant explained that,

" they will be able to work with your mother, there will be a programme of speech therapy, physiotherapy and any other therapy she needs".

That was the aspiration.

The reality was that Mum was not really getting any better. In fact she was getting worse.

The reality was that Mum was 81, completely independent until her stroke. The last time she had been admitted to hospital was to give birth to Graham in 1969.

She just wanted to get back home. It was as simple as that but no one seemed to understand her and she understood less of us.

The move to Ayrshire Central appeared to set her back and to us confirmed that she was regarded as a 'geriatric'. The Hospital did not seem to have some of the basic resources never mind the range of therapies referred to.

It was not that the staff did not care, they all did, but some cared better than others. In effect the geriatric tab really determined the care Mum got – she and many more others like her were not a priority or certainly not the highest priority.

At Ayrshire Central Mum had lots of visitors. There were the older ones – Aunt Rhoda, then 85 herself and the Wilsons, and there were younger ones like Gary, Kevin McKie and Jim Richmond.

Amongst the younger ones who went to see their Gran was Paul Rodgers, our Bobby's eldest son. A slim blonde-haired handsome 22 year old young man whose looks belied the fact that he had been having a trouble-some time.

A trouble-some and really 'unsaid / un-talked' about time – that was the soft approach to a hard problem.

The unsaid / un-talked about problems that had broken the surface and substance of family life were that Paul had problems with drink and drugs. He had served time in prison mainly for breach of the peace whilst under the influence of drink and or drugs.

But now he was out of prison and had journeyed from Dumfries where Bobby now lived to see his Gran Rodgers.

No matter how hard prison had been and how hardened he'd become to life and death through drink and drugs he could not handle the changes he saw first-hand in his Gran. She was not how he remembered her or wanted to remember her and he left her room holding back his tears and fears.

We all saw further deterioration in her condition and sought the views of the Senior Nurse.

Her view was pretty clear,

" your mother has now been here for eight weeks and in general terms recovery should be evident and take place by 12 weeks. It is looking more likely that the best state your mother will be in is the condition she currently exhibits".

It was a long-worded way of telling us, 'this is as good as it gets'!

Mum remained in this 'best state' for another few weeks and at 2.55pm on Friday 28 October 2005 I took a call from Mum's Consultant.

He was calling to give us an update on what the views of the Hospital were and what the future for Mum would be.

He was straight-forward and to the point,

" The damage the stroke has done to your mother is permanent and there will be no practical improvement.

There is no evidence of other infections. Your mother is going to remain dependent indefinitely. This does not mean she cannot go home but you need to know that this means a high level of care.

Nursing home accommodation is the other option."

I jotted down notes of the Consultant's views so that I could accurately update everyone and only asked one question – when do you need a decision from the family?

The answer and time was shorter than I had been imagining,

"Next week, a week today.

It will take time to implement and have a discharge planning meeting. If the decision is a Nursing Home then we need to look for a placement and involves Social Work for a place and funding.

Until then your mother stays in hospital.

The patient's wishes are a key consideration, but

A Nursing Home may be the better option".

I arranged a family meeting for that evening.

I had been scheduled to attend an Advanced Employment Law module on Employment Tribunals on Monday 31

October 2005 in London but decided to postpone this module. I had been thinking about doing this for the last few days and had not been feeling too great. A trip to London was the last thing I really wanted with the news and issues we now all had to deal with.

The reality was that the news and issues we had to deal with were not a shock to anyone in the family – we had all seen it coming and knew what the options were.

We met at Mum's house and all had our say on the options and the best way forward and we made our decision.

Nancy and I also made a decision – we decided to buy Mum a pair of green velour sleeping shorts and matching top with a small brown bear motif. We took it into the hospital the next afternoon and fitted Mum fine; she liked the green colour, she had always like the colour green and shades of green.

Nancy and I visited Mum on Sunday 30 October from 7 to 8pm. We shared the visiting with Elaine and Marlene.

Mum was sitting up in her bed propped up with pillows and when she would slip down a bit I would lift her up to make her more comfortable.

She sat fresh and resplendent in her new, bear motif pyjama set and she was as lucid and bright as she had been for a while. Sometimes she would go back in time but all the time she knew who we were and where she was and more-so why she was here. I lifted mum up on the pillows to make her more comfortable and she held my hand in hers and asked 'Who's hand is this?'

I was a bit taken aback and hesitatingly replied, 'It's my hand'.

'Yes I know,' Mum said, 'but it's more than your hand – it is Robert's hand.'

I tried not to look surprised by Mum's comment and tried to get a sense of what she was really thinking.

" Mum I know you know what's going on this evening. You do know you are in hospital and you need to drink and eat to get better to be able to come home – you know, don't you."

Mum looked at me and Nancy with her soft but serious eyes and declared,

" I know I am in the Home and I've been in Hospital',

mildly correcting me as to her Irvine Central was known as 'The Home' due to its previous history as a Maternity Hospital.

She continued, *" but sometimes it's better if I'm not here and I know that too and you need to remember that".*

With that the soft eyes remained as symbols of love but the serious mind and the mind to be serious had left for a better place – for now she was already twenty years back with Robert, her Robert.

It was heartening to see Mum with her old sparkle back in her eyes which even without words spoke of her love and affection for us all. She was back as the wise old owl who spoke softly but so clearly. She understood us and we understood her. Mum had said what she wanted to say and we said cheerio in the knowledge that she was as clear, calm and comfortable as she had ever been since going into hospital.

We had a couple of glasses of wine and slept soundly that night with thoughts that maybe, just maybe things were changing for the better.

With London now off my travel plans I worked from home on Monday 31 October and I got the opportunity to catch up on my workload.

The catch up was cut short as our Davy called at around 9.30am.

"Kenny, I'm just phoning to let you know the hospital have just called me to say that Mum has taken a turn for the worse.

They said she was up early and in the big chair in the Day Room where they left her as the sun was coming up and into the room. When they next went back to her she was slumped forward in the chair – they said it looks as though she has had a heart attack and the Doctor from Crosshouse is with her now.

It's not looking good and they've told me that no one should break the speed limit to get there. I'll phone round the others and if you pick up Jim and Jessie I'll take Elaine and Marlene.

See you down there."

I didn't struggle to break the thinly- coded message, it was hardly the enigma code.

Don't break the speed limit, in other words forget it, your mother has already passed away and the hospitals don't need you as another patient as a result of un-necessary speeding and a car crash.

Your mother is dead- not disabled or discharged – Dead.

We made our way to Ayrshire Central and observed all the speed limits.

We all reluctantly agreed,

' this was the best outcome , she had made up her mind last night , she had gone to join Dad , she knew last night , SHE KNEW LAST NIGHT, yes she knew , I bet she did'.

As ever Mum in the end made our decision easy for us, she decided to take our pain and died on the morning of 31 October 2005.

She died but lived up to everything we ever thought and wrote about her,

" Mum is the most practical, honest, caring and beautiful person. Mrs Baxter hasn't a look in when it comes to making soup as Mum's is the best in the world. She cares so much for the family that it hurts. She would like to take any pain and hurt suffered by her children and shoulder them. She would have your cold flu or broken bones, your tears and grief and what do you get in return? A real Mum without comparison"

These words were even more true on 31 October 2005.

We all felt a huge sadness at Mum's death, but this was tempered by relief that she was not suffering and was at peace and with the love of her life.

We all had Mum's funeral to get through. Those that wanted to go and see Mum at Jimmy Dykes (George Collin's) 'Parlour went and saw Mum.

She was peaceful but she was where she had decided to be, with Dad. It had only been 16 months since they had been parted.

We all put into the coffin what we wanted to put in in memory of Mum.

There were bears, books and momentos.

Nancy and I decided it would be appropriate to put in a Thank You Note and a 'Luck Penny'.

The Note simply read,

" Mum, Just a wee Luck Penny for you (and Dad) on your final journey. Love Always and Thanks for Everything.

Till we meet again, Love, Nancy, Kenny, Gary and Greg."

Following the Service in the Central Church it was a cold day on 4 November 2005 at Hillcrest and it was only warmed by the tearful memories of Mum.

The family took Mum's cords and lowered her gently down to Dad. There was no inexplicable turning of windmills this time only the sad, respectful silence and a lot more tears.

The assembled mourners were invited back to the Masonic Hall in Darvel for something to eat and drink.

On behalf of the family I made a speech. Not off the top of my head but prepared and on paper to give me focus.

" OUR MUM – A TRIBUTE – IN REMEMBRANCE '

Everybody's Mum is special but our Mum was extra special and we think unique.

.

HERE'S WHY.

As a young girl Mum walked about 6 miles from Quarter, outside of Hamilton to school and back. You might think this was not exceptional but she walked barefoot to ensure her shoes were kept good for longer.

She went into service as a 16 year old young woman and helped Jean Deans bring up her family.

Mum was a beautiful young woman but that extended in life to her personality.

On 31 March 1948 Mum and Dad married and brought up 6 sons and five daughters. We were not just brought up but brought up the right and loving way.

At Saltcoats, Dreghorn and finally Darvel we never had a lot of material things (possessions they now call them) but we had everything we needed and more.

We were all well clothed and fed although it was a case of 'first out best dressed'. It was OK, but in the midst of winter you could find yourself in a flowery summer dress – OK that is if you were Lilian , Marlene , Elaine , Yvonne or Avril but not if it was Jim , Bobby , me , David , Colin or Graham.

11 kids all brought up by Mum and Dad – very special if not unique.

Mum was the wise owl of the family- she was the mother, mother in law, sister, aunt , counsellor , confidant and friend to all.

BUT.

She didn't like change – she needed a constant like Dad.

When we bought them a twin tub washing machine she kept the old boiler, wringer and washing board – just in case.

When we bought them an automatic washing machine she kept the twin tub – just in case.

We referred to Mum as loving and giving in the notice of her death and that's just what she was.

She loved us all and gave her all. From a smile, a kind greeting, a wee remembrance, a bowl of soup, a luck penny.

We and you had it all.

Every one of us (and our children and grandchildren) got luck pennies when it was our birthday, our anniversary, our holidays or simply just that we needed a luck penny.

Mum was the Boss (no change there then guys). Dad handed over his un-broken pay packet every Friday and Mum made it last and last to this day.

Mum was special.

Special people draw special people – there's our Aunt Rhoda there (dad's sister) but more like a sister to Mum .

There's William Kerr – our cousin but like a son to Mum.

There's The Nurse, Nurse Ogilvy – a friend for life.

There's all of you – specially here for a special person.

It takes a special Mum to be with Dad for over 56 years to bring up 11 children, to be a granny to 19 grand-children and a great grandmother to 16 great grandchildren.

Towards the end Mum was hurting and she knew it was hurting us.

She knew the prospect of dependency on us at home or in a Nursing home was all that she did not want.

She consulted with Dad and confirmed to Lilian, Marlene and Yvonne that 'Dad had visited the Hospital and said this was not for him', and evidently Mum agreed as without fuss she left on Monday 31 October.

She left Hospital but she will never, ever leave us.

Love and Thanks to you all on behalf of all the Family and Mum and Dad."

The day ended with a mild drowning of sorrows and all the young ones drowning their pints in tears.

Looking back it was a bit weird.

A few months before Mum took ill she had started to give back presents we had given her. She said she had not used them and she was tidying up a bit and it would be better for us to have them back.

At first it made little sense and then every sense – she was clearing up for the future and returning personal gifts to their 'owners'.

Long before Mum died it had been made very clear that her and Dad's wishes were that 'Davy was to have the house', 44 Glen Crescent, Darvel, was to be his home. The home Mum and Dad had already paid for whilst Davy was the remaining occupant.

As Executor of the will I had to arrange with the aid of the Kilmarnock solicitors, Bell & Co. that Davy got the house.

Everybody knew that was what was to happen and everyone signed over their share of the house to Davy.

Apart from the house Mum's will was pretty simple – we were all to get equal shares of Mum and Dad's savings – the estate.

There was 'nothing on tick' – not one debt to pay. In time – honoured fashion Mum had seen to that.

In amongst the piles of papers and photos was the start of a compensation claim Mum had started – 'John Allan v British Coal'. I scanned the document but put it back in the pile – I had enough to do for now without taking on British Coal on behalf of our Grandfather, Mum's Dad.

After a few weeks of legal and administrative proceedings we all got a substantial cheque as our equal parts of the estate. It was quite incredible that from their pensions they had managed to save for our futures and paid off their mortgage. Money they had saved but typically not spent on themselves.

Typically selfless and typical of them.

It was also literally the end of an era, gone but never to be forgotten.

We all held on to our heart-ache of losing Mum but were warmed by the fact that we had been blessed and proud to have her as Our Mum in the first place.

CHAPTER EIGHT

Wee Jock – Unfinished Business

Although Mum and Dad's ' estate ' was settled and shared out equally there were a few bits and pieces which came up and still needed to be sorted out. These were things like over-paid community tax and any income tax refunds due which generally took more time to deal with than things like outstanding Bank and Building Society accounts.

To find and identify these things and get them sorted I had to rummage through piles of old documents and photos. What should have taken me a few hours ended up taking days as I tried to identify the people in the old photos and read old letters and post-cards.

To move things forward I was repeatedly drawn back into the past.

In an old box I came across a photo of 'Wee Jock', our grandfather and Mum's dad and alongside it was the start of the compensation claim headed, **' John Allan v British Coal'** which I had put back in the box when I had first found it weeks ago.

At first I thought nothing of it and nothing had come of it after all this time. I was tempted just to bin it but instead decided to see the claim through in Wee Jock's and Mum's memory.

I phoned a few numbers, provided copies of any documents, birth certificates requested by the Solicitors and generally made a nuisance of myself - I was pretty good at that.

I became the amateur fighter for John Allan the amateur boxer who had been wounded five times by the Germans but never knocked out and here we were , 'Wee Jock ' and ' Wee

Kenny ' in the white corner taking on British Coal in the black corner.

Surprisingly we punched above our weight and after a very long wait we got a result. We got compensation for 'Wee Jock' and the toll years of working down the mine had taken on his health.

On 7 October 2006 , almost a year since Mum died I was able to write out to Lilian , Jim , Marlene , Elaine , Bobby , Yvonne , Davy , Colin , Avril and Graham and send them a cheque to take account of additional monies received including their share of the British Coal compensation in respect of John Allan aka ' Wee Jock'.

It wasn't about the money – it was about the memory and finishing something Mum and Dad had started because it was important to them.

The sense of achievement and justice was worth more than the money.

It was also a fitting tribute to Mum and Dad and in remembrance of the veteran of World War I, the Battle of the Somme and who used to love coming to visit Mum and Dad in Darvel with wee bits of cheese in his pocket.

It seemed to me that this was a final victory for ' Wee Jock ' and all that he had fought for in World War 1.

But like stages in the war it turned out that the compensation victory was not the end but 'the end of the beginning'.

Wee Jock died on 3 April 1973 and that was a known fact.

That was the end of his life but not of his memory – our cousin William Kerr would see to that.

What William had researched and confirmed from official War records and extracts from local papers back in 1915 was that Wee Jock (like most men and women who served their country in the First World War) was an ' unsung hero'.

His working life began in 1907 at age 13 at Quarter Collieries and in 1913 he joined the Territorial Branch of The Cameronians (Scottish Rifles) , part of the 6th Battalion.

After the declaration of War on 3 August 1914 the 6th Battalion was mobilised and sent to Falkirk for months of intensive training after which they were sent on ' active service ' on 19 March 1915.

I would have thought the only thing that Falkirk , France and Flanders have in common was the letter 'F' but there you are they were sent to Falkirk for training.

After their months of training in Falkirk they were fit for fighting and fighting is what they did as far as you could say the wholesale slaughter of men could be described as fighting.

After landing at Le Harve they went to the front and took part in the attack on Aubers Ridge ; were then transferred to the 154th Brigade of the 51st (Highland) Division and fought at Festubert ; were then reorganised and accompanied the 51st Division to the Battle of the Somme.

You wonder why did they transfer the 6th Battalion and reorganise so often?

It was not like they were a Business reorganising to cut costs and increase efficiency.

The simple fact was that on-going transfers and reorganisations were necessary because so many of their colleagues had been cut down and killed in action against bloody bombing and machine gun fire.

At Festubert alone there were 16,000 casualties.

Of the four companies of the 6th Territorial Battalion Scottish Rifles, less than half had survived to answer the roll call.

99 were dead or wounded and Wee Jock was one of the 80 survivors.

An account of the action at Festubert gives you an insight into the reality of the war, the fighting and the dying,

' ' The following evening , precisely at zero hour, Captain Brown led the men over the top into the caldron of war shouting ' Come on Blantyre ' . Immediately the soldiers came under murderous artillery and machine – gun fire and were mown down, almost as soon as they climbed out of the trenches.

When they finally reached the German trenches the men of 'A' Company frantically hacked at the barbed wire with cutters in an attempt to cut their way through it. The Blantyre men got through by running up a communications trench where the bodies of the German dead lay so thick on the bottom that they had to run over the top of them. The Blantyre men took three lines of trenches and then managed to get themselves into a village where they dug themselves in.'

But this was not an anonymous war and fighting, this was Wee Jock, our grand-father fighting for his life and the report in the Hamilton Advertiser in 1915 confirmed this reality,

" Private John Allan, 13 Low Quarter, Hamilton, a well-known local amateur boxer received a body wound with the bayonet (third time wounded). He is in hospital in France'.

By the end of the war in addition to the bayonet wound his body had a total of five bullet / shrapnel wounds to show for his service; he also had three medals. The 1914 – 15 Star, the British War Medal and the Victory Medal affectionately known as Pip, Squeak and Wilfred.

Wee Jock, an unsung hero of the past had no memorial stone or plaque to mark his present resting place in Larkhall Cemetery and that was William's concern.

So we got our heads and the families together to get a memorial stone for 'Wee Jock '.

William and I visited Bobby Main, a Sculptor in Cambuslang and we tried to choose a memorial stone that spoke a bit about him and his times as a coal miner, an amateur boxer and a First World War soldier. We needed something natural, strong and hard as Wee Jock had been.

We found it - a blue marble memorial stone in the shape of a book.

Until the memorial stone was in place Larkhall Cemetery could not speak for us to remind us where this old soldier lay. There was no marker and even if he had died in France as an unknown soldier he would have had a cross.

The memorial stone we selected and had inscribed was all and everything that was needed to mark the grave of our unsung hero and keep his memory more alive than ever. Bobby Main delivered and sited the stone at Larkhall Cemetery on Wednesday 25 July 2012 – over 39 years since Wee Jock died and nearly a century since he had fought and nearly been killed in action on the 'Western Front'.

'Wee Jock 'finally had his 'book – mark 'on history and a fitting marker for the grave of a known soldier – our Grandfather.

On Sunday 29 July 2012 William, Nancy and I paid a belated tribute to John Allan as William laid a wreath at his newly marked grave in Larkhall Cemetery.

After marking time for nearly forty years 'Wee Jock' ex 1-6th The Cameronians (Scottish Rifles) has his and our marker of respect and remembrance.

"In Memory of our Dear Grandfather, John Allan, ex 1st – 6thBat The Cameronians (Scottish Rifles), Died 3 April 1973, Aged 79."

'Wee Jock, Business Finished'.

Our cousin William Kerr at the newly-marked grave of our grandfather – Wee Jock

Wee Jock's commemorative stone

CHAPTER NINE

'Working Daze'

By 2004 I had racked up some 23 years of experience working in Human Resources within Scottish Power (SP) – a one Company boy and man but with 13 different jobs in that time.

In the next 6 years I had another 6 jobs as the pace of Business change meant that the tendency was to embark on yet another restructure before the last one had been bedded down.

In 23 years I had seen quite a few momentous events but was not naïve enough to think I had seen everything.

I had been involved in dealing with the impact of the Fuel Crisis in 2000; a bout of industrial / strike action in December 2001 / January 2002 ; the Foot and Mouth outbreak in 2002 and the Pandemic Flu preparations in 2004/ 2005.

National events that were as big a challenge as you could get in your day. But there were more national, regulatory and competitive challenges to come and with the aspirations for ScottishPower to be a 'Global Power Player 'came the Global challenges.

On St. Andrew's Day (30 November) 1999 ScottishPower acquired Pacificorp in America. The £4.7 billion deal was then the biggest takeover of a foreign company by a Scottish firm. There was a clear sense of national pride and achievement with high fives all round and the pipes and drums playing loudly.

By 2005 whilst Pacificorp wasn't quite 'going down the pan' the State energy regulations (in Utah ; Idaho ; Wyoming ; Oregon and Washington) and the management of Pacificorp in itself proved to be even more challenging than the Company Directors had anticipated.

In May 2005 SP announced its intention to sell off Pacificorp and by 21 March 2006 a deal was struck with Mid

American Energy Holdings Company (a Company controlled by the legendary US investor Warren Buffet.)

The deal was 'successfully' completed at a reported loss of nearly £1billion !

The pipes and drums played a lament and ScottishPower beat a retreat from the American Market.

The deal solved an American 'problem' for ScottishPower but at the same time created a European one. We were seen by some European Energy industry giants as ripe for takeover.

The first on the scene was the German Energy Group E.ON in 2005 with an offer of 570 pence per share.

The response to this takeover bid was a defensive strategy.

E.ON had already acquired other electricity companies in the UK and the thinking of the day was that SP would be ' amalgamated ' and' rationalised ' to cut out duplication of services and support. In short under this offer it was fully anticipated that there would be a considerable loss of ScottishPower jobs.

The defensive strategy itself though meant a restructure to take out some Business costs and make more efficiencies across all the ScottishPower Businesses. Under David Rutherford, the Energy Networks Director we delivered 250 manpower reductions and cost savings as part of this overall Company defence strategy.

That defensive strategy was successful as the bid by E.ON was rejected by the Board on 22 November 2005 but left the Company open to other acquisitive Energy Companies who were true global players.

By 20 November 2006 the Board of Directors of ScottishPower agreed an £11.6 billion takeover by the Spanish Energy Company Iberdrola.

As part of the HR Integration Team I attended meetings with our Iberdrola counter-parts (Alvaro, Armando and Teresa) at the ScottishPower Head Offices in London.

Effectively we were involved in HR due diligence and preparations for the integration of SP into Iberdrola as the parent Company. Each part of ScottishPower was reviewed and new structures and initial plans and processes to control the integration and the development of these new structures were prepared.

Back then due diligence was hardly ever heard about or understood outwith Company and Commercial circles.

That was until February 2012 when the once mighty Glasgow Rangers effectively failed in their due diligence and a Whyte Knight turned into their blackest of days in their 140 year history.

In 2006 out-with private companies due diligence was a relatively unknown business chore and not many punters would have heard the words let alone understood what was involved and why should or would they.

Now it seems 'due diligence' is the order of the day or disorder of the day and everybody knows something about it.

Peculiar how it takes the plight of a once mighty football club to bring home the commercial realities and pitfalls of Business life to a much wider community.

The punters would have understood the next part in the 'integration' process though – it was a trip to Spain in February 2007.

I joined a Trade Union delegation to Spain.

This delegation was for the full time officials and a number of lay trade union representatives to meet with their Spanish counter-parts to exchange information on both Companies and to gather information on Iberdrola's record on dealing with trade unions and in particular their approach to major restructures and takeovers.

There was also to be an opportunity to meet with Senior Iberdrola Executives who would present and explain their Business Plans for ScottishPower and Iberdrola worldwide.

In effect the visit was a fact – finding visit and cultural exchange all rolled into one.

The meeting with a range of Senior Iberdrola Executives in their Offices in Madrid was serious but not sombre and all of the Spanish Executives spoke English which helped a lot. It was a bit of a relief that everyone left the meeting relatively pleased by the professional and positive way it had gone.

The joint trade union meeting with the aid of interpreters also went well although the Spanish Trade Union Officials were clearly surprised that the ScottishPower Trade Union representatives were quite comfortable for me to sit in on their meeting.

I was the only ScottishPower or Iberdrola Manager to attend this meeting. They simply couldn't understand why and how the ScottishPower Trade Unions trusted me (a senior HR Executive) to sit in on a joint Trade Union meeting.

Out-with the main business of the meetings we had the opportunity to visit a gas –fired Power Station outside of Madrid and a major control Centre in Madrid before flying to Valencia. There were further visits to Iberdrola Business Centres before we were shown Spain's entry to the America's Cup which was centred in Valencia and was being sponsored by Iberdrola.

.

In this 'cultural exchange' we brought diaries; a range of trade union leaflets; pens; rulers; everything but 'wampum' and whisky.

We also brought a confusing array of UK 'accents' which some of us couldn't understand never mind the Spanish.

In return, we learned how to greet our female Spanish colleagues with a ' peck ' on both cheeks , we ate paella , had a glass or two of Rioja and 'enjoyed' a night of traditional Flamenco dancing before returning home on the third day.

The Flamenco dancing was very professional but I had developed sinusitis and a thumping head which was definitely not helped by what appeared like steel – reinforced heels and toes being thumped repeatedly and vigorously for well over an hour on bare wooden floor-boards.

Then to steel toe cap it all for the Flamenco dancers to return for a 15 minute encore due to the diplomatic but over enthusiastic ovation they had been given by the UK trade union delegation.

During the Flamenco dancing we talked in sign language and developed our lip-reading skills – the decibel levels must have been on a par with a 1970's disco and come to think about it the Flamenco dancing was pretty much the same with John Travolta moves aplenty.

The full time trade union officials from UNISON, the AEEU (AMICUS), PROSPECT and the GMB along with their lay representatives whilst not entirely convinced that Iberdrola were the ' best thing since sliced bread ' were sufficiently reassured that Iberdrola represented a much better fit that some of the other Energy giants who could have taken over ScottishPower.

The culture shock of being taken over and not just taken over, but taken over by a foreign company had really only just begun when ScottishPower was officially taken over by Iberdrola on 23 April 2007.

Iberdrola had a fundamentally different approach to Company structures than ScottishPower and the management and control of these structures. Their focus was on the central control of all of the key levers of ScottishPower.

For me all this meant I had another 6 jobs in 7 years as restructure followed restructure from 2004 onwards. My job titles reflected the nature of the restructures and the changes in the Human Resources function.

In 2004 I was HR Business Partner, Power Systems and then moved into a more central role as Head of Employment Policy, Employee Relations and Projects in 2005. At this point I was tempted to put in a claim for an up-grading based on the length of my new Job Title ?!

Eventually I started what was to be my final role as Director of HR Management in 2009.

In a sense employees got used to restructuring as with each new Chief Executive; Director or owner they knew change would be on the cards.

But change went beyond the structures on paper. Employees often had to compete for jobs within these new structures with fewer jobs in them than before.

At times, most times the workload was at best heavy and at worst horrendous.

During a particularly hectic work period I was driving to work and listening to ' Radio Scotland ' for road reports and business updates – not Radio 1 , not West Sound or Radio Clyde but a definite sign and sound of the times and the fact I was getting older.

I listened to 'The Thought for the Day 'and was impressed enough to write it down when I got into work on 19 October 2005:-

'Thought for the Day.

WORRY why WORRY ?

40 % of Worries don't happen.

30 % of Worries have happened.

12 % of Worries are not within your control.

10 % of Worries are about health and only make you worry more.

ONLY 8 % of Worries are ' REAL'.

I don't know if the percentages are scientific calculations but the whole thing rang true for me and from then on in I didn't care less about work but I did worry less.

The centralisation and restructure of HR also meant that some of the ' older ', more experienced HR employees left or were made redundant.

For some time new posts had been and were being filled by external candidates who were presumed to have ' better skills ' than the existing talent within ScottishPower.

To be fair some of them actually did have the skills and talents for the new roles in Human Resources and were ahead of the internal candidates.

But as usual there were a quite a few who had an impressive paper CV and for these people their CVs could and should have included claims that they were professional musicians as well because they certainly could ' blow their own trumpet'.

The reality was that there were a number of particularly poor appointments – HR Directors / HR Managers who confirmed to their Teams that they would only be with ScottishPower as a stepping stone to their next career development out-with the Company within 18 months or so.

One HR Managerial appointment was openly of 'the fake it till you make it' school of HR.

In other words 'a pure chancer' who had chanced his arm and stretched his CV to get a job with ScottishPower.

It was of little surprise that he was found out. His bloated and over-blown CV was found out as much by the full time and lay trade union officials as by his HR colleagues. The trade union officials clearly rumbled him as someone who didn't know what he was talking about and his HR colleagues rumbled him as they didn't know what he was talking about either.

With some others the 'Peter Principle' clearly applied as they had been promoted well beyond their level of competence and were now displaying their full range of incompetence. Still favoured by those who had appointed them but not favoured by those they now blamed for their failings.

Finally there were those who lacked the emotional intelligence and knowledge to man-manage their Teams without giving orders and instruction in a ' command and control ' style that was as far away from a more modern and progressive coaching style as you could get. To them their behaviour was strong and driving leadership, to others it was bullish at best and bullying at worst.

All of these developments had consequences –the better HR appointments succeeded and moved their part of the Business forward and successfully lead their Team and were well – regarded.

The poor appointments failed and left to pursue a career out-with ScottishPower with another 'notch' added to their impressive paper CV. They also left other Managers to 'pick up the pieces'.

Their's, though was not the only fall-out – the internal HR talent – those employees who had been passed over for appointments and promotions saw all of this and got fed up and left when the opportunity arose.

Some senior HR employees also left ScottishPower and amongst these was John Stewart, the UK HR Director who had succeeded Steve Dunn and left on 30 June 2009 after 16 years with SP.

The significance of this for me was that it was a bit of 'a sign of the times '.There was a big amber light flashing at the last crossroads of my career.

I had a lot of respect for John and had hoped he would have been in his role for some time to come as he worked with integrity, honesty and professionally telling it as it was and trying positively to find solutions to the challenges ScottishPower faced under its new owners.

It was not to be as John left to become HR Director with ScottishPower's old industry rival Scottish and Southern Energy.

It was also not to be for some other long-standing HR colleagues like Joe Fitzpatrick and Kim Stevenson who left on 31 December 2009.

There were and are still a great many talented HR professionals in ScottishPower but somehow the latest change had got to me.

In the run up to Christmas and New Year it was again the case of looking back and also trying to look forward to see what the future would bring.

Effectively it brought an end to my ScottishPower career after nearly 29 years of service. I had lost part of my job in the latest restructure and lost part of motivation to be a part of ScottishPower.

I was finding it professionally and personally hard to live with some of the Business and people changes and reckoned if I couldn't live with them I would be ' better off ' living without them.

In short I decided I was not 100% committed to what I was now doing or being required to do and that was not good enough for me – it was time to go.

By February 2010 further changes were made to the Human Resources function and these changes impacted my job and in effect sealed my fate in leaving.

When I looked back at my time with ScottishPower I had had about 19 different jobs – 18 in Human Resources but also one as a ' Construction Manager ' – a real eye opener of an experience for someone with no technical qualifications.

During my time with SP I had studied for and been awarded an M.Sc in Human Resources Management at Stirling University and completed a Chartered Institute of Personnel and Development Advanced Certificate in Employment Law (CIPD ACEL) between May 2005 and November 2007.

I had received a Merit Award for the Advanced Employment Law Certificate but that one piece of paper only told a fraction of the story.

There was an Induction and 10 training / learning ' Modules ' which I had to attend – all in London; I had an assignment to complete and an exam to pass – all whilst going through some of the most difficult professional and personal times I had ever experienced – so much so that I had to re-submit my assessment , postpone my exam once and failed it the first time.

I was nothing if not determined.

A lot of people would have relished the opportunity to go to London and see the 'sights' but for me it meant getting up about 4am and getting to Glasgow Airport for a 6.30 am flight to Heathrow, catching the Heathrow Express to Paddington and then a shared taxi to Great Queen Street in central London and then doing all of this in reverse to get home about 8 or 9pm.

At the actual training / learning modules I had to check my e mails on my Blackberry and respond to Business calls during breaks.

But I did it even if I did have to pass on the opportunity and expense of being presented with my Certificate at The Ivy in London.

My experience had included some of the worst times and working relationships and some of the best times and working relationships.

The worst and best of times are opposite extremes and most of the time I simply enjoyed my work and I can honestly say that every working day I enjoyed a laugh with one work colleague or another.

I experienced the worst of times in the Power Systems Business during the strike days of December 2001 and January 2002 and having to miss out on a family holiday in October 2001 to stay at work trying to figure out a way to avoid the industrial action in the first place.

The worst of times on a personal basis when accompanying David Rutherford on 27 September 2004 to explain to a Mum and Dad and two daughters that their son / father had been killed in an accident at work and he would not be coming home.

No job title or text book could prepare you for that tragedy and task. Big Davy gave a very professional explanation of what we thought had happened and drew diagrams to help with his explanation of the tragedy.

We had always to look the parents and daughters in the eye as human nature was such that if you didn't there was a suspicion you were hiding something. But the only thing we were hiding was our fear that we were not coping with this tragedy.

We did our best to explain what had happened and what would happen next and the parents were shocked ,very understanding and appreciative and the daughters were understandably stressed and emotional.

With a great deal of humanity, integrity and honesty we could give a reasonable answer to what had happened but we could not answer the question they screamed at us in silence – WHY ?

I experienced the best of times in Energy Networks with the HR Business Team I picked and developed and at the Head Office with the Employment Policy, Employee Relations, Projects and Heads of HR Teams who were professional and fun to work with – in the main ?!

The best of times when I managed to get support and approval for a five year (2002 – 2007) manpower and skills plan which actually focussed on apprentice and graduate recruitment and skills development as opposed to the trend and pressure for manpower reductions.

All in all ScottishPower had given me great opportunities and I had taken them and had a great career – the positives far, far outweighed the negatives.

I officially left ScottishPower on 30 June 2010 after a night out with what was to be former colleagues on 18 June 2010 at All Bar One in Glasgow.

During all my time with ScottishPower I had always tried to be professional, honest and act with integrity.

I also did my best to form good working relationships with fellow employees , senior managers , customers , consultants and full time trade union officials and lay representatives to help solve Business challenges on as positive a basis as possible.

Basically it was about treating everybody fairly and with dignity and respect.

A particularly satisfying end to my career was detailed in the HR Organisational Announcement by Sheila Duncan, UK Director of HR which read,

' .. after nearly 30 years with the Company, Kenny Rodgers has decided to move on to new challenges in his career. Over the years Kenny has held a number of senior roles in HR and has made a

significant contribution to the development of the function in that time. Kenny's reputation as the " ultimate HR professional" goes far beyond ScottishPower and he is very well respected by our Trade Unions as well. Furthermore Kenny has been a key contributor in supporting the Business change agenda and has been integral in enabling the business success of ScottishPower".

I was not sure about ever being the ' Ultimate HR professional ' but I did strive to be professional at all times and I think I did form very good working relationships with the Trade Unions, so much so that I was enormously sad when the full time official of the AEEU, Danny Keeney died on 14 July 2006.

I had and have no regrets about leaving.

I miss some of my work colleagues – like Paul, Mark, Steven, Peter, Guy, Gordon, Joan, Fiona , Elaine, Lindsey, Gayle , Sarah, Joyce, Debbie , Karen , Linsey, Connie , Jayne, Irene, Gillian , Pamela, Jane, Suzanne and many others; I miss my dealings with full time trade union officials and shop stewards to try and jointly move the Business forward but I don't miss my work.

My 'Working Daze' had started with the old South of Scotland Electricity Board (SSEB) way back in 1981 and then the names of colleagues reflected this Scottish Public Utility as Jimmies , Wullies and Marys predominated.

The names changed with the times as a privatised ScottishPower took over MANWEB (Merseyside and North Wales geographical area) and Southern Water and this added the Georges , Edwards and Elizabeths.

When we crossed the Atlantic we said howdy to Hank, Roy and Justine at Pacificorp and said bye (missing you already) in almost indecent haste when we sold up.

Then there were new Spanish names like Alvaro, Armando and Teresa to meet and greet but that was only part of the 'new world ' of Iberdrola with interests in America , South America and beyond .

It was a new world of names and faces I was destined not to be part of as the biggest part of my working career had gone into the previous 29 years.

In all of my time at ScottishPower the professionalism and talent of the many far out-weighed the failings of the few. The vast majority of my time and people at ScottishPower were good and I had had a fantastic career.

Occasionally I have a meal and a drink with others HR colleagues who left ScottishPower (Jim Moore , Joe Fitzpatrick and Kim Stevenson) but like a football supporter no longer resident locally and unable to continue to support his Team I still look out every day for the 'ScottishPower Results ' ; the Iberdrola share price and the Pensions Updates

Before I left Nancy and I had worked out if I could ' afford ' to leave and what was I going to do with myself especially after all the years with ScottishPower and regularly working 12 hours plus working days and more hours in the evening and weekends.

We talked things over even more when I was on 'Garden Leave' from April to June 2010.

I've always liked a gamble and on 12 April 2010 whilst on Garden Leave I spied a horse called Garden Leave. It was a big outsider but I decided not on form but based on the coincidence of the name and my position to have a punt on this horse.

It was till then the most money I had put on a horse but still only about £20 and sure enough this 'donkey' strolls in to win and I leave the bookies about £500 better off thanks to 'Garden Leave'.

To this day I have never heard of another race this horse has been in let alone has won so it's probably ended up in the ' knackers' yard'.

To avoid me ending up in the ' knackers' yard' as well I had to think about what I was going to do , what was I going to be now ?

I could be a Consultant – I could have been but I reckoned this was an 'out of the frying pan into the fire' move and decided to go into the Floristry business and become a Florist instead!

On occasions talking to work colleagues before I left ScottishPower about career change the reference to ' floristry ' was interpreted as ' forestry' but the bottom line was it was something the Monty Python team would introduce as , 'and now for something completely different' but not as different as being a ' lumber-jack'.

Becoming a florist was not an automatic process and although I had helped Dad make holly wreaths for years that was a long time ago and flowers were a different proposition all-together.

I signed up for some training at the Scottish School of Floristry and signed on at the ' buroo' on 16 July 2010.

It was a bit disconcerting at the 'buroo' – not because of some of the unemployed people with their ' dugs ' tethered to the railings at the 'Job Centre' but because technically I wasn't even a statistic for the 'buroo'.

I had paid over 30 years national insurance; I could not and did not receive any benefits (not even to get myself a ' dug') and I was about to enter the world of self – employment.

In short the Job Centre Adviser told me there was no real reason to 'sign on' every two weeks so I signed off.

At the Scottish School of Floristry in Bearsden Glasgow I attended practical one or two day courses lead by Carole Pike on making floral wreaths, hand-tied bouquets and sheafs and sprays and by September 2010 my training was completed.

I devised a Business Plan for the next three years and against Greg's advice and better judgement set up in business on 1 November 2010 a 'Forgetmenotfloristryandcemetery-careservices'.

Despite the dubiety about the name I did reasonable Business selling holly wreaths and floral bouquets over the Christmas period 2010 but the cemetery care services (cemetery plot maintenance and headstone cleaning services) were a' dead loss'.

I had done my market research and no one really provided these specific services, clearly there was a gap in the market which I could fill and make some money.

Then it dawns on you, the reality is that although there is a gap in the market and filling that gap is a good idea in theory the reality is that the gap in the market is there because there are few people who really want this service and even fewer who want to pay for it.

'Dragon's Den 'here I come – aye right!

Another reality was that 'word of mouth' in floristry is more effective than a website for local business and I spent too little time in promoting and marketing my Business.

In effect I worked from home and had no 'shop front 'to display my work. The upside of working legitimately from home was that you did not have the overheads of a shop and the downside you had no presence in town. In fact for a while it seemed like I had more presence in Leeds than in Darvel as helping our old friends the Bullers became the centre of my attention and time.

After hearing that Robert was having some problems at work I made an initial and spontaneous offer to help but this help took up much more time than I had ever anticipated from around July 2010 to November 2011.

Just what was it that took up all this huge amount of time and effort and resulted in a 'David and Goliath' struggle?

New kids on the block who Robert was absolutely convinced were bullying and harassing him - only the kids were not kids.

Kids can be really cruel but adults can be infinitely more cruel.

Bullying by kids is hard to deal with but alleged bullying by adults is even harder to deal with and so it proved in Robert's case.

According to the ACAS definition , " Bullying may be characterised by offensive , intimidating , malicious, or insulting behaviour, an abuse or misuse of power through means intended to undermine, humiliate , denigrate or injure the recipient".

There are hundreds even thousands of workers who will not recognise this definition but they will still know that they are being bullied or have been bullied.

They will know they are being picked upon; being criticised unjustly; having their work undermined; being spoken to or at as if they didn't really exist; being accused of not doing things they should have and doing things they shouldn't have; having their confidence eroded; feeling powerless to stop the bullying and generally suffering in silence or feeling compelled to leave their job to get away from it all.

Robert was probably the least likely type of person you would think would be subject to bullying and harassment. He was a big guy from the North East of England (Leeds) , an ex HGV driver who had played football in his day and now enjoyed a game of snooker with his mates at the Ackroyd Street Working Mens Club on Wednesday nights. He smoked, he drank, he was really a man's man and was well capable of standing up for himself – with men at any rate.

His 'problem' though turned out not to be a man or even one woman.

To Robert he was 'snookered' by two women.

As Robert eventually lost confidence in his Trade Union I ultimately became his ' pro bono' doubles partner and representative. I quickly found out there were no trick and quick shots to be played to get Robert out of his 'snooker'.

He had been employed as the Caretaker at Seven Hills Primary School in Morley since 24 March 1994 and as part of his job stayed in the School House directly opposite the School. He had over 15 years of excellent service with the School but according to Robert and his wife Gill who also worked at the School things began to change in 2007 with the appointment of a new headteacher and later a new business support manager at the school.

At first the change of management at the school did not seem to affect Robert but in 2009 it all started to go 'Pete Tong'. Robert felt he was being picked upon by the new management duo at the School. This feeling grew through various actions and meetings with these senior staff members and eventually and on his Trade Union's advice he submitted an informal grievance on 14 January 2010 referring to harassment and perceived victimisation by the headteacher and business support manager.

The shit hit the fan three months later but not as a result of investigations into Robert's grievance but as a result of disciplinary investigations into allegations against him. It all seemed a bit odd.

Prior to my real involvement in Robert's case some staff and parents had already voiced their concerns about events at the School. This had resulted in a meeting of these concerned staff and parents with David Dewhirst, the Chair of School Governors and Ed Balls, the M.P. for Morley and Outwood in July 2010.

It was also about this time that the local press and TV had taken an interest in what was happening at the School and a brief televised report from the School had sparked a bit of interest in Robert's plight at the time but most of the staff 'did not want to get involved'.

It was after these events that I really became more and more involved and agreed to represent Robert.

For about the next 18 months I became immersed in a whole series of hearings, appeals, investigations and meetings in an attempt to get justice for Robert and get his case fully and properly heard on the basis of all the available and relevant evidence.

Two School Governors were appointed to investigate the formal bullying and harassment grievance he had submitted in

September 2010 and report back on their findings and conclusions.

On 25 November 2010 the findings of the Report were quite clear and were effectively that Robert had not been appropriately managed and that both the headteacher and the business support manager could have been more constructive in their dealings with Robert; that he had been treated in an oppressive manner; written to in quite an aggressive tone ; been dealt with in a fairly inflexible and heavy handed manner and that the headteacher had contradicted herself on two occasions.

But despite these findings the Report concluded that the Governors were not satisfied that the behaviour amounted to bullying and harassment and they thought there was insufficient evidence to fully substantiate the allegations.

Robert submitted an Appeal and a series of further grievances over how he had been treated. At one point we had his Disciplinary Appeal, the Bullying and Harassment Appeal and about four other grievances running. It effectively meant I was working full time on Robert's case and Education Leeds / Leeds City Council had about six to eight HR staff engaged in dealing with the various appeals and grievances.

We used and escalated all the School's internal policies and procedures to make Robert's case but effectively it was to no avail. In the main his appeals and further grievances failed and as a last resort and more in hope than expectation we used the School's Whistle-blowing Policy and Procedures to disclose genuine concerns about mal-practice and misuse of the School's Policies.

Things had gone pretty quiet from around March 2011 and then 'out of the blue 'Mr Dewhirst the chair of the school governors issued a communication dated 6 June 2011 to Governors, Parents and Staff which confirmed the headteacher had brought forward her plans to retire.

Did she jump or was she pushed was the question most people would ask in such circumstances but the fact of the matter was very few people actually knew all the circumstances.

For Robert it had all got too much and as the pressure of the cases had intensified he moved from being stressed to being depressed. In January 2011 he had had a heart procedure to deal with an abnormal electrical pathway in his heart. And this procedure had to be repeated in July later that year.

It was now fully two years since Robert's woes had begun and in August he and Gill decided they wanted to explore the possibility of a settlement.

Eventually after a great deal of to'ing and fro'ing Robert was given a final offer of a financial settlement by the School to consider and decide upon.

My direct involvement in Robert's case really came to an end in early November 2011 as Robert was required to get independent legal advice on the potential settlement of his case and the ultimate signing of any agreement.

He chose a lawyer with offices in Morley and I attended the first meeting with him to help explain Robert's position, what we had done to date and where we were now.

The decision to sign any agreement was Robert's. His lawyer explained her view and the options going forward. She actually seemed positively surprised at how much we had done and how far we had taken the case and the proposed settlement in the face of the power and resources at the School's disposal.

Robert signed the agreement at his next meeting with his lawyer and he has been bound by that Agreement since then.

But out of adversity often comes strength and determination as they say to 'not let the b's get you down '.

As the song goes, 'what doesn't kill you makes you stronger '.

In all of this my attitude and approach is summed up in three quotes,

" It's never too late .... To take a stand,
Sometimes we need to draw the line
Because we know it's right

And for our own self-respect.
Your heart will tell you when the time is right.
When it does, listen.
Then fight hard.
You will respect yourself.
So will others."
And,
'It's never too late to tell the truth,
Lies are a burden,
They entangle us and weigh us down.
Truth always fights to break out.
It usually succeeds anyway.
It's not worth the struggle.
Telling the truth clears the air.
Lifts the burden.
Liberates.
And,
"Justice is truth in action". Benjamin Disraeli.

From around July 2010 to November 2011 I had made about 20 two-day, 500 mile round trips to Morley just outside of Leeds and spent hour upon hour at home drafting numerous reports and responses to help Robert.

I had gathered and retained over 1,000 documents including e mails, correspondence, reports, notes of meetings and also a number of tape recordings and CD recordings of joint meetings.

I think I must be the only over 50 something who effectively had a 'gap year' in Leeds but what happened to Robert was just not right and I could not stand by and watch him unravel through unfolding injustice.

Robert and Gill moved to Majorca where their daughters Sofie and Katie worked and we met up with them on a few occasions in Majorca but somehow after the great struggle to get justice and a settlement for Robert and in the move to Majorca our friendship got lost. It was not the same and despite getting together in Majorca we sadly grew apart.

Apart from taking ' a year out ' to help the Bullers there was also a stark realisation that to break into the floristry business was no easy task and if anything the market was probably shrinking and at the same time being eaten up by the large supermarkets.

The market was shrinking as more and more people expressed a wish for 'No Flowers' and 'Donations to Charity' or 'Family Flowers Only' when a loved one died.

The big supermarkets ate into the market as their purchasing power meant they could buy flowers as cheap if not cheaper than most florists and each Supermarket had floral bouquets and plants conveniently situated within their Stores which shoppers could pick up relatively cheaply and with ease.

What these Supermarkets have not offered (to date) are the more specialised floral products like hand- tied bouquets, wreaths (floral and holly) and special occasion flowers and arrangements (weddings etc) and so there is still a vibrant and competitive market for these products and services.

My Business Plan 'B' was to rename the Business - 'Lily of the Valley' – not quite as lengthy as before but more focussed ; target advertising within the Irvine Valley and look to larger Florists to contract for in making holly wreaths in particular.

Result business nearly doubled over the Christmas period compared with last year. Along with a new website I at last found a very positive use for the social media of the day. Friends and existing customers Face-booked the flowers and extended my personal contacts and recommendations that brought in more business.

Floristry is a Business that focusses on key events in people's lives, like Birthdays, St. Valentine's Day, Mothers' Day; Christmas, Weddings and Wedding Anniversaries, Births and ultimately Illness and Deaths.

I had not really anticipated putting my new found skills to use just yet for those saddest of occasions on a personal and family basis but it was inevitable that that day would come – the only question was who would it come for?

CHAPTER TEN

A Lost Soul

Drink and drugs are the scourge of every town and city in Scotland.

The drinking culture is well established and the friendly Scottish drunk is an accepted and yet unacceptable stereotype.

The drugs culture is also pretty well established but thankfully there is no accepted 'druggy stereotype 'or acceptable 'druggy stereotype.'

These twin addictive evils separately or combined are a force of absolutely no good.

Addiction produces waste and wasters but it is still a choice of whether or not to be wasted.

The drug culture has a cancerous form – it eats at the individual who begs, borrows and steals to feed a habit. It destroys individual brain cells, personal relationships and the social fabric of a community and towns.

It also steals any work ethic a person may ever have had and leaves in its place dependency.

The past norm of working, of being employed and earning a living is now for too many people third generation deceased. There appears to be no shame in not working and never wanting.

Instead of a job and a work ethic you get methadone and 'a dug '.

Methadone is the druggies allowance for an addiction and they also get an allowance for 'a dug'.

Irony of ironies – they can hardly look after themselves and what do we do, we give them money to look after a 'wee dog'.

But usually it is not a ' wee dog ' , usually and stereotypically it's a ' pit-bull ' or some other dangerous or semi – dangerous breed of 'dug' who shit like pit ponies on the pavements of every town and loo and behold this is not the type of ' shit ' their owners will pick up.

My apologies to pit ponies for this reference as they were hard-working animals with a real purpose in life – pit- bulls?

If we even try to query the reasons or sense of why druggies should get an allowance then they play the Human Rights card. They have a right to their canine company, it will make them better and accepted citizens – aye right.

The headlines in February 2012 highlight the ultimate impact of drugs on individuals, but say nothing of the 'dugs',

" Drug Death Toll Soars to Nine a Week'

More than nine people die every week from drug abuse, according to shock figures released in late 2011.

And the number of drug-related deaths has risen by two-thirds in the past decade says a report for the Scottish Government.

The vast majority of victims are men in their late 20s and 30s.

The study revealed there were 485 drug-related deaths last year – 66% higher than ten years ago.

Although the number has dropped slightly compared with the previous year it still remains one of the highest drug death tolls on record.

The report was compiled by the National Forum on Drug- Related Deaths in Scotland."

In 2011 prescribed methadone cost Scottish taxpayers £28million.

This is the two – fold legacy of drug abuse –financial costs of £28 million in methadone alone and the human costs of producing human parasites, piles of dog shit and premature deaths.

Suppliers and users of drugs are human parasites – human none the less.

Unless you are very, very fortunate you will know and be related to one or more of these parasites.

Suppliers and users – someone's son, daughter, nephew, niece, cousin , uncle , aunt , even someone's mother , father or grandmother or grandfather.

The human drug cycle is pretty much complete as we enter third generation of family suppliers and users. Whole families from gran and papa to daughter and son and grandson and grand-daughter have become part of the drug culture - all hooked on 'their drug of choice' or a pusher's drug of choice.

Hooked on drugs and hacked off work as the drug culture replaces the work ethic once so prevalent in the first and even the second generation.

Paul Rodgers is Bobby and Linda's eldest son, our nephew, Gary and Greg's cousin. He stays in Dumfries but is too close for that drug comfort.

He is our personal, social and cultural reality of the impact of drugs.

There are some like him in Darvel and the Irvine Valley and close by in Kilmarnock.

The BBC's BAFTA- award winning documentary series 'The Scheme 'was produced and shown by the BBC in 2010 / 2011.

It highlighted all the worst elements of drug addiction in its focus on some of the lives of a very small section of the Knockinlaw / Onthank community in Kilmarnock.

It was labelled 'poverty porn 'by some but was more akin to 'druggie dross' or ' heroin hell' to me.

People and a programme too close for comfort and for some only too ripe for exploitation.

The BBC could have picked any town in Scotland or England or Wales for that matter but it came across as a Scottish, an Ayrshire shame with more emphasis on heroin than hope.

It was perhaps also a reality check, a junkie needle to jab our conscience , an unwelcome reminder of the human drug-infected flotsam and jetsam that we would all probably rather ignore in the hope that it would go away.

For us and Paul his problems with drugs and drink did go away - but he went with them.

Until 3 October 2011 Paul was not a statistic but he was a troubled soul.

Paul did not set out to waste his life but by his mid to late teens drink and drugs took over his life.

His 'drugs of choice' were 'vallies' and maybe a bit of ' skunk'.

He was in and out of prison and prison almost became more of a home than his home in Dumfries. In prison he had a regulated life, a TV, a radio, a mobile phone and none of the hassle that got him into prison in the first place.

At 29 years of age he was close to being 'institutionalised' but he didn't quite 'make it'.

On 31 December 2011 he would be 30. No longer the blonde haired young man who was still fresh – faced when he had visited his Gran Rodgers in Ayrshire Central Hospital.

At aged 29 he was a veteran drug user.

He had the scars of his war with drugs but no medals.

He was a veteran drug user until early on the morning of 3 October 2011 when his veteran status ceased – he died of a drug overdose.

Paul was barely cold when the cold fact of his death was 'announced' on Facebook on the afternoon of 3 October 2011.

The 'wonders' of electronic – communication never cease – is it the age of the modern gossip or of information and intellectual exchange?

'Modern gossip' has my vote.

You now don't need to hang out of your tenement window and have a 'blether' with your neighbours.

Now you can simply sit on your big fat arse and 'poke 'people on Facebook.

It might be just as well because hanging out a tenement window will now probably be a ' health and safety hazard ' and be ' out-lawed.!

On 4th October 2011 the day after Paul's death had been confirmed on ' Facebook' Bobby gave me and the rest of the family a first- hand account of what had happened.

He had gone to his work with the Council's Refuse Collection Service at about 6.45am that morning and had left Paul, his brother Stephen and two friends sleeping.

Stephen had come down the stairs at around 9am and found Paul 'blue and freezing' in the living room. He had tried to resuscitate Paul but the hospital reckoned he died between 6 and 9am that morning.

These were the cold facts that consigned Paul to the world of statistics – another number for the drug death count.

But before Paul could be buried there needed to be an autopsy and that autopsy had to be in Glasgow where the skills and resources and toxicology specialist could determine the cause of death and whether or not there had been any 'foul play'.

All of this took weeks to happen and confirm that Paul had died of a drug overdose.

By the time Paul's body had been returned to Dumfries it was late October and left Bobby in a quandary about when to arrange to lay Paul to rest.

It was the 6th anniversary of Mum's death on 31 October.

It was his brother Stephen's birthday on 2 November.

It was the 6th anniversary of Mum's funeral on 4 November.

The date chosen for Paul's funeral was Thursday 3 November.

Those in the family who could attend the funeral arranged to travel down on the morning of the funeral to be at Bobby's for about 11.45am in time for the service at St. Matthew's Chapel of Rest at 12.15pm.

As the new florist in the family I made the family wreaths for Paul's funeral. A traditional round wreath of blue irises , large and small white carnations and blue thistles from all his cousins and a ' pillow ' of white chrysanthemum blooms , blue ribbons for the cushion edge and an offset centre of a few red roses and blue thistles.

It was an unwelcome professional 'first for the family'.

We arrived at Dumfries as planned and Jim, Jessie, Marlene, Elaine, Jimmy, Yvonne and their Iain (Paul's cousin) and Nancy and me all went to see Bobby and pay our last respects to Paul.

The others could not make it and Lilian had been seriously ill in hospital but it was a good family representation on a bad family day.

We were introduced to the Social Worker, David who was to drive Bobby and Stephen to St. Matthews where the 'Service' would take place and from where the hearse would leave for the cemetery.

We all had a drink of tea, coffee or juice and as we drank Bobby nervously told a joke or two and we laughed nervously.

Stephen arrived back home just in time after going out for a haircut.

Linda was still in hospital, where she was recuperating from a brain condition which had stemmed from a viral infection. She had lost some of her short term memory but intermittently regained it only to lose it again. There was no rhyme or reason for her condition and she required care and support on a twenty four hour basis.

Bobby had managed to break the news to her that Paul had died but to Linda some days he was still alive and other days she was certain that he had died.

The medical advice was that she was not fit enough to attend her eldest son's funeral. Maybe it was better that way.

There were no more jokes and the time came to go to St. Matthews for what was to be a unique celebration of Paul's shortened life.

In effect there was to be no Service as such, no signing of hymns, and no reciting of scriptures.

Paul wasn't religious so Bobby and Stephen had picked out music and songs that Paul liked and these were to be played at the Chapel of Rest.

We entered the Chapel of Rest last after a good number of youngish people had gathered and sat down.

We entered and went to the front pews as the Eagles played *'Desperado'*.

The Chaplain welcomed us all to the celebration of Paul's life and explained the format of this celebration.

Next on the 'play-list' was,'*The Drugs Don't Work ' by The Verve*.

To be frank there were a few examples of people in the chapel that confirmed ' drugs don't work ' but today was about respect for Paul.

The Chaplain interspersed the music with a prayer or two and a short summary of Paul's shortened life - warts and all.

The tear-jerker as Bobby had put it was *REM's 'Everybody Hurts Sometime '*.

This was especially poignant for me and Nancy as it was and is our anthem for Marion and Davy.

At the end of the Service the Chaplain thanked everyone for attending and invited them to join the family at the cemetery. He also invited them to take away photographs of Paul which had been left along the pews in his memory.

The photograph of Paul had been taken in happier times but to me there was no real happiness in his eyes and he seemed to be smiling 'on the outside'.

On the back of the photographs there were two versions of the memorial to Paul.

One read :- " In Loving Memory of Paul S. Rodgers ' and the other read :-

'In Loving Memory of Paul (POD)'

and then both had his personal details :-

'Born 31.12.81.

Died 3.10.11.

God Rest His Soul '.

It was as if one had been written by Bobby and the other by Stephen with Stephen's reflecting Paul's nickname of POD rather than his full name.

The finale was a song I didn't recognise and during which Paul's coffin was placed on the 'trolley' and placed in the hearse.

The family flowers were placed on top of the coffin along with the two other floral tributes for Paul. There were then enough flowers to provide a floral cover over the wooden coffin.

We followed the funeral cortege to its slow and inevitable journey to the cemetery and joined a good number of people paying their last respects there.

I was called to hold and lower Cord 3 and Colin was called for Cord 5. In my place at Cord 3 I bent down and gently touched the coffin to say goodbye to Paul.

The mourners were silent and respectful and the silence was only broken by a heart- broken Stephen who stared bleakly at his elder brother's grave –

'see you man' were his last words for Paul at the graveside.

A Lost Soul.

Paul in happier times before his tragic death

CHAPTER ELEVEN

'Old Cronies'

The pace of life in the twenty first century has increased but in the last nine years it seems to have moved up yet another gear or perhaps even 'warp factor'.

The earth has been wracked by a heady mix of natural disasters; numerous examples of man's continuing inhumanity to man; political, economic, environmental, social and technological upheavals and a fair smattering of scandals and man – made disasters.

The world we lived in changed even more in the nine years since 2004 and we changed with it.

Changes ranged from the cosmic to the microscopic, from the sublime to the ridiculous and from the benevolent to the absolutely malevolent.

Scientists on 15th March 2004 discovered the most distant object ever identified in our Solar System.

The TSUNAMI devastated Asia on 26th December 2004.

On 19th January 2005 it was reported that Cancer had replaced heart disease as the number one cause of death for people aged 85 and under.

Pope John Paul(2nd) died on 2nd April 2005.

7th July 2005 became Britain's worst attack since World War 11 when Islamic terrorists bombed London and killed 52 people and wounded about 700.

On a more peaceful note the Irish Republican Army announced on 27th July 2005 that it was officially ending its violent campaign for a united Ireland and would instead pursue its goals politically.

Saddam Hussein was convicted of crimes against humanity by an Iraqi court and hanged in Baghdad on 30th December 2006.

1 January 2007 Romania and Bulgaria joined the European Union bringing the number of member nations to 27.

Gordon Brown replaced Tony Blair as the Prime Minister of Great Britain on 27 June 2007.

Terrorist had the audacity to attack Glasgow Airport on 30 June 2007.

Buenos Aires, the capital of Argentina experienced its first snowfall in 89 years on 10 July 2007.

On 28th August 2008 Barack Obama accepted the Democratic presidential nomination and became the first African American to be selected by a major Party as its nominee for President.

In October 2008 Britain recorded its worst day of trading since 'Black Monday ' in 1987 - £90 billion pounds was wiped off the value of Britain's companies. In the USA Lehman Brothers bank collapsed and in the UK HBOS; Royal Bank of Scotland, Bradford and Bingley and the Alliance and Leicester all had to be rescued.

On 20th January 2009 Barack Obama was sworn in as the President of the United States of America.

Sweden became the fifth European country to legalise same-sex marriage on 1 April 2009.

Swine Flu (H1N1) killed over 100 people in Mexico on 26 April 2009.

Drugs killed Michael Jackson on 25th June 2009.

Abdel Bassett Ali al – Megrahi (the terrorist convicted of the Lockerbie bombing of Pan Am Flight 103) was freed from prison on compassionate grounds on 20th August 2009 – he was suffering from terminal prostate cancer and was expected to die within 3 months – his death was eventually confirmed on 20 May 2012.

Volcanic ash from the Eyjafjallajokull volcano eruption disrupted European flights from 14 to 21 April 2010.

David Cameron took over from Gordon Brown as Prime Minister on 11 May 2010.

Spain beat Holland to win the football World Cup on 11th July 2010.

Over the 12th and 13th of October 2010 33 Chilean miners trapped underground for over two months were all pulled to safety one by one.

Prince William and Catherine Middleton married at Westminster Abbey in April 2011.

Spring 2011 – revolt spread across the Middle East and North Africa.

March 2011 Japan was shaken by a 9.0 earthquake and tsunamis that triggered a nuclear meltdown at three of the reactors at the Fukushima Daiichi nuclear plant.

77 people were killed at a youth leadership camp by lone gunman Anders Breivik on 22 July 2011 in Oslo , Norway.

Osama Bin Laden and Colonel Gadhafi were killed on 2 May and 20 October 2011 respectively.

Huge changes and events across the world that made history but often it was and is the smaller changes that have a personal impact on the pace and face of life.

Smaller things like mobile phones.

From their origins as one kilogramme metallic bricks that were marginally more receptive than two tin cans held by a piece of string they have developed into web-enabled miniature video camera-phones which can now be linked to and by ' 4G' wireless applications – whatever they are ??

Now we don't just have mobile phones we have smart phones ; i-pods and android devices which kids can work with what seems like a sixth sense that is alien to their parents. Most of the parents don't even know what an android looks like never mind how to work it unless it had been on 'Doctor Who'.

Most changes that affected people were not the dramatic and earth shattering changes.

Time alone changed you, your perception of you and other people's perception of you.

These changes bring home the fact that we are getting older and maybe wiser but definitely older.

There are seminal moments in life for everyone :-

First tooth.

First word.

First step.

First Birthday.

First day at School/ College/University.

Graduation.

First job.

First love.

Marriage.

First , second , third ....child.

16th Birthday.

18th birthday.

21st birthday.

30th, 40th, 50th 60th, 65th...70th......80th.........90th...........100th birthdays.

Retiral.

Many changes and developments naturally revolve around age and it is nothing new.

Even in Shakespeare's time he identified 'seven ages of man'.

These ages were / are:-

*'**Infancy** – in this stage of life he is a baby.*

***Childhood** – It is in this stage that he begins to go to school. He is reluctant to leave the protected environment of his home as he is not confident enough to exercise his own discretion.*

***The Lover** – In this stage he is always remorseful due to some reason or other, especially the loss of love. He tries to express feelings through song or some other cultural activity.*

***The Soldier** – It is in this age that he thinks less of himself and begins to think more of others. He is very easily aroused and is hot headed. He is always working towards making a reputation for himself* *and gaining recognition, however short lived it may be, even at the cost of his own life.*

The Justice *– In this stage he has acquired wisdom through many experiences he has had in life. He has reached a stage where he has gained prosperity and social status. He becomes very attentive of his looks and begins to enjoy the finer things of life.*

Old Age *– He begins to lose his charm – both physical and mental. He begins to become the brunt of others' jokes. He loses his firmness and assertiveness, and shrinks in stature and personality.*

Mental dementia and Death *– He loses his status and he becomes a non-entity. He becomes dependent on others like a child and is in constant need of support before finally dying.'*

Pretty descriptive or depressing depending on your point of view or even your stage of life.

The monologue detailed in 'All the World's a Stage 'from Shakespeare's 'As you Like It ' is even more descriptive and depressing in its final line ,

"Sans teeth, sans eyes, sans taste, sans everything.'

There may well be 'seven ages of man (and Woman – although we won't talk about their ages) 'but to me, like cats, I think we have the potential to have nine lives or at least nine stages of the one life.

All these stages of life are pretty much like Shakespeare's ' seven ages of man 'only a bit more ' pram-centric '.

In fairness to Shakespeare I don't suppose there were a hellava lot of prams about in the late 16th and early 17^{Th} centuries.

Each stage of life (SOL) can be characterised as follows:-

SOL 1 – you are the infant, safe and secure in your pram, you probably experience your first memories. You are snug ,warm , supported and protected.

SOL 2 – you are out of the pram and in nursery / school uniform .These are your formative years through childhood, adolescence, into early maturity and even marriage.

SOL 3 – You acquire a pram for your child / children and run yourself ragged over the child years. You visit your parents more often

than before and leave your offspring with them at weekends and on special occasions – they are literally 'grand – parents'.

SOL 4 – Your children are now out of their prams and you are relieved of pram duty for a wee while. Your pram is sold off or put up in the loft in the expectation that 'it will do someone sometime'. You look forward to pushing your grandchildren in their prams.

SOL 5 – your wish is granted, probably sooner and more often than you had anticipated, as you get to push the grandchildren in their prams. Your old pram stays in the loft and new- fangled buggies are all the rage. This pram pushing grandparent routine becomes part of your new keep fit regime that you did not know you were entering.

SOL 6 – Your grandchildren leave the pram and you are relieved of pram duty.

SOL 7 – Your great grandchildren come along and what looked like a pram in your day looks more like a space capsule or three-wheeled moon buggy. In fact it is not actually called a pram anymore – it is an 'MPS Travel System ' and you are thoroughly confused and wonder what ever happened to prams. You only get to look at the grandchildren in the ' MPS Travel System ' because you cannot fathom out how to ' erect ' the MPS never mind be trusted to use its guidance controls in the streets on your own.

SOL 8 – at best you can walk unaided and are fairly spritely; at worst you are in a wheel – chair being talked at and shuffled from your ward to the day room and back again.

SOL 9 – everybody gets to 'enjoy' SOL nine, well nearly everybody. You, in your box are wheeled on a 'trolley in and out of the Church or into the Crematorium.

According to my' Pram theory' Nancy and I are somewhat unbelievably in SOL 4 – with reasonable prospects of reaching SOL 5 sometime in the future.

What does this fourth stage of life actually mean?

It means that you have a more acute realisation of age – your age and that of everyone around you.

It means fewer invites to 18th and 21st Birthday Parties and if you are invited it is as an Aunt or Uncle. The very terminology reflects your age – Aunt Nancy and Uncle Kenny.

Secretly and you won't know it but you may be the 'mad uncle or mad aunt' which every family has.

If you even suspect you may be in contention for the 'mad uncle /mad aunt' award then the secret is to exaggerate the eccentricities of another family member so that they appear to be even madder than you.

This may take a bit of doing especially if you actually are the mad Aunt or Uncle but it's well worth a try.

Apart from trying to avoid the title of ' the ' mad uncle / mad aunt ' it also means that you celebrate anniversaries and birthdays that you thought were for other people of a different age and now you are that age!

Silver, Pearl and Golden Wedding Anniversaries replace 18th, 21st Birthdays and the pre marriage Stag and Hen nights.

But with age friends or pals become buddies and with even more age buddies mature and become 'old cronies'.

Almost by definition you cannot be a 'young crony' but through a ' time-served apprenticeship' close friendships can be forged by shared experience and companionship which produces cronies.

It is a kind of metamorphism only in reverse – you start as a young, lonely swan and end up as an old duck in the pond with other old ducks.

Almost by definition you also cannot be a crony if you are 'tea-total'.

Furthermore cronies by definition are male; there are no female cronies. 'Crones' – yes but 'Cronies' – no.

In the French language ' crony ' would be a male word ; one crony would be ' Le Crony' and the plural would be ' Les Cronies ' , a bit like ' Les Miserables ' but a bit happier – probably the drink that does it.

For a good many of Scottish men the tradition of having a pint after playing football extends well beyond the years in which you actually play football and so it is with a few of us 'old cronies' / 'les cronies' who meet regularly on a Thursday night and on Saturdays after 'the football' to have a blether and a few pints.

The Darvel 'old cronies Team Meetings' take place in the Black Bull where mine host , Albert Anderson greets customers like a stand-up comic treats hecklers.

He has honed his customer service skills since his days as a ' Bouncer ' at the Covenanters in Newmilns many years ago and can now despatch undesirable customers from the pub with a smile through clenched teeth but no clenched fists.

In fairness you are always assured of a warm welcome from Albert and Janet and you will get the best pint in the town but please take your sense of humour with you.

Most 'old cronies' have their place in society and also their place in the pub.

A regular seat where they are 'Regulars'.

Our Team seats are to the right immediately you enter the pub with a good view of at least two of the flat screen TVs in the pub.

The seats are recognised as where we prefer to sit by other punters in the pub but they are not reserved for our motley crew of cronies.

The most senior and most revered of the cronies is Guy Collins – at over 80 years of age he takes his place at the head of the table and doles out words of wisdom, observations and four-fingered karate –like blows to the ribs of those who don't listen or respond to the patter of the day.

There is John Collins, Guy's eldest son and a Principal Teacher at the centre for learning excellence that is Auchinleck Academy. An ex 'drillie' (physical education teacher) he has progressed through the ranks at Auchinleck and his ' specialist subject' is sport and has played both Junior and Amateur football. He is a Darvel Vics veteran and a Celtic fan who was there in Milan in 1970 when Celtic fell at the final hurdle and failed to beat Feyenord in the European Cup Final. His 'specialist' drink is McCallan malt whisky.

Jack McKie was also a teacher at Auchinleck and ex Darvel Vics player. Cool, calm and thoughtful and now getting to grips with life beyond teaching as he retired on 30 June 2012. He comes from a big family but he is also one of a few – he is a Killie supporter.

John Dixon is the third teacher in the Team or ex-teacher of Mathematics at Auchinleck. An engineer to trade, a fellow Kilmarnock Football Club supporter and Loudoun Gowf Club golfer.

Alistair McKie (my brother in law and Jack's brother) is a regular Thursday night member. Since being paralysed in a car accident he has become a talented artist, a bird – watcher and also a watcher of Killie – he suffers with us on Saturdays.

Bobby McDill is the local SNP Councillor but we don't hold that against him. His favourite 'tipple 'is water, more frozen water with a little whisky in it. Politics apart he is well regarded and works really hard for the communities he represents.

The communities themselves have in turn come a long way politically from the days when it was felt and stated that a 'monkey' could and would win the local election in Darvel as long as it was a 'Labour monkey'.

Occasionally the old cronies are augmented by 'The McAllisters' (brothers James , Ian and Alex) , Billy , big Scooby and Gerry and when that happens we are usually late home and on the wrong side of sober.

On other occasions Hugh (John's brother) and Derek (John's brother in law) and Gavin Collins(John's son) and Gavin T (young Gavin's brother in law) join us for a pint or two.

Nearly everybody in the company of cronies is related to somebody else – there are brothers, brothers in law, cousins, nieces, nephews and a whole lot more besides. In America the banjos would definitely be playing but we all have 5 fingers on each hand and 5 toes on each foot – except maybe for the mad uncle ….. !

In our ranks we can muster 5 Killie football fans – me, Alistair, Bobby, Jack, and John Dixon and we attend all or most of the home games.

Before the arrival of Mixu Paatelanien as the new Manager and his Assistant Kenny Shiels, Killie were going nowhere.

Nowhere near the top of the Scottish Premier League after a final day reprieve of a Nil – Nil draw with Falkirk in season 2009 / 2010 to stay up and avoid relegation.

We were and are not ' diehards ' , not even ' fanatics ' but we are supporters and we did our bit for the club by buying season tickets and going to the home games even when Killie were going nowhere.

One such game to fill Killie fans with dread was a midweek fixture at home to Celtic.

Wednesday 20 April 2011 saw us all there for the 7.45 pm kick off and as usual we made our donation to Killie's funds in the shape of buying 12 tickets for the half time draw.

The top prize was £200 with the opportunity to lift another £2,000 if you could kick a football from about 25 yards and hit the crossbar.

Easy for some but the fact was the Crossbar Challenge prize was at its maximum of £2,000 because no one had been able to hit the crossbar for some time and the prize fund had gone up by £200 at every home game until it had reached and stayed at £2,000.

The game was a typical Killie v Celtic game; we played some good stuff but Celtic stuffed us with two goals before half time. Every Killie fan knew that Lazerus or even Gary Glitter had a better chance of a come-back than Killie.

Another three points were heading home to Parkhead with little to cheer for by the Killie fans.

At half time we took our usual position on the walkway just above the centre of the pitch and had our usual discussion about Killie's inability to score.

John looked out the half time draw tickets – he was the recognised custodian and checker of the tickets.

It was all the more important that night as he silently checked the numbers which were read off the randomly drawn first ticket and which appeared on the big screen on a delayed reaction basis and sometimes not in the right order.

Amazingly - tonight we have the right ticket and the right numbers in the right order.

John broke the news and we all looked at each other and he turned to me and he says,

" *You're on* ".

I looked at Bobby, John and Jack and I said, '*you sure ?*' – it was a double- barrelled ' you sure' question – are you sure we have the winning ticket and are you sure you want me to have a go??

'*Yip*',was the singular answer .

I tied my shoelaces and handed the boys my jacket and made my way to a Steward to show him the winning ticket and gain access to the football field.

Once the Steward has vetted me and my ticket I was free to make my way to the spot from where I would be given the chance to hit the crossbar.

Before that though the PR guy / announcer asked me my name off mike and I told him, it's Kenny Rodgers '.

To my surprise he queries whether or not this is my real name and asks if I have any proof that it is my real name. It was not the best of starts to what was becoming a bit of a nervy occasion.

The Killie cheer-leaders danced away in the background as I produced my driving licence with my name, John Kenneth Rodgers (aka Kenny) .

'That's fine', he says, *'now do you want to kick the ball or do you want the youth team player to hit it for you'*.

I was a bit taken aback by this and in my head I'm thinking does this guy not think I'm fit enough to kick a ball 25 / 30 yards and this is a bit of a blow to the old confidence.

I confirm that I'll have a go myself and the youth team player somewhat reluctantly gives me the ball and a look that says, 'I don't think so, mister '. But when I feel the ball and bounce it three times and move a bit nearer the goals each time the youth team player confirms the modern balls do appear light but I'll still need a good contact on it.

We chat a bit more and the PR guy heaps some more pressure on me by making sure I know the game is being televised live on ESPN it is being beamed all over the world .

No pressure then.

Surprisingly, I remained calm if not cool and when the Killie Cheer-leaders dance routine was finished I'm on.

My one shot at the crossbar is towards the Celtic fans in the Moffat Stand and all I'm thinking about is not falling on my arse and striking through the ball to give it some lift and height.

My focus is all on the ball as I've never seen the crossbar move with the exception of at Wembley in 1977, when it had a bit of 'help' from the Scottish football fans.

The PR guy then declares,

'I'll count you down from 3, 2, 1, and then you hit the ball, OK'.

'OK' , I say and I look at the crossbar in the distance and with the floodlights on, it all seems a bit surreal – what the f… am I doing out here , remember just concentrate on the ball and hit through it.

I've played football but not for years and it's too late to think back to the games of ' borrie ' we used to play as kids down at the Darvel Juniors Park as 3, 2, 1 rings out in my ears and a bit of a murmur breaks out as I step forward the four paces to the ball and make a good contact with it and also avoid falling on my arse.

The PR guy lets out an involuntary gasp of *'OOH'*, as the ball actually rises as it leaves my foot and the Celtic supporters directly behind the goal have the best view of the ball speeding through the air.

I had already lost sight of it in the glare of the floodlights and my glasses but I have a feeling it is flying well as I didn't really feel the ball leave my foot – usually a good sign you have struck it sweetly.

Sweetly or not the ball still had to be at the right height to hit the crossbar and the mounting noise from the Celtic supporters told me my guided missile was on its way.

The gasps from the Celtic and Killie fans grew louder but not too loud for me to hear the thump of the ball on the bar and a huge cheer going up all round the ground.

This was my 'You Tube 'moment as I jumped about like a 'daftie' and strode forward to the Celtic fans and clapped my hands in their direction.

I had been pleasantly surprised at their loud cheering and clapping and wanted to recognise that. It was as if they just really appreciated a 'football punter 'actually winning the two grand with one kick of a ball.

I turned towards the PR guy and the Killie fans and gave them and Bobby, Jack , and John a wave – as much to say,

'hey, I did it , I f…ing did it '.

The youth team member collected the ball and left the field with his moment of glory stolen by an old punter.

The PR guy stepped forward and shook my hand as did Nuts – the Killie Mascot – I gave the Killie fans a clenched fist salute as the PR guy confirmed,

'Kenny Rodgers, from Darvel has won the two grand, fantastic',

and strolled off to his position to the left of the field.

The steward who escorted me on the field escorted me off it and a few fans shook my hand as I made my way back to the guys.

One Killie fan, a bit forlornly or desperately declared,

'Get stripped, you should be on '.

Back with the guys there was a general shaking of hands and heads as they recovered from the surprise that I didn't fall on my arse and had avoided total humiliation – in fact they were as they say ' gob-smacked ' - nearly lost for words but not quite.

Word and pictures started to get around as Joanne 's partner Thomas was in Amsterdam and he'd just phoned her to say ,

'I've just seen Kenny and some of the guys on the telly, I think they've won the crossbar competition.'

John and I go to collect the £200 half time draw money and the £2,000 Crossbar Challenge cheque after Celtic score another two goals and win 4 – nil.

What a result – not the 4 – nil but the winning of £2,200 – unbelievable but true.

I get the cheque to share out and also get a blue shirt which on the front has printed in white letters,

' **Killie Crossbar Challenge – I took a shot and** ….

' - on the back of the shirt was printed –

' **Hit It'** !!!

We walked back to the car, animated by adrenalin that has now started to flow with the realisation that I was now in a league with the English Premier League superstars in terms of earnings from the beautiful game – after all I've just earned £2,000 from one kick, contact of about one tenth of a second, if that – all I need is a contract for about 10 minutes of crossbar hitting and I reckon I'm onto about £12 million and then I can retire?!

High as a kite I struggled more than the ball did to come back down to earth but I had the very people to bring me back down to earth.

In the car I half – jokingly said,

'I think I would rather Killie had won three points than we had won the Crossbar Challenge'.

Almost in unison the cry went up,' *ya lying wee shite* '.

Well it was the thought that counted.

In the days that followed more people confirmed they had seen yours truly and young Barrie McCrindle had captured it on his mobile phone and by electronic wizardry and Greg and

Gary's help ' Kenny Rodgers' Crossbar Challenge was on 'You Tube '.

The Thursday night crew of cronies are back in the Black Bull from about 9pm on the Thursday and the Crossbar Challenge gets a re-run and is even funnier now hearing the guys and having it confirmed that their biggest fear was that they thought I would fall on my arse.

I wore my blue Killie shirt which confirmed - not just did I not fall on my arse but I hit the crossbar.

To this day and probably for years to come I'll be 'living' on this football story.

The forty-seater bus left from the Railway Inn to go to the semi-final of the Scottish Communities League Cup at Hampden on 28 January 2012. Nothing unusual in that ; football buses leave towns and cities all over Scotland to take the fans to support their Teams.

What was unusual is that this was a joint Ayr United and Killie bus , with a smattering of Rangers and Celtic fans thrown in for good measure.

Ian McAllister (ex-captain of Ayr United) had it all organised and the bus arrived at the Railway Inn and left on time for the 1pm kick off. There was even time to go to the Bowling Club near Hampden where Ian has booked in thirty of the punters – the rest, the younger ones would go to a pub.

We queued up at the Bowling Club in an orderly fashion and give the details of the 'booking'. The Committee Man checked the list and contrary to our expectation says,

'You are not on the list, you can't come in '.

He was met by cries of *'you must have made a mistake, it might be under Ian McAllister if not Darvel Bowling Club'.*

Another check was made and sure enough a mistake has been made – big Ian had booked us in for the Celtic game on Sunday!!

Even further checks were made with more Committee Men and the decision was that we could come in as there was still capacity in the Club. That was about the most eventful part of the day, that and an obligatory fish supper before the game and the obligatory staying at the pub too late on our return from Hampden.

The actual game was pretty dire and Killie won 1- 0 after extra time and now had the chance to win the Cup if they could beat Celtic at Hampden on Mothers'Day – Sunday 18 March 2012.

In 2001 Henrik Larrson scored all three goals in the 3 – 0 defeat to Celtic on Sunday 18 March 2001 and on the same day in 2007 Hibs crushed Killie 5 – 1.

This was the third time this century Killie have been in the Scottish League Cup Final and coincidently all three finals on Mothers Day – Sunday 18 March .

This time the result will surely be different?

The football signs under new Manager, Kenny Shiels were good or at least encouraging.

On 15 October 2011 Killie had lead Celtic 3 – 0 at half time and the Killie fans' winning bets looked assured - not.

The only thing you could be assured about was that Celtic would not play worse in the second half and Neil Lennon would have ripped his players even more apart than Killie did in the first half.

That game was the 'turnaround' game for Neil Lennon as Celtic improved and scored three goals in about seventeen minutes to draw the game and 'turnaround' their Championship winning season.

On 18 March 2012, Mothers' Day, Killie's prayers were answered by the players as they played with pride , passion and a fair bit of skill to beat the mighty Celtic one nil.

We beat Celtic and we beat the bookies with a £10 bet placed in September 2011 for Killie to win the Cup at 7 to 1 and another £10 on the day of the final for Killie to beat Celtic at 7 to 1.

It was hardly a hammering for the bookies but as it was Mothers' Day Nancy also had £5 on Killie to beat Celtic.

We all had a few drinks to celebrate the historic victory which made the players immortal legends.

The celebrations were muted later as we learned the father of Killie's midfield dynamo Liam Kelly had had a heart attack at the end of the game and died later that evening.

Liam Kelly – now Immortal as a player but having to live with the mortality of his dad on a day that should have been one of the best in his life.

A wonderful time and result marred by a shocking ending of a life.

The old cronies 'meetings' in the pub continue with all the usual patter.

It's a scene and stage of life that is replicated throughout Scotland and a part of Scottish culture that may be under threat as more and more pubs go out of business and close their door to customers and cronies alike.

For the time being we'll take our places in the Black Bull on most Thursdays and Saturday evenings until we get to about SOL 8 if Albert doesn't bar us before then.

Gary, Greg, Nancy and I celebrating our silver wedding anniversary

BANK OF SCOTLAND

KILMARNOCK
30-34 KING STREET
KILMARNOCK

80-08-53

Date 20.4.11

Pay JOHN RODGERS

Two Thousand pounds only

A/C Payee

£2000-00

KILMARNOCK FOOTBALL CLUB LTD

SIGNATORY

CHEQUE NO SORT CODE ACCOUNT NO

⑈020004⑈ 80⑉08531⑆ 00310921⑈ 10

Proof positive that I did hit the bar in the KFC Crossbar Challenge

CHAPTER TWELVE

Princess Lorraine

Well before Marlene's second husband Mike had died on 11 April 2003, Lorraine, her only daughter had made her way back to the UK. But she was not on her own.

Her soul mate and husband was J.D. aka Jan Daniel Van Aswegan.

His name was quite a mouthful and if in South Africa you had given JD a mouthful of cheek you were liable to be arrested – he had been a member of the South African Police Force.

They had met when Lorraine was 17 and had gone to College in Johannesburg.

JD left the Police Force but not before he had performed his most notable duty of being part of Nelson Mandela's security entourage when he took the final steps in his " long walk to freedom ' when he was released from prison in 1990.

That year (1990) the ANC was 'unbanned' and in 1991 became embroiled in fighting between their members and the ZULU Inkatha Movement.

Nelson Mandela eventually became President of the Government of National Unity in 1994 as the ANC won the first non- racial elections in the new South Africa.

It would be fair to say that at this time South Africa was not as stable a country as most would have liked – black and white alike.

A Truth and National Reconciliation Commission was established and chaired by Archbishop Desmond Tutu (the outcome of my first University Honours Degree – a 2-2).

From 1996 and up to the time the Commission reported in 1998 it appeared to reconcile no one – it branded apartheid as a crime against humanity but also found that the ANC itself accountable for Human Rights abuses. But on the plus side the 16th of December was declared a Public Holiday in South Africa and was known as the 'Day of Reconciliation'.

Thabo Mbeki took over as President when the ANC won the second general election in 1999 but the huge challenges of poverty, corruption, aids and all too frequent bouts of extremist violence remained.

Freedom had been a long road but for some that long road had a turning.

Lorraine and JD had married on 23 February 1991 in Standerton in South Africa about a year after Nelson Mandela had taken his long walk to freedom

Their turning was to the UK as freedom and the ballot box in South Africa was interspersed with violence and bullets but there was no 'magic bullet' to transform the country into a successful and stable integrated, multi-racial society.

To many in South Africa the ballot box at that time was dominated by 'tribal allegiances' rather than 'national conscience'.

In short Lorraine and JD made the conscious decision to be 'out of Africa'. JD left his mother, father and three sisters (Annemarie, Hannie, and Mercia) to be with Lorraine and start another life in the UK.

In South Africa Lorraine had qualified as a hair dresser and after gaining experience in salons in Johannesburg she worked on a 'freelance basis '. Effectively she had a 'chair' in a well – known salon. She paid 'rent' for it but attracted her own customers through her own talents.

In the UK she worked on the same basis and got 'a chair ' in Harvey Nichols in Manchester when she and JD moved to West Houghton near Bolton.

Lorraine was confident in her abilities to get on in 'Harvey Nics'.

Even as a young girl in Galston she was pretty confident with an impish sense of humour. She would go for walks with her dad, Frank and when he occasionally nipped into the local pubs for a pint on the way home she would sit down and have a game of dominoes with the local worthies.

It started as a bit of a laugh and something to do while she was waiting for Frank but when she regularly beat the locals at their own game there were less visits to the pub to spare the locals further domino drubbings and embarrassment!

Lorraine was very attractive, bright and quick witted but no matter what, she treated everyone the same. She was not embarrassed to tell us that one day this guy had come into Harvey Nics for a haircut.

"He didn't have an appointment so I said hi and offered him a seat at the window - it was about the only one available anyway.

He was quite young – looking, tanned and had dark hair and I thought I'm not going into the stereotypical hairdressing holiday conversation so I simply said to him,

" This is a good seat by the window and I think you'll be comfortable here until we are ready for you. You just never know if you are lucky you might see someone rich and famous go by

.

Would you like a tea or coffee while you are waiting"?

He gave me a sort of puzzled look with a hint of a smile and opted for a black coffee.

"As I was returning to the main salon I was conscious that a good few of the hairdressers and their customers were looking towards me and the customer waiting at the window.

Then two or three of the hairdressers said in unison,

" Lorraine, do you not know who that is " ?

I hadn't a clue and was put out of my misery when I was told,

" That's Ryan Giggs."

" Oh well I might remember him the next time he comes in.

Who is Ryan Giggs anyway "?

There was an answer to that but it really didn't matter to Lorraine – she treated everyone the same and as they say, 'what you see is what you get'.

West Houghton, just outside of Bolton became Lorraine and JD's new home town. It was a relatively easy commute for both to Manchester – Lorraine to Harvey Nics and JD to his job in ' IT ' but it had a bit of a village feel to it.

It was only really on special occasions Lorraine and JD would meet the rest of the wider family but whenever you saw them they were lively, bright, and positive – they never complained about anything.

Both were intelligent without necessarily being academic. They were keen learners and JD progressed to more challenging and rewarding IT roles through training and personal application.

Lorraine not one to shirk a challenge started a B.Sc. (Honours) Open University Degree. It was a continuation and combination of a Scottish and South African work ethic that served them well in some 4 years since Mike's death.

In Marlene's world those four years had seen her buy and set up her own home in Darvel and take on two part time cleaning jobs to ensure she had enough money to pay the bills and live a little.

Nothing earth – shattering seemed to happen during these years but to Marlene she had had her fill of earth-shattering experiences and stability in her life was more welcomed .

Regular contact with Lorraine and JD became part of that established stability and so too did a positive personal relationship with Robert (Bobby) Cox, great grandson of the legendary Sammy Cox of Rangers and Scotland fame.

Bobby was divorced and he and Marlene had known each other since away back in secondary school – it was a bit of a re-acquaintance that was good for both of them.

From dismal days of the past came one of the proudest days in Marlene and JD's lives as Lorraine completed her

Open University Degree Course. Graduation was set for 24 May 2008 in Glasgow.

Nancy and I drove Marlene and Bobby to Glasgow that morning as we had arranged to stay there overnight in a visit to see Gary at his flat in Charing Cross.

We met them the next day to take them back home and although bleary eyed Marlene and Bobby talked excitedly about the Graduation Ceremony, their celebration dinner and celebrating into the early hours of the morning.

Marlene was still over-flowing with pride in her little Princess who was now an Honours Graduate.

Lorraine and JD were as bright as ever or at least looked and talked as bright as ever. They would get the train back to Manchester later that day.

It had been a great achievement and a wonderful occasion for them, captured forever in their minds and on camera.

Nancy and I met Lorraine and JD almost exactly one year later on 23 May 2009 and there could have been no bigger contrast between the occasions.

Lorraine had been admitted to hospital – she had suffered a brain haemorrhage and a stroke.

When we arranged to see her, Lorraine, as usual , made it all seem so light –hearted and positive from her room at Hope Hospital in Bolton.

" We had been out the evening before with friends and I only had a few drinks but felt a bit 'woozy' when we arrived back at West Houghton

.

We went to bed and I didn't think much more about the wooziness .JD got up and left for work early and I decided I'd have a bit of a lie in.

About 9am I decided it was time to get my arse in gear and jumped out of bed only to land myself flat on the floor as my right leg went from under me

.

It was weird, I was all ready to kick start the day and I couldn't stand up and it got worse from there in.

I knew I had to call someone for help and could only crawl to get my mobile from the bedside table as my right arm was now feeling very numb.

Anyway I thought I've got my mobile now and I'll give JD a call and he'll arrange to get help and come home. That should be simple enough I thought.

It was simple enough to get JD's number and press the call button but when he spoke – well I didn't answer as the words I heard in my head did not come out of my mouth.

I also managed to dial 999 and they managed to trace my call as the same thing happened again – I went to speak and no words came out.

JD must have known it was my mobile number and that something was wrong – it must have been horrendous for him knowing it was me but not knowing what I was trying to tell him.

The next thing I really know was that I'm in Hospital and can't really move my right arm and right leg very well – well not really at all.

That was bad enough - I was getting my head round the fact that I seemed to be partly paralysed but worst still I thought I was in a parallel universe where I was speaking and no one could hear me.

I soon realised the fact was that the rest of the world was not deaf it was me who could not speak.

I never thought I would be lost for words but I had lost them completely and that silent fact was brought home to me as porters took me back and forward from the ward for tests and scans.

The ones who knew about my partial paralysis would work to my good leg and arm but new ones didn't know about it and when they tried to speak to me and tell me to move this way or that I couldn't tell them about my arm or leg so as often as not I fell off the bloody trolley bed whilst trying to get back on my ward bed.

I could not say a word to them but I could hear them and they didn't know that I could hear them. For some of them (not all) it was as if they were dealing with a drunk , a drunk that was not listening to what they were telling the drunk to do. They got pissed off with the 'drunk' who did not listen to them, speak to them and kept falling over which would be understandable if I were a drunk but it got even worse.

They assumed I couldn't hear or understand them and started talking about me as if I was not there. They thought I was a drunk and no – user and that I was Eastern European with a name like , 'Van Aswegan'.

" What kind of name is that, she doesn't understand or want to understand and they come over here and get the best of treatment."

It was only a few who were like this but it made me desperate to be able to speak and get out of the hospital.

Lorraine paused as if to let us take in her experience and words which now free-flow to describe events since she simply 'fell out of bed'.

Her mind and her voice had been screaming but no one heard her – it was her most surreal and unreal experience. She had a mind to speak her mind but no voice. It was as if she didn't exist or if she did it was as a mute drunk or east European drunk.

Her experience reminded me of a picture, a horrifying picture – the 'Silent Scream '.

Lorraine really made light of the situation that at the time had made her desperate to get out of the hospital and she never blamed the attendants who could not hear her silent scream – she reasoned that they did not know and how could they know.

A situation that would have terrified most people was a big challenge to Lorraine.

So what did she do?

" I realised that I needed to learn to speak again , so I watched the TV all the time it was on and I listened to words and repeated them in my head over and over again and sometimes I tried to say them out loud but nothing came out. So I practiced more and more during the night. I watched old black and white films which were repeated day into night and I built myself up to make the staff aware that I could speak and I wanted to go home.

My big chance came when the Ward Sister was hovering near my bed in the early hours of the morning and I went for it

,

" Hey, I did not sign up for this, what's going on "?

I don't know who got the biggest fright but it worked as they realised I could speak.

I wasn't a drunk or east European drunk, I was English – well Scottish with a bit of a South African accent.

I was elated and even phoned JD to come and get me – he was a bit taken aback to say the least."

Incredible but true and Lorraine just told as it was, no blame, no malice just thanks that she was alive and thanks for the treatment she had received.

Lorraine had found her voice but before JD could come and get her from Hospital she had to hear someone else's voice – it was the voice of her Consultant.

" You've had a brain haemorrhage and it has affected your mobility in your right arm and leg."

Lorraine pretty much knew this much but not the answer to her question,

'

" But what has caused this?"

The Consultant's answer was 'we don't know at this stage, 'but it came out as ,

" You are young and fit and with physiotherapy and speech therapy you should get all your speech back and hopefully a good deal of the mobility in both your limbs".

Lorraine literally threw herself into her therapies- her speech returned fully and quickly and she used it in her frustration at her slower progress in regaining mobility in her arm and leg especially when she would fall over.

She got a bit of feeling back in her hand and arm and slowly got better walking with a stick. They perhaps did not seem like big changes in the scale of things but they were really significant improvements and although progress was slow it seemed pretty sure.

Most notable of all was that Lorraine never complained, she coped with every challenge and made light of her situation. She joked about the time it took her to get ready in the morning and her early attempts at putting lipstick on after she had got out of hospital.

The house had been rearranged to accommodate her return home. The living room became a bedroom on the ground floor until Lorraine progressed enough to be able to get upstairs.

Her first jaunt up the stairs was shuffling on her backside all the way and then back down again. It took a lot of time and effort to do what other people would take for-granted – getting ready in the morning, going to the shops, washing and eating.

She pushed herself hard and made baby step progress – small but noticeable progress and all part of Lorraine ultimate aim of walking on her own without the aid of sticks or other aids.

The baby steps of progress then seemed to stop and reverse. Was Lorraine pushing herself too hard? The effort never let up but the progress did and so much so that the consultants decided another brain scan was now required.

The scan results explained the halting of Lorraine's progress – she had a brain tumour, a large brain tumour.

The Consultant explained the position and his proposal to operate and remove the tumour.

" It is a fairly lengthy operation to remove the tumour but because of the position it is in and the potential for growth it has to be removed and I would like to remove it as soon as possible".

It takes the surgeon and his team six hours to remove the tumour.

Lorraine came round in hospital and she was able to speak and was as bright as anyone could be after six hours of brain surgery.

Her progress continued and we visited her at Hope Hospital where she showed us the copies of the brain scans she had obtained from her consultant.

She showed us the big dark space on the scan where part of her brain had once been.

The space is bigger than a golf ball but smaller than a tennis ball.

But clearly her brain was still working and working well as she joked as usual,

" well there you are then I must not have been using that bit of my brain and I haven't got it now so I don't need it".

There is a popular myth that humans only use 20 % of their brains and here was Lorraine just about making a virtue of losing about 20% of her brain.

Lorraine's recovery was back on track in more ways that medical.

She joined a stroke victims group. But this was not a sit about all day talking and having coffee group – this was a group with guts and determination to recover or make the most of the abilities they had limited by their strokes.

Lorraine went quad biking and quad racing .They all knew what it was like and they liked Lorraine and her determination to recover and in the process brighten up the support group through her attitude, smiles and sense of humour.

Lorraine was positive, the operation appeared to be positive but the one thing no one was yet positive about was, 'Did they get and remove all of the tumour and was it benign or malignant' ?

In Lorraine's mind and probably everybody's mind were these vital questions but no one raised them for fear of getting an answer that would be at odds with Lorraine's recovery.

No one really asked the awkward questions but tests and scans were completed to complete the picture of Lorraine's health and future prognosis.

The fairy-tale recovery would not be an outcome as Lorraine's and everybody's worse fears were realised and crystallised by the consultant in news that broke both hearts and minds.

" We got most of the tumour out but there is a cancerous growth in your brain which is inoperable. We can treat it to arrest the spread but it will not cure the cancer as it is a very aggressive type. We will give you some information on the cancer you have and the radiotherapy and chemotherapy treatment we can commence. I'll speak to you again once you are able to take this in, "

and with that the Consultant left to visit another patient and give out more good or bad news.

His news for Lorraine, Marlene and JD just confirmed life's not fair – she survives a brain haemorrhage, comes through a six hour operation to remove a tumour in her brain and does everything possible to regain her mobility and her speech, learn to walk with a stick and then without a stick to get driving again and get back to work – life's not fair.

She never lost sight of her aims which would get her back to work but they receded into a different horizon with the confirmation of cancer. A bombshell for us and a time bomb for a thirty eight year old young woman who dared to still count time in years and months.

There were no survival rates for Lorraine's type of cancer only ' survival times' – for most months not years and depending on the patient's reaction to radiotherapy and chemotherapy treatment the months could be counted on one hand.

Radiotherapy, chemotherapy, blood tests, anti – sickness tablets and steroids were Lorraine's defences against an invading and aggressive cancer.

She took the treatments, tests and pills in her stride and if pushed in a telephone conversation she would say,

"Yeh, I have been a bit tired today, so have watched more TV than usual. You know I've had the best of treatment and everybody has been great".

Her positivity shone out like a beacon of hope and for months she more than held her own with her cancer.

Her colleagues at Harvey Nics were fantastic and arranged a fund raising day when they worked for nothing and then extended into the evening with drinks for colleagues and customers. Marlene went to Harvey Nics with Lorraine and was nervous about the occasion and how it could affect Lorraine – she needn't have bothered.

Lorraine's work colleagues were probably more nervous than them but put on a fantastic occasion. Her colleagues and her customers were also fantastically generous with gifts, vouchers for holidays and cash raised on the day.

It was all that was good in people to help when all was bad with Lorraine.

The usual effects of chemotherapy eventually hit Lorraine and as a hair-dresser the most poignant one was the loss of some of her hair. It did not deter her,

"Mum, we're going shopping today".

"Lorraine we've already done a big shop, we don't really need to go shopping and you must be tired so why don't we just stay home ", was Marlene's plea.

" No, we're going shopping for a wig and not just any old wig but one I really like ".

She found one and it really suited her. She looked good, she looked healthy.

Her appetite was not healthy. After treatment food would taste like 'mush '. So when she felt bad and had little appetite JD learned to make meals that were good for her but which she didn't really like anyway.

His reasoning was simple there was no point in making Lorraine her favourite meals when they were going to taste like insipid mush but instead to make these meals when she felt better and they would taste like she remembered them.

The first course of chemotherapy treatment was really hard but Lorraine completed it with her usual fortitude, forthrightness and sense of humour.

This was how we all wanted Lorraine to be. She had made a special visit to Darvel to see us all for Christmas and celebrate New Year 2009. She laughed and joked about her days out with the Stroke Support Group. She asked after everyone in the family out of genuine interest and made light of her own illness.

That type of attitude and approach was not a one off – this was Lorraine and her approach to life.

Nancy would call Lorraine on a fairly regular basis and it was only as the effects of the chemotherapy wore on that on occasions she was too tired to speak but if that was the case then the next day or day after her chirpy voice would be recorded on the answer machine when we were out ,

" Sorry I couldn't speak to you yesterday, will catch up with you when you get back, Take care, bye for now."

The second course of chemotherapy was scheduled for 13th November 2010 – it is a second course of treatment that most patients with Lorraine's condition never actually receive.

Lorraine's blood test results delayed the commencement of the second course of chemotherapy.

She waited for news of better blood tests but better news never came – she became gravely ill and was hospitalised.

Marlene got time off work and shared the hospital vigil with JD. The vigil lead up to Christmas and it was clear that Lorraine's time was running out – in telephone conversations Marlene never really said this – it's as if she lets us know this that she was accepting that Lorraine was going – was dying.

Lorraine's spirit, strength and determination saw her through Christmas and into another New Year.

Still thinking about everyone else she got through Christmas and New Year without a fuss and then 9 days short of her 40th birthday she slipped away.

Nearly two years after falling ill Marlene's Little Princess fell asleep on Monday 3 January 2011.

She was thirty nine years of age but more like a perpetual twenty something year old with a zest for life that had been wrestled from her in an uneven and unfair battle for life.

The year was barely 3 days old and it had dealt Marlene another shit hand.

For Marlene and JD there was no miracle cure for Lorraine, no fairy-tale ending for a precious Princess.

After a few days with JD and attempting to come to terms with an end that they knew had to come Marlene returned to Darvel to prepare to return to West Haughton to prepare for a funeral.

On 9th January 2011 I drove Marlene to JD's in West Haughton on my way to see our old family friends, 'the Bullers' in Leeds.

It was about a three and a half hour journey and although Marlene sat next to me in the passenger seat she was not close to me as she recalled tales of her Lorraine. Tales that took her back to the warm and sunshine days in South Africa and tales that brought Lorraine back to life as a seventeen year old going to College in Jo'burg and meeting JD – 22 years ago – so alive , so vibrant and so much to look forward to.

" It has been said that, when you lose your parents you lose your past.

When you lose your child you lose your future."

While it is not totally true we all did lose a bit of our future when Lorraine left us. Those closest to her lost the biggest piece with the biggest heartache to get over and somehow move on to their future with the focal point of the jigsaw missing. Only cherished memories of the past and love were left to fill the future gap.

The funeral was arranged for Friday 14 January 2011 and all the family that were fit to attend made their way to JDs and Lorraine's – JDs - to meet up and follow the funeral cortege to the crematorium.

Those who wanted to go and see Lorraine for a last time went to the funeral parlour. At the parlour we witnessed Lorraine, a sleeping beauty that no soft touches or kisses could awaken.

We joined the funeral cortege that wound its way out of West Houghton towards Bolton through traffic lights that threatened temporarily to split the cortege in two distinct parts.

By the time the cortege reached the crematorium the cortege arrived in its entirety as the traffic lights shone green and the Bolton traffic respected the slow cortege convoy.

We awaited our turn to take our places in the 'Church' at the crematorium. Awkward and nervous conversations were taking place between family members and others gathered to pay their last respects to Lorraine. Everybody was 'sussing out 'who everybody was in a nice way and there were acknowledging nods to people you had seen before and knew you better than you knew them.

As we waited two turtle doves landed on the road about 4/5 feet from Nancy and I and despite cars passing close by on the way to car parking at the rear of the crematorium they refused to be flustered or fly away. They strutted up and down and bobbed and weaved their heads to get a good look at Lorraine's funeral entourage. Having checked us all out they nonchalantly flew up to the bow of the nearest tree and continued their vigil over us until we were called for Lorraine's service.

Two turtle doves probably just waiting to be thrown a few crumbs of bread and instead offering us crumbs of comfort and some connection to Lorraine. Whatever their purpose they like Lorraine had gone when the service was over and we viewed the floral tributes for Lorraine.

The Church Service was conducted by Rev. Graham Culter, a Hospital Chaplain Lorraine and JD had met on a few occasions and had also visited his Church in Brinscall.

He had befriended them in hospital and as he spoke it was easy to see how Lorraine and JD had warmed to him.

He himself was a warm spiritual yet practical man; he was religious but not zealous and he practiced rather than preached.

It was obvious that he had taken to Lorraine and JD as he gave a resume of Lorraine's life with Marlene, JD in Scotland, South Africa and then back in England.

He spoke with personal conviction,

"In Hospital I met the most inspirational lady.

.

I have never met someone so positive as Lorraine and so thankful for everything that everyone did for her "

.

He spoke some more about Lorraine's exploits with the Stroke Support Team and then it all seemed to get to him, get to his core as a human being and his religious beliefs.

Lorraine's positivity and humanity had shone through all of her illnesses and set – backs and the realisation that if ever someone did not deserve to die – it was Lorraine.

That thought and his memories of his 'most inspirational lady' seemed to hit him like a marathon runner hitting the ' wall ' and his strong and positive voice trailed and toiled as he seemed to struggle with his words, his emotions and probably his god.

He was as close to tears as I have seen any minister and it only further brought home Lorraine's impact in life and death.

Here was a man who had only really known Lorraine for a short period of her life and here he was struggling to come to terms with her death despite all his faith and spirituality.

It hit everyone in the room and we all struggled to cope as the Minister won his struggle to regain his composure and conveyed Lorraine's last wish,

" You are to enjoy yourself and have a party".

The 'kick –off 'time for Lorraine's party was two o'clock at the Reebok Stadium in Bolton.

The funeral entourage had been invited by the Minister and all followed on. It was a lovely big room on the second floor of the Hospitality Suite within the Stadium and the room like the waiters and waitresses was warm and inviting.

The entourage arrived in their own little parties to have a bigger party – there were the colourful crimpers from Harvey Nics ; the stroke support group ; the South African friends ; friends and neighbours from West Houghton and the family – 5 or 6 car loads of us.

The food, drink, hospitality and conversation flowed within the Reebok Stadium and when time was politely called there we called into another pub to remember another time with the closest of family and friends.

There was Karen and Philip Daft and Karen's Mum Audrey who didn't have a Daft name but a drinks name – she was a Tennant.

There was Diane, a friend in South Africa and now back in Edinburgh. There was JD and Marlene and the family – Rodgers, McKies, Potts, Richmonds and Bobby Cox. A bigger ' family' brought together by tragedy and held together by the warmth of glowing memories of the missing family member.

We cried some and laughed some more and woke up bleary – eyed the next morning to the reality of a wet and windy Bolton.

We woke up to the reality that we were returning to our families back home but for Marlene and JD the most significant and the most precious part of their family had gone – *LORRAINE.*

Lorraine's graduation with a proud mum, Marlene and Bobby Cox

Lorraine and JD at Lorraine's graduation

CHAPTER THIRTEEN

The Next Generation(s)

Lorraine and Paul although of the next generation were destined not to be part of it. Their lives and deaths were poles apart but both their lives ended well before their allotted three score and ten years.

Other lives in the next generation marched on with time into their next 'SOL'. Their lives and experiences were at least as varied as the previous generation but lived at a faster pace than ever.

Some events and experiences were pretty commonplace and reflected the same type of experiences as the previous generation but other events were beyond ' our ken ' and by definition belonged to that next generation as part of their time and age.

Weddings were commonplace events – not to the bride and groom but in the general scheme of things. But in Darvel it was not uncommon for a simple wedding to have a complex pattern of families and friendships.

It may happen in every small town but in Darvel it seemed to be accentuated.

In Darvel weddings were and are the equivalent of knitting the fabric of the town and community and when a wedding involved an incomer to the town it only served to vary the pattern with a different coloured thread.

And so it was that the community and family fabric of Darvel was knitted in a spate of weddings. It resulted in a 'lace tapestry' of inter-twined relatives and friends that the Eglington Fox Hunt could not have followed even before the Scottish Parliament banned fox hunting.

In short it was not simple – almost everybody in the town was related to some degree or other – nearly everyone was a 'country cousin'.

If the weather had been better in Scotland there may well have been bango players strumming their stuff in their porches but thankfully the rain kept them in-doors.

It was no exaggeration and one particular example will suffice –

Mark Lyons married Marlene Richmond.

Simple enough.

Mark is the eldest son of our next door neighbours – Derek and Bobbi – Bobbi is John Collins' sister and John's wife Trisha is Nancy's sister.

On the Richmond side Marlene is the daughter of Tom and Ellen. Tom is the older brother of Jimmy who is married to my sister Yvonne.

Simple !?

With each wedding the 'multiplier' relationship effects went on and on.

Our latest of the 'inter – Darvel marriages' was Gavin Collins to Nicola Thomson, in the Thistle Hotel at Irvine on 30 June 2007. An auspicious day for them and also for Glasgow Airport as terrorists had the audacity to attack the Airport. The TV reports updated us on how the terrorists had been ' smitten' by big John Smeaton and a few other brave souls.

It wasn't quite like the Egyptian and Syrian forces attack on Israel on 'Yom Kippur ' – 6 October 1973 – the holiest day in Judaism.But attacking Glasgow Airport at the start of the 'Glesca Fair' and interfering with punters' holidays was not the best of plans.

It all added a sense of 'uniqueness' to the wedding.

For all of the 'inter-Darvel marriages' there were also 'extra – Darvel marriages and partnerships' which meant that the Darvel genes and connections extended well beyond the town and into wider and widespread communities.

Perhaps not surprising in this group were the 'soldier sons' Bobby and Jim Rodgers who had been ' posted' throughout the UK and beyond.

Bobby Rodgers and Chrissy in Warminster.

Jim Rodgers and Nadine who moved to Inverness.

There was also,

Claire Rodgers and John in Belfast.

Lilian Rodgers and Jamie in Kilmarnock.

Kevin McKie and Laura in Kilmarnock.

This was not a new phenomenon it simply reflected the reality of people's circumstances and stage of life.

These were the normal 'Intimations' in the local newspaper but there were other events in the lives of the next generation , some of them went to print and some of them were unprintable.

It was unprintable and unforgettable when we celebrated Trisha's 50th birthday in Dundee in early January 2008. Dundee was the 'City of Discovery' and the ' discovery ' of Thomas – Joanne's boyfriend from Glasgow and his introduction to the world of the Collins' immediate and wider family.

It was a daunting task , not so much for remembering people's names as about 80% of us came by the names of John , Hugh , Gavin or Kenneth but in terms of the impression he would make as a ' boy ' from the East End of Glasgow.

The big man did himself proud and at 6 feet four inches tall was last seen carrying Gary (6 feet two) on his shoulders around a meeting room table in the basement of the Hilton Hotel in Dundee.

A long trench coat over Thomas's shoulders was all that was needed to create the world's tallest man and recreate a sketch from the Beano comic which was ' born' in Dundee the home of ' Jam , Jute and Journalism'.

It was not a normal part of the family initiation test but it had the desired effect 'the big man was welcomed to the family '. Anyone who was 6 feet four and could carry Gary on his shoulders was a welcome addition to a family which had more than its fair share of vertically-challenged 'borrowers' in it.

Thomas had made a good impression on everyone and when he and Joanne went to stay in Manchester in June 2008 we all thought the going away party would be a hoot.

It was a hoot but mainly because Thomas had booked the only pub in Glasgow which ran out of alcohol until the barman ran out himself and restored normal supplies.

Unbelievable but enjoyable.

From one tall person making a name for himself we move to another tall person making a name for himself in the world of Junior Football.

We were there on 31 May 2009 when Auchinleck Talbot won the Scottish Junior Cup 2-1.

We were there on 29 May 2011 when Auchinleck Talbot won the Scottish Junior Cup 2 – 1 after extra time.

We were there on 7 January 2011 when Hearts narrowly defeated Auchinleck Talbot 1 – 0 in the fourth round of the William Hill Scottish Cup.

We were there to watch Auchinleck Talbot and in particular Gavin Collins (John and Trisha's son) who was described in the Heart's Official Programme as ,

'Gavin Collins , Defender, joined Talbot in 2005 after impressing the then Talbot manager Tam McDonald, is mooted to be the best centre-half in the Junior game which proved to be more than right after being capped at Scotland level. Gavin is talented and reads the game better than anyone in the Juniors and he has established a formidable and effective partnership with MartinMcGoldrick.'

We were there on 27 May 2012 with Gavin and Nicola's son Sam all decked out in the Auchinleck black and yellow colours when unfortunately Auchinleck Talbot lost 2 – 1 to Shotts Bon Accord in the final of the Scottish Junior Cup.

Beyond the 'simple' fact of life - births, weddings, anniversaries and deaths, were the facts of living – experiences of life at school, university, work and leisure.

Our next generation had their experiences and their time which we lived with them as their family.

It was their lives and they were different from us but they experienced many of the same things we had experienced and we also shared these experiences and emotions from a parent perspective as they 'grew up'. We were now the Mum and Dad or the Aunt and Uncle that were the 'support acts' in helping our own achieve their potential and live their lives to the full.

Nancy and I knew things were changing and going to be different when Greg asked for a lift to a 'Hymn Concert' in Edinburgh in October 2004.

It puzzled us as Greg was not religious and didn't attend the church but the riddle was solved as it turned out that ' Him' was a rock band rather than a ' song of religious praise '.

Like Gary before him Greg started in May 2006 working at the tomatoes – a few months seasonal work to help pick the tomatoes and get a bit of discipline , work ethic and a wee bit of money.

Before and beyond work was education. Greg embarked on and completed an HNC in Multi-Media Computing: Web Development at Ayr College on14 July 2008.

In late July 2009 he received a different type of education. He learned that wet roads can be treacherous as he rounded a bend on the A719 Ayr to Galston road at Carnell Estate, Fiveways only for the car to slide onto the grass verge, demolish a BT pole and return to the road facing back the way he had come.

The call home could have been our nightmare call but he and his travelling companion were unscathed – shocked but unhurt.

Greg was and is a good driver and he was unlucky and lucky at the same time. There was little we could say but 'be careful' and be grateful that the accident was fatal for the car and fateful for Greg. I could really appreciate what had happened and it was the road conditions which were a major contributor to the accident after all I had done exactly the same thing twenty five years ago on the Coal Plant Road on my way to work at Cockenzie Power Station!

Greg at 23 years of age still skate-boarding through life and loving his ' unconventional 'sport whilst many of his age have already given up playing football and are now ' Sky Sports' enthusiasts. He's been to Barcelona in 2011with his skateboarding friends and mixed with skateboarders from around the world who gather at the ' Parallel ' and the Barcelona bus station to showcase their skills and enjoy their sport.

With his HNC in Multi Media Computing he has also tried his hand at ' DJ'ing ' but mostly mixes music for fun.

After a year in University accommodation Gary decided that he wanted to get a flat and share it with three friends – three female friends. We thought it might make a good investment rather than pay rent for at least 4 years and have nothing to show for it so we went ' flat hunting' in Glasgow.

We looked at flats in the West End and some were absolutely dire and in poor condition but most were over our budget. We moved our search area further away from the university out to the West of the West end and also in the other direction a bit nearer to Charing Cross.

On 30 June 2005 after two or three viewings of a large ground floor apartment we bought 74 Kent Road in Glasgow with the aid of Munn and Co. Solicitors. It was about 100 yards from the Mitchell Library and about a fifteen minute walk from Glasgow Uni – it suited Gary and his friends fine.

Gary's plan was to complete his Honours degree in Bio-medical Sciences and then do his medical degree to become a Doctor – four years of studying followed by another five years of studying and practical experience in hospitals. That was the plan and part one of the plan was delivered when Gary graduated with a 2-1 Honours Degree on 1 July 2008.

As usual Gary had the assistance of a women to be organised for his Graduation but this time it was not Nancy but Felicity (Flic) Arthur who had completed the same degree as Gary and who had got his arse in gear to hire his gown and arrange for graduation photos.

We met Flic , her sister Hattie and Mum (Jerry) and Dad (Neil) on the day of their graduation and they were all very bright and we had a good chat about university life , the next steps to becoming a Doctor and small things like the cost of all this. We enjoyed their company but thought little more of the acquaintance at that time although Nancy as perceptive as ever told Gary she thought Flic would be' a good catch'. But to Gary then Flic had a boyfriend and they were just good friends.

Gary had 4 conditional offers for medical degrees at Aberdeen, Dundee, Glasgow and Norwich. Conditional on getting at least a 2-1 Honours Degree which had been confirmed on 29 May 2008.

As Mum would have said, he was on the next rung of the ladder to become a doctor but there were a hell of a lot of rungs still to climb as he selected Glasgow University for his next period of study. But in climbing these rungs it became clear that he would have more help and support from Flic as she became Gary's girlfriend and yet again was taking the same course of study as Gary.

Gary has always enjoyed playing football and football is a big feature in the lives of a great many people in Scotland. It is the National game but is not generally a matter of 'life and death'.

Tragically though the football field can be and has been a scene of sudden and unexpected deaths. Davy Cooper was 39 when he collapsed and died of a brain haemorrhage on 23 March 1995 while he was filming a coaching video.

More recently Phil O'Donnell died on 29 December 2007 after suffering a cardiac arrest on the football pitch while playing for Motherwell against Dundee United. Phil was 35 years of age and had played for Motherwell, Celtic, Sheffield United and then again with Motherwell.

His brother Jim worked for ScottishPower in the Energy Networks Finance Function and we often talked about football but there was very little anyone could say to ease the pain of losing his brother.

People and fans could not say very much that would really help but they voted with their feet on 25 May 2008 as 60,000 Celtic, Motherwell and Phil O'Donnell supporters turned out for a benefit match held at Celtic Park in Phil's memory. It is a match that I can proudly and genuinely say we were there (me, Nancy and Jeanette).

The latest football star to experience a cardiac arrest on the football pitch was Bolton's Fabrice Muamba on 17 March 2012 and fortunately he was released from intensive care in April 2012 and on his way to recovery after collapsing from a cardiac arrest and being ' dead ' for 78 minutes.

It is almost certain that on 9 April 2009 the Glasgow University football fields at Garscube Sports Centre would have been the scene of the death of a young man but for the actions of Gary and his mate Dev.

Fraser Thomas was and is not a famous footballer but he was as precious to his family as any famous footballer when he took part in the football trials for the Glasgow University football teams.

When he collapsed during these trials it was the actions of Gary and Dev which led to their nomination for the 'Unsung Hero' category of the Sunday Mail Young Scot Awards in 2009.

The Programme for the Presentations on Thursday 9 April 2009 read,

"Gary Rodgers 21 & Devin Chetty, 21 Glasgow.

Friends Gary and Devin are responsible for saving the life of a teenager whose heart stopped beating on the football pitch.

In September 2008 Fraser Thomas, 20, tried out for the Glasgow University football team at the Garscube Sports Centre. He went along hoping to use this as a good way of

keeping fit while studying at University but he collapsed in the middle of the match.

Gary and Devin, who are 1st and 3rd year medical students, realised right away that Fraser had stopped breathing and had no pulse. They took turns in administering CPR.

Another fortunate turn of events revealed a portable heart defibulator was in the first aid kit at the Sports Centre.

Gary and Devin decided to use it despite never having used one before and Fraser's heart started beating again. Both the boys followed Fraser, who suffers from the heart condition hypertrophic cardiomyopathy, the same condition suffered by Phil O'Donnell, in the ambulance to make sure he was all right and were allowed to see him briefly before going on their way.

Kathryn Thomas said,

" There is no doubt Gary and Devin saved Fraser's life and I am sure they are exactly the type of young people we would like to see graduate as doctors in the future. I am sure they will save many more lives and I believe they are an inspiration to all young Scots."

Nancy and I attended the Award Reception and Ceremony but Gary and Dev did not win the Award as they were 'out-sung ' by two young boys from Inverness who had prevented the School bus from becoming involved in a serious accident when the driver collapsed and was unable to control the bus.

In this case it was really and truly not about the winning of the Award.

Fraser had won his fight for life with the aid of Gary and Dev and that was good enough for them.

Gary talked us through what he and Dev had done and how it was that their life-guard training had given them the practical skills to administer CPR.

But what people don't generally know or realise is that CPR is a messy and hard business. They had to take it in turns to compress Fraser's chest and give him ' mouth to mouth' but it was absolutely necessary and they did without a thought other than to save a boy they did not really know.

Gary and Dev got a letter from the University thanking them for their prompt and effective action and somewhat quizzically to Gary they were offered counselling. It was an offer they both declined but Gary admitted later it might have been different if Fraser had died that day - it certainly would have been different for Fraser and his family.

Nancy and I met Fraser and Fraser's Mum and Dad at a Glasgow University Football Club Sportsman Dinner in March 2010.

Before any words were actually spoken Fraser's mum 's eyes were filling up with her emotional recall and knowing just how close she came to losing her son.

It was a mother's love to a mother's love as she met and embraced Nancy. It was hard not to be emotional as we all enjoyed the night and thought about the ifs and buts of that heart-stopping and thank-fully heart-starting day in September.

Dev has since graduated as a Doctor and has all but completed his 'Junior Doctor 'year in Dumfries.

Gary has been part of a cancer research project in Germany in July 2010 and a year later spent about 8 weeks in Australia in an Adelaide trauma ward as part of his course and completed his practical training at Crosshouse, Ayr, the Southern General Hospitals and Stornoway Hospital before he had to face his finals in 2013.

But despite all the positives aspects and contributions of the ' youth of today ' this 'next generation' probably gets as bad a press as the last generation did.

The perennial cries are of , 'that did'nae happen in my day' ; ' would you credit it , he's just spent £300 on an i- phone and he has'nae got a bean to his name';' he's never worked and never wanted and he's got a bloody pitbull'.

Like in every generation some of the criticism of the youth of today will be justified and some will be a continuing stereotyping of youth but in all of this it should never be forgotten that the youth of today are the products of ' the youth of yesterday' - their parents.

The mirror does not lie.

For all the negativity spawned by social depravation and unemployment and darkness and despair associated with a drugs, drink and crime culture it is attitude, the attitude of the next generation and the last that will determine our future.

Thomas Jefferson, the third President of the United States once said,

" Nothing can stop the man with the right mental attitude from achieving his goals; nothing can help a man with the wrong mental attitude."

Much has changed since Jefferson was President of the United States (1801 - 1809) – but for the next generation like the last generation's attitude if not everything remains absolutely essential.

Criticism of 'the youth of today' by every previous generation seems like 'a given'. It also seems to having taken on if not biblical proportions then 'Dads Army' proportions – ' We're Doomed ' seems to be the constant cry.

It is as if each generation forgets the old Scots saying ,' We are all Jock Tamson's bairns ' , not literally , not even in Darvel, but we all share the same humanity and no one person or generation is innately better than another.

There are enough 'youths of today' in our family and beyond with 'attitude' to help ensure that they achieve their goals and that we avoid a ' Darvel 'Doomsday'.

Gary Rogers, 21, & Devin Chetty, 21 Glasgow

Friends Gary and Devin are responsible for saving the life of a teenager whose heart stopped beating on the football pitch. In September 2008 Fraser Thomas, 20, tried out for the Glasgow University football team at the Garscube Sports Centre. He went along hoping to use this as a good way of keeping fit while studying at University but he collapsed in the middle of the match.

Gary and Devin, who are 1st and 3rd year medical students, realised right away that Fraser had stopped breathing and had no pulse. They took turns in administering CPR. Another fortunate turn of events revealed a portable heart defibrillator was in the first aid kit at the sports centre. Gary and Devin decided to use it, despite never having used one before and Fraser's heart started beating again. Both the boys followed Fraser, who suffers from the heart condition hypertrophic cardiomyopathy, the same condition suffered by Phil O'Donnell, in the ambulance to make sure he was all right and were allowed to see him briefly before going on their way.

Kathryn Thomas said: "There is no doubt Gary and Devin saved Fraser's life and I am sure they are exactly the type of young people we would like to see graduate as doctors in the future. I am sure they will save many more and believe they are an inspiration to all young Scots."

Dev and Gary – the unsung heroes

Gavin and Nicola's first son – Sam Collins

Gary's graduation – honours degree in Bio-medical Sciences - July 2008

CHAPTER FOURTEEN

Old Endings - New Beginnings

The family and people have changed and will continue to change.

People move from one stage of life to the next. For a few this will be a seamless transition but for most there will be a struggle with the past before acceptance of the changes and moving to the present.

Everybody has to adapt to change and accept that with age change is a given. It does not mean lying down to advancing years and becoming old before your time.

It's a bit like men going bald ; there are options – do they attempt a comb-over like Bobby Charlton of old ; a comb forward ; buy a syrup of figs (a wig) ; cut it all off or buy a hat.

There are big changes like job changes – me a florist after 29 years with ScottishPower in Human Resources, now that's a change!

But other activities represent a transition; a change in lifestyle brought about by changing circumstances.

Playing football, running marathons and half marathons and weight training are all gone and in their place are playing golf or more accurately trying to play golf ; cycling and three sessions a week at the gym with runs of about two or three miles at each session.

The old saying of 'The older I get the faster I was ' rings even more true.

For me and Nancy walking becomes a more regular joint activity and form of exercise. Whilst I have the gym Nancy's focus on keeping fit becomes 'Zumba' twice weekly.

Family and lifestyle changes also mean that family holidays with the ' kids' have gone and my redundancy gives us the opportunity to ' re-invent ' the family holiday by buying an apartment in Majorca.

For some time Nancy and I had realised like most folk that our savings in the UK were making next to nothing in interest and in fact when you took account of the relatively high rate of inflation the real value of our savings was decreasing.

According to the experts higher returns could be had from investing in antiques, gold and even fine wines but we passed on these investment opportunities in favour of the 'safer haven' of a holiday apartment abroad.

We looked for an apartment in Tossa De Mar on Spain's Costa Brava but its relatively close proximity to Barcelona meant that holiday homes were expensive and pretty much the preserve of wealthy Catalans.

We visited and holidayed in Majorca and looked at buying an apartment in Santa Ponsa and Cala D'Or but eventually we bought an apartment in Son Caliu, just outside Palmanova in April 2010 and this gives us and our wider family the opportunity to holiday there on a flexible basis.

People face physical changes as they grow older but the physical landscape of the town has also changed.

Darvel has changed and with it the attitude in and to the town of Darvel itself has changed and that in turn brings further change for the people of Darvel.

Still the birthplace of Sir Alexander Fleming and of Sammy Cox of Rangers and Scotland but the fabric of the town has literally changed.

The fabric of the town is no longer textiles and in particular lace with only one factory remaining. Darvel's history and heritage is recorded as a 'Lace Town' and the entrances on the A71 road from the West and East reflect this in the road signs,

' Darvel, A Lace Town', but that reflects the history not the current reality.

'John (Jock) Aird's factory on East Main Street has been demolished and remains derelict ,doubtless awaiting the pick-up in the housing market before this manufacturing site becomes an estate and is renamed ' John Aird Avenue or John Aird Drive or John Aird Way or even all of these.

Also gone the way of Jock Airds is the last of the industrial lace looms in Darvel with the closure of Basfords and Johnstone Shields. The sites that were the home to looms have already been transformed into homes for the residents of Darvel.

Only the names of the new streets like' Lace Mill Wynd 'leave a clue as to the town's heritage before the arrival of these homes.

The factories were made of brick but their life-blood was people. Factory closures took on a very personal note for not just those affected by redundancies but also their families and friends.

Yvonne's big Jimmy had to find new work and new skills – he went back to school – not as a seat of learning but as a job – he became 'Jimmy the Janny'.

A world away from the factory but the reality of life away from a factory.

At its peak in the early 1900's there were about twenty lace and textile mills in the Irvine Valley employing thousands of people and producing about 50% of all lace furnishings in Britain.

By the 1960s and 1970s half of the mills in the Valley had closed and the textile industry in Darvel aka ' a Lace Town ' was reduced to a handful of factories and a few hundred employees. The last Darvel lace weaver standing was Michael Kay at Johnstone Shields.

Morton, Young and Borland (MYB) in the next door town of Newmilns is now the last lace producer of its kind not only in the Valley but in the world. The original Nottingham lace looms weave Scottish lace for a world market that was originally 'normal' but is now a 'niche' – albeit a 'niche' that

MYB are intent on developing and expanding in the face of recession and the long-established trend of mill closures.

Lanfine Weaving Company where Nancy still works continues to prosper but not without changing the nature of its work and focussing on what the customer really wants. They import more materials from abroad but retain both a manufacturing and finishing capability that retains good customers like John Lewis and gains new customers with new needs like the National Health Service and Laura Ashley.

Just as the lace industry holds onto its presence in the Valley by a thread the old Co-operative building in the centre of the town holds precariously onto its presence in the street. It is partly demolished and partly 'listed' but it is hard to see how it can remain safe given its long period of neglect.

A new Co-operative convenience store was built and opened on 5 January 2012 just about 20 yards from the original CO-OP buildings which amount to no more than modern ruins.

The old cardboard – backed books with hand-written weekly orders and records of the Store quarter and the 'Dividend' have long gone along with our old Store numbers of 902 and 3902. They have been replaced by plastic membership cards with eighteen numbers to identify you and automatically tally up your dividend and send out your dividend vouchers.

This new CO-OP appears like the 'prodigal son' and although it offers some employment it also presents a threat to those employed in the other convenience stores in the town. They are a competitive threat to other Traders and Shop Owners who had remained in the town and refurbished old shops in an attempt to increase local trade and survive on this trade.

It is literally a 'trade-off' – some new employment but the likely loss of some old employment. The inevitable consequences of free competition but for some locals the return of the 'prodigal CO-OP' gets a luke-warm reception.

Time and competition will tell if the CO-OP is taken back into the Darvel family.

Further afield but with a sizeable impact on Darvel and the wider Irvine Valley and beyond Johnnie Walkers in Kilmarnock has closed. After nearly 190 years Diageo walked out on Kilmarnock and Johnnie Walker walked to Fife to be bottled and distributed.

Some 700 workers were affected by a decision Diageo announced on 1 July 2009 to restructure and, cease production at Kilmarnock and shift production to Leven in Fife.

Workers at Kilmarnock who were willing and able to relocate were redeployed to the Fife depot. They were leaving for Leven and leaving behind almost 190 years of history.

It was about much more than the change of the wording on whisky bottle labels that was required as workers and their families were up-rooted, re-routed to Fife and re-rooted in Leven and the surrounding area.

Effectively it was the end of an era at Kilmarnock but Diageo insisted they were not making an error and moving to Fife and enlarging that base made economic sense.

Fife's gain was literally Kilmarnock's loss.

Vesevius Crucible also crumbled under the competition and closed with the loss of hundreds of jobs.

Another bitter blow for the Valley.

The Newmilns Vesevius Amateur Football Team like some broken – hearted partner of the factory also died and is no more.

The Team that beat the mighty ' Tiber ' in 1974 , with me and Tony Wright as seventeen year olds has gone – the pitch and the changing rooms remain but there is no team to grace the park.

Darvel Juniors Social Club is long gone and demolished and in 2011 the Darvel Juniors football team almost followed as it had few followers and little funds.

Darvel Football Club founded in 1889 is nearly 124 years old and it seems like its Secretary James(Jim) MacLachlan and other long-term Committee Members and supporters like Robert (Bobby) Dempster have been there since about its foundation or at least have about that amount of service to the Football Club between them. Remarkable guys who get no financial reward and a lot of hassle for all their efforts in Junior football.

I now have a £20 Season Ticket for 2012/ 2013 which is valid for League games only. A small contribution which may not get the Juniors back to their glory year of 1975 at Hampden but at least help with other contributions to get a decent team back on the park as a start on the road to recovery.

There are other 'junior '/ new developments in the town – Darvel Junior Secondary School's extension to accommodate nursery children was completed in June 2012.

Some of the old has gone in the form of the old 'school dining hall' and 'Class 13' - originally a temporary out-building it became pretty permanent given that I had been taught in it well over 40 years ago.

The Nursery School moved from the 20th century building in Ranoldcoup Road to 'a new build at the primary school campus '. That is the modern stance to the age old challenge of education.

Councillor Douglas Reid's view was that,

" It will give the primary school children much-improved facilities, while retaining the grandeur of the old school building'.

It is an investment in the Town and in the Town's future with some 309 children on the Primary School roll and the nursery offering about 120 early year places.

The previous investment of time effort and money to design and build a skate park had paid off by 2008 and what was yesterday's 'mis-understood' has become today's norm.

There is a new attitude to the ' hoodies ' – there is a recognition that this is their sport ; it keeps them fit and they get the same sort of enjoyment out of it that footballers get out of playing football ; golfers get out of playing golf and runners get out of running.

It is now a norm even if a relatively new norm.

Ironically and sadly Larry Stevenson, 'The Godfather of Skateboarding' died on 25 March 2012.

His obituary in the Glasgow Herald was a statement of how he as a skateboard maker helped take the sport from an early 1960's children's gimmick to a respectable and professional sport.

'He basically was the godfather of skate culture. Before him skateboards were toys.'

Not that it helped that much in Scotland but in the USA his big idea was to get public acceptance of skateboards by linking them to surfing. Surfing at Carnoustie does not quite equate to surfing in California but it was in California as a lifeguard on Venice Beach that Larry had begun to design and sell skateboards out of his garage.

The rest is as they say history – even if it is little known history.

'He commercially produced the Makaha Surf and Ski Skateboard and by 1965 his Company had sold $4million worth of skateboards. But by about this time the sport went through a drop-off. Politicians and police spread fear about the dangerous skate-board menace on the city streets and the industry all but collapsed.

I think about 40 years later Scottish skateboarders had the same ' hoodie 'reputation to overcome but overcome they did.

Larry did not lie down and while, 'everyone in the skateboard industry at the time was wondering if skateboarding was the next hula hoop ', he ' still had a feeling that it would come back and it did'.

'His most lasting mark on the design of skateboards was the 'kicktail ' (an upward curve at the end of the previously flat board) that is now used to do almost every modern trick.'

'Larry Stevenson, The Godfather of Skateboarding'.

Darvel is well after California in the alphabet and well behind the times but the Darvel Skatepark was officially and successfully opened on 22 November 2008 and has been welcomed and well – used.

The lesson from Larry was don't give up in what you believe in.

The next stage in this particular development process is to fund and erect floodlights so that kids and adult skaters, boarders and bikers can use and enjoy the facility safely in the evenings.

The town's Morton Park was also revamped and has a variety of children's play areas that are up to date and safer than the old ' shoot ' and wooden swings where many a kid was scarred or scared for life.

Almost inevitably in the face of cheaper supermarket alcohol and a developing culture of drinking at home the local pubs had begun to feel the pinch and in 2006' The Turf 'closed and shuttered it doors.

The days and boozy nights of' Miss Young ', George Menzies and the inimitable Eric were eclipsed as cheap supermarket alcohol and lack of customers called time on The Turf.

The Town also has a new Surgery. It was named, 'Loudoun Medical Centre '. Perhaps Sir Alexander Flemings name could have been used in addition to the recognition previously accorded to him in the form of the Town's ' Fleming Street ' ?

Since 2008 the talk has been of recession and 'double – dip recession and has signalled the end of Darvel as a major textile centre in the UK.

The industry set up by the Morton's in 1876 has effectively all but gone but that does not mean there is no 'industry' in the Town.

The demise of the lace industry had been coming for a while and in its wake industry, endeavour, initiative and development was required to change the fabric of the town.

Two major Festivals are now part of the new fabric of the Town.

Darvel features strongly in The Irvine Valley Walking Festival – the tenth Annual Walking Festival took place on 11th, 12th and 13th May 2012.

Notable walks include :-

'The Two Hills which are Cairnsaigh in Galston and Loudoun Hill in Darvel – a strenuous walk of some ten miles.

The ' Big Power Walk ' , following a visit to ScottishPower's Whitelee Wind Farm walkers take the old weavers trail over the moors from Eaglesham to High Overmuir Farm above Darvel and then return to Galston on the country roads on the north side of Darvel and Newmilns.

The Lanfine House walk / visit is highlighted by the hospitality of the Sasse family barbecue and refreshments.

The ' Cross the Border ' walk is a strenuous ten mile walk back to Darvel over moorland , forest and farm track from the Lanarkshire border.

The ' Highways and Byways ' is a circular walk around Darvel starting from the ' Bankers ' along the Brandsfield Path at the Gower Burn. This walk has declined in popularity since 2008 and the recession caused by the Banking collapse. ?!

The 'Sir Alexander Fleming Walk ' commemorated the 80th anniversary of the discovery of penicillin by Darvel's greatest son. It is better known as the ' Five Miles '.

The ' Music Festival Walk ' leaves from Hurlford on a ten mile walk via Loudoun Kirk and Loudoun Castle up the country roads on the upper Irvine Valley to reach Darvel.

Of late the Darvel Music Company have provided entertainment in the Black Bull after the walk has finished (local musicians Alex McAllister and Davy Paterson are the leading lights on this entertainment and are entertainers in themselves).

And so seamlessly to the second Festival in Darvel which is really the major festival – it is the Music Festival.

Much as Wigton has become 'Book Town' Darvel can lay very good claim to be Scotland's ' Music Town '.

According to the Darvel Music Festival website- www.darvelmusicfestival.org –

" Over 164 acts have performed at Darvel Town Hall since the Festival first got under way in 2002 and audience numbers have increased year on year. Top performers have included; Phil Cunningham and Aly Bain ; Hue and Cry ; the Bluetones, Eddi Reader and Capercaillie."

From inauspicious beginnings the Music Festival has ' hit the right note ' and continues to develop. In 2009 , " The Darvel Music Company was formed to promote music culture , music development and ' live' musical performance within Darvel and other communities within East Ayrshire.

The inaugural meeting was held on 30 April 2009 and took over the running of the prestigious Darvel Music Festival. The Company is not for profit and run by music – loving volunteers – no one gets paid !"

Darvel – Scotland's Music Town *!*

The fabric of the Town has changed.

The high – walled, white-washed brick Factories have in the main gone and in their place are houses at 'Glen Brig ', and 'Lace Mill Wynd'.

The 'chatter 'of the textile and lace looms which I could hear as a boy at the ' Observation Post ' high on the hill above Darvel on a sunny day when the factory doors were left open is as they say ' no more ' and in part of its place is the sound for part of the year of musicians from all over the world.'

'Heritage rocks and rolls with culture' – who would have thought?

The town's Latin motto , ' Non sibi sed cunctis' – **' Not for ourselves , but for others '** seems particularly apt as more and more people out of town visit and enjoy the music Festival.

We also try and contribute to the 'Not for Ourselves,but for Others' theme by going on a Sponsored Walk.

Some of the ' old ones ' and not so old ones at Nancy's work had decided to do their bit for Charity – The Ayrshire Hospice Trek around Cumbrae / Millport on Sunday 11 September 2011.

It's an early start with Stewart Neil's mini bus to Kilmarnock and then an organised Bus from there to Largs to catch the ferry to the Isle of Cumbrae. All the 'girls' turn up , Lilian, Mags, Lynsey, Marianne , Fiona and Gillian

All the 'girls'– I am the only guy in our walking party but it all in a good cause.

The walk itself is a round trip of 10 miles round the island with the first stopping point at Fintray Bay and the second at Newton Bar for refreshments, karaoke and the Raffle.

Nancy and I are quick walkers and after a slow departure from the ferry we brave the Cumbrae elements – it was windy and was raining but everyone was in good spirits – some more than others and there was even the offer of a wee wine or a beer at the first stop. We have juice and a sandwich and pressed on to the second stop.

Everybody went at their own pace – the only race was the race to get your sponsor money in to support the running of the Ayrshire Hospice.

We were the first to arrive from our group at the Newton Bar and the new arrivals got our seats as we move on to the final leg of the sponsored walk – our plan was to get back to the finishing / starting point , get the ferry back to Largs , have a look about the shops and have a meal in a pub.

Job done, everyone arrives back at Largs and have a drink in a local pub before the bus returns to collect the now somewhat motley crew.

At Kilmarnock we manage to get another drink while waiting for Stewart and when we are dropped off in Darvel a few of us manage to have another wee drink in the Masonic Club.

Not quite the Sunday I had envisaged but another example of the best of people doing their best for people who have had the worst of fortune as far as health was concerned.

Think we might do it again and we did in 2012.

Like every town in Scotland Darvel has its challenges but it also has the potential to meet these challenges and be a different Darvel.

A Darvel that respects and literally builds on its past on the road to its future.

Nearly nine years on the 'face and fabric' of Darvel has changed significantly and so have the faces and fate of the family and friends.

Mum and Dad's generation are still represented by Rhoda and William. Rhoda is now in her nineties and William over seventy.

We watched Aunt Rhoda blow out her candles on her ninetieth birthday cake without the aid of a fireman and make her secret wish – not so secret really, her wish was to have another party when she is one hundred. That would be amazing and fantastic so here's hoping.

Nurse Ogilvie is still going strong at 90 years of age on 22 February 2012 and still regarded as one of the family.

Nancy's Aunt Jen is the stalwart in the McCulloch / Moodie family. In the face of considerable adversity and the loss of her husband at a relatively young age she has had the determination and perseverance to bring up her own family and then repeat it all as an ever – helpful and present granny and great gran.

Trisha and John walk their way and graduate into ' grandparent-hood ' as Gavin and Nicola's son Sam takes his first steps and heads into his second year of life and then greet the arrival of his wee brother Adam.

Gavin also takes a different career path from the music of West Sound to the pounding of his initial beat as a new 'Copper ' in Cumnock. Someone was 'having a laugh' when they allocated Gavin, the well-known Auchinleck Talbot centre half to police the streets of their bitter football rivals in Cumnock.

To make then doubly proud Joanne graduated with a degree in Speech Therapy in July 2012 and she and Thomas became engaged on 2 July 2012.

Jeanette has the challenge of change at her work with the GMB Trade Union as she endeavours to become an Officer.

There are no surviving members of Mum's direct family.

All the rest of the family are thankfully still progressing through their lives and their own respective stages of life.

The Rodgers' family tree of life has acquired a few more 'roots' but it also has more branches.

We have our main contact with the Allan's and Kerr's on my mother's side via William Kerr in Paisley. William is not rooted in the past but is very proud of his roots particularly John Allan ('Wee Jock') our grandfather and his hero.

In the main the McTavish branch of the family flourishes but on occasions flag a little bit as my eldest sister Lilian and husband Duncan get beyond retiral age.

Lilian had been extremely ill and admitted to Monklands Hospital with a suspected kidney infection.

On 31 October 2011 (6years to the day Mum had died) Nancy and I visited Lilian in Monklands Hospital or at least we tried to. After fighting our way through the maze of off-street parking we sought out her ward and found her bed. Only problem was there was no Lilian and none of the patients were fit enough to tell us why her bed was empty and there was very little sign left of her having been here.

It was as if lightening had struck twice on the same day but 6 years apart, another Lilian gone.

Lilian had gone and gone to a 'better place'.

The nurse explained Lilian had in fact gone to Hairmyres Hospital in East Kilbride to have a heart procedure – the insertion of a stent. We rested a bit easier with this news but decided not to rest on our laurels as the nurse also confirmed her expected return time could be anytime between about 4 and 10pm.

We waited a wee while and the nurse returned with the flowers which we had brought for Lilian in a vase. We left our card and best wishes after about an hour and it was just as well as it was about midnight before she returned to Monklands.

She has still not returned to full health but with medication is getting there.

Lilian and Duncan's sons and daughters have made them proud grand-parents many times over as Shona and Martin have Ross, Rachael and Rebbekah; Roddy and Elizabeth have Melissa , Aaron, Rory and Bethan ; Lorna and Douglas have Emma , Amanda and Elise and Alisdair and Ashley have Millan and Hannah.

We had never been to a hundredth birthday party (although Aunt Rhoda is the closest at over ninety and still going strong) and it was a bit of a surprise to receive an invitation from Shona to come to a hundredth birthday party on 1 September 2012.

The mystery of whose 100th birthday it was soon became clear as we read the invite – it was a combined 100th Birthday for Shona, her husband Martin and daughter Rebekah. It was a great idea and a great night of fun and celebration in Hamilton.

The senior branch of the Rodgers family has also grown Jim and Jessie are grandparents to Aidan, Allan, Andrew, Jack, Tiegan , Kyle , Katie and Katy. All these kids are growing up fast and young Jack is also driving in the fast lane with his own website to record his trials and tribulations as a boy racer. Both of the soldier sons (Bobby and Jim) now out of uniform and back in 'civvy street' as their lives change and develop.

Marlene's immediate family has reduced once again with the tragic loss of her 'wee Princess', Lorraine.

Elaine and Alistair have their hands full helping with Kevin and Laura's son Finlay.

Bobby and Linda have one less Rodgers in their family as the 'Lost Soul 'that was Paul has found peace.

Bobby with his son Stephen still trying to 're-find' Linda and facing up to the fact that he might never as her mind flits like furniture of an older age and stays more solidly in a solid past.

Nancy and I have Gary and Greg as different as chalk and cheese but all the more valuable and precious for that. Gary awaiting his graduation as a Doctor along with his girlfriend and fellow Doctor ,Flic. Greg taking the opportunity to change jobs and make use of his HNC in Multi Media Computing : Web Development and mixing music , skate-boarding and time with his girlfriend Rhia.

The Richmond's in the form of Jimmy and Yvonne are also static in family numbers terms as Jim and Iain continue to make their way in the world.

David has a new job and is content in his own house and with the company of his mates playing golf and darts as it suits him.

Colin still working for ScottishPower and married to his Elaine.

We decided to have a family get-together on 27 April 2013 to celebrate both Gary and his girlfriend Flic passing their final exams and getting their first appointments as Doctors.

It turned out to be a double celebration as without fanfare or a fuss Colin and Elaine got married in Kilmarnock on that very afternoon. The surprise was shared and declared to all the family as confirmation of their marriage duly arrived in the mail on Monday 30 April 2013.

The message was clear and simple, 'We are delighted to announce :

On Saturday 27th April 2013, at the Burns' Wedding Venue in the presence of two witnesses Colin Rodgers and Elaine Milne became husband and wife.'

Avril and Andy in Middleton, Manchester have the challenges and joys of proud parents as Aidan and Vhairi develop from 'tots' to ' teens'.

Graham, the youngest of the immediate Rodgers family is now over 40 but has cut out his forty a day smoking habit. In

Mikayla their daughter they have a huge talent to nurture and develop.

Mikayla is a wee mite like her mum wee Elaine but with the might in her voice to sing like 'Subo' – Susan Boyle.

Darvel's got talent - watch out!

The last nine years have in a sense brought what most families would get by way of good and bad fortune.

We have no big lottery or Euro-millions winners – or if we have they have kept it very quiet.

We have the tragic loss of family – Lorraine to cancer and Paul to drugs.

We have new family members with new Christian and Surnames.

The experiences over these nine years may be no different than those of other families but they remain unique to our family. Unique but at the same time universal as, ***'Everybody has to Cry Sometime'***.

Me and Nancy cruising on our 30th wedding anniversary

Mikayla – the youngest born of the youngest born – nine years on

Musical Epilogue

The musical score to this book pretty much speaks for itself and reflects events and emotions to the full.

Elvis	All Shook Up	Infancy
Royal Scots Dragoon Guards	Amazing Grace	Hillcrest
Paul McCartney & Wings	Mull of Kintyre	Hillcrest
10cc	I'm Not in Love	Adolescence
Elton John	Daniel	Big Danny
Joan Armatrading	Love & Devotion	Uni
John Lennon	Imagine	Uni
David Bowie	Life on Mars	Uni
Sex Pistols	We're So Pretty	Uni
Whitney Houston	The Greatest Love Of All	Gary
Tina Turner	Simply the Best	Greg
REM	Everybody Hurts (Sometimes)	Davy
East 17	Stay Another Day	Marion
Robbie Williams	Angels	Mavis
Ronan Keating	If Tomorrow Never Comes	Nancy
Frank Sinatra	My Way	Determination
U2	It's a Beautiful Day	Hope
Westlife	You lift me Up.	Love/Support.
Jessie J	Price Tag.	Materialism /Happiness.
Kelly Clarkson	Stronger	Strength of Character.
James Morrison	One Life	Honesty/ Integrity

There is no end.

'Happy is the man who can recall his fathers with joy, who with their deeds and greatness can regale a bearer , and with quiet pleasure beholds himself at the close of that fair succession'.
Goethe.

'Better to write for yourself and have no public, than to write for the public and have no self'.
Cyril Connolly.

"This above all: to thine own self be true".
Polonius in Shakespear's Hamlet.

In Memory of:

Big Danny, Davy Clements , Marion Clements , Patricia (Mavis) McCulloch, Harry McCulloch, Robert (Bobby) Rodgers, Lilian (Lily) Rodgers , Paul Rodgers , Lorraine Van Aswegan and all the other friends and relatives we have lost along the way.

ND - #0241 - 080726 - C0 - 197/132/26 - PB - 9781780356501 - Gloss Lamination